Play and Learning
in the Early Years

Play and Learning in the Early Years

From Research to Practice

Edited by Pat Broadhead, Justine Howard
and Elizabeth Wood

Los Angeles | London | New Delhi
Singapore | Washington DC

SAGE Publications Ltd
1 Oliver's Yard
55 City Road
London EC1Y 1SP

SAGE Publications Inc.
2455 Teller Road
Thousand Oaks, California 91320

SAGE Publications India Pvt Ltd
B 1/I 1 Mohan Cooperative Industrial Area
Mathura Road
New Delhi 110 044

SAGE Publications Asia-Pacific Pte Ltd
33 Pekin Street #02–01
Far East Square
Singapore 048763

Library of Congress Control Number: 2009933842

British Library Cataloguing in Publication data
A catalogue record for this book is available from the British Library

ISBN 978-1-84920-005-9
ISBN 978-1-84920-006-6 (pbk)

Typeset by Dorwyn, Wells, Somerset
Printed in Great Britain by MPG Group, Bodmin, Cornwall
Printed on paper from sustainable resources

Mixed Sources
Product group from well-managed
forests and other controlled sources
www.fsc.org Cert no. SA-COC-1565
© 1996 Forest Stewardship Council
FSC

Contents

Acknowledgements

The editors would like to thank the Vicky Hurst Trust for supporting this work in its early stages; the book is dedicated to the memory of Vicky Hurst and her deep commitment to the importance of play in young children's learning.

About the Editors and Contributors

Editors

Pat Broadhead PhD is Professor of Playful Learning at Leeds Metropolitan University. She has been an early years and primary teacher and has researched play and learning in early years settings for over 20 years with a number of related publications.

Justine Howard PhD leads the MA in Developmental and Therapeutic Play at the Centre for Child Research, Swansea University. She is a Chartered Psychologist and Developmental and Therapeutic Play Specialist. Her research is concerned with children's perceptions of play, how perceptions are influenced by social and environmental interaction and the characteristics inherent in play that render it valuable for children's development.

Elizabeth Wood PhD is Professor of Education at the University of Exeter. Her research interests include teachers' professional knowledge and practice, play and learning in early childhood, children's choices in free choice time, and the policy–practice interface.

Contributors

Liz Brooker PhD is a Senior Lecturer in Early Childhood at the Institute of Education in London. As a former early years teacher, her research interests have focused on children's perceptions of the environments of home, pre-school and school, and the transitions they make between these cultural worlds.

Emese Hall is currently writing her PhD. After gaining a PGCE from Exeter University, Emese taught for two years before returning to full-time study. During her Masters work, she had developed the interest that led on to her doctoral research into the communicative potential of young children's drawings.

Pam Jarvis PhD is Early Years Professional Status academic programme coordinator at Bradford College University Centre. Her PhD, awarded by Leeds Metropolitan University, focuses on children's play-based learning.

Kathy Ring PhD is a Senior Lecturer at York St John University. She contributes to Initial Teacher Training, supervises PhD students, and is currently working with a range of Local Authorities and early years practitioners developing young children's use of drawing as a tool for making meaning. With Angela Anning she co-authored *Making Sense of Children's Drawings* (OUP, 2003) and she contributed to *Mark Making Matters* (DCSF, 2008).

Helen Tovey is a Principal Lecturer in Early Childhood Studies at Roehampton University, London. She teaches on BA, MA and CPD programmes, focusing particularly on aspects of play and environments for young children. She has had extensive experience of working with young children including 10 years as a nursery school head teacher.

David Whitebread PhD is a Senior Lecturer in Psychology and Education at the University of Cambridge Faculty of Education. His research interests include metacognition and self-regulation in young children, children learning through play, and the cognitive neuroscience of early learning. His publications include *Teaching and Learning in the Early Years* (3rd edn, RoutledgeFalmer, 2008).

Maulfry Worthington is engaged in doctoral research on *children's mathematical graphics* and its origins in imaginative, multi-modal play (Free University, Amsterdam). She has many publications including *Children's Mathematics*: *Making Marks, Making Meaning* (SAGE Publications, 2006), co-authored with Elizabeth Carruthers. Their work is featured in the *Williams Maths Review* (DCSF, 2008). See www.childrens-mathematics.net

Foreword

Janet Moyles, Professor Emeritus, Anglia Ruskin University

Play is currently receiving a high profile in government thinking and funding, making this book timely and welcome in enabling us to extend our knowledge of play and the links between play and learning in early years educational settings from a research-informed perspective. Play should be accepted as a legitimate approach to children's learning throughout their early (and primary) years through the pedagogy of early childhood education. Play and learning are intrinsically linked to the young child's sense of self, their identity and their efficacy as independent learners (Bowman et al., 2000).

Although the word 'play' is used in early years documents and policies in England, it is neither clearly defined, nor well understood by practitioners or policy makers in this or many other countries. The word 'play' is used loosely to mean anything that is undertaken 'playfully', be that children's self-chosen activities or playful teaching by the adults. Often, it implies 'playing about', in the sense of 'messing around'. The phrase 'learning through planned purposeful play' in the Early Years Foundation Stage (EYFS), (DfES, 2007: 11) is perhaps designed to allay adult fears that young children are not working hard enough. However, it risks confusing the plans and purposes of adults relating to their goals for children's achievements with the authentic, but different, intentions of playful children. It also represents conflicting views in the discourse related to play: contradictory use of terminology and the conflation of teaching/instruction/planned with the word 'play' is problematic for both practitioners and parents – as well as society as whole – in terms of our expectations of children, education and schooling.

There are different modes of learning and teaching through play and these important aspects are ably explored within this exciting new book by a range of writers, all experts in play research and in early childhood education. The three editors have skilfully brought together a range of papers espousing the value of play to children in educational contexts, and illustrating its complexities. The editors encompass many years of reputable and valuable play research, not least Pat Broadhead's studies on the links between cooperative play and intellectual challenge (Broadhead, 2004, 2006), Elizabeth Wood's seminal research on play, children's experiences and practitioners' roles (Wood, 2007; Wood and

Attfield, 2005) and Justine Howard's investigations into children's perceptions of their play and the important role of practitioners as play professionals in supporting children's experiences (Howard, 2002, 2009; Howard et al., 2006).

The research that has been undertaken by the play scholars contributing to this edited collection confirms that play is a powerful medium for learning in the early years and is not inferior to teacher-directed activities. To be effective in their role, early years practitioners must understand the complexity of play and not perceive it as simply a way of occupying children while they get on with seemingly more important 'teaching' and assessments (Rogers and Evans, 2008).

This book is also significant because it makes research and theoretical perspectives readily accessible to practitioners to support them in adopting and developing research-informed play and learning practices. Greater knowledge will not only enable practitioners to become more confident in providing appropriate curriculum experiences for young children, but will support them in making rational and informed decisions about the development of children's play in learning contexts.

It has been a long time in coming but it is encouraging to see that play in early years settings, for children from birth to five or six years of age, is now perceived to be a vital part of education and care. However, many of us have substantial concerns that play is still conceived very narrowly by some involved in early childhood education as something that can be 'used' as a teaching tool, and that it is not accorded the status that research shows to be vital. The research examined within this book shows indisputably that play is a deeply intellectual and meaningful activity for children, closely linked to their self-regulated learning and metacognition, and vital to the development of appropriate self-knowledge and dispositions towards learning. The researchers offer clear evidence of children's competence in understanding their own learning and their need for extended play experiences, which should be recognised, respected and built upon by practitioners.

Neither play nor learning for young children can be rushed. They are processes which take time to evolve into deeper learning and understanding (Moyles, 2008). Play is also antithetical to outcome-based education because it is flexible, extremely creative, sometimes messy and always under the control of the learners. This means that it is a powerful source of evidence for assessment: analysis of children's choices provides the evidence base for effective extension of their learning. Confident young players become lifelong learners who are capable of independent, abstract thought and who feel able to take risks in order to solve problems and gain understanding (Elkind, 2007).

Children (and practitioners) have been put under great pressure to reach externally imposed goals: neither children nor adults perform well under pressure because it narrows thinking, rather than encouraging divergent, creative responses. Play also promotes the concrete experiences which lead to abstract thinking and the ability to use symbols (Worthington, 2010).

Practitioners who fully understand children's play are able to plan environments and experiences which foster learning through play. Such practitioners understand the learning environment from the perspective of the child. They know how to listen to children and respect and trust their judgements, making time and space for play. They are concerned for children's well-being and observe individuals and groups carefully in order to learn about children's existing knowledge, dispositions and skills. The research in this book emphasises children's voices and children's choices: however, early years pedagogies stem from adults and their engagement with children and their deep understanding of why children play as they do. The book is unique in illustrating, through empirical research, children's intentions, motivations, meanings and modes of engagement, as well as exemplifying the adults' roles.

These chapters offer significant evidence of the long-term positive implications for practitioners who are educated to understand pedagogies of play. Networks of good play practice can support practitioners through involvement in action research and advanced study: by reflecting deeply on play, pedagogy and learning, they can achieve a greater sensitivity to, and understanding of, young children. This level of professionalism enables practitioners to reflect on their own thinking and practices and, in so doing, articulate their beliefs, values, theories and views of play. The thinking professional is then more able to seize 'teachable moments', understand children's developing capacity for self-regulation and become more sensitive and flexible in extending children's learning and development, through play and playful teaching.

This book provides theoretical and practical support for reflective professionals who wish to understand the complexity of children's play and learning, and build on this to develop their own pedagogies.

References

Bowman, B., Donovan, S. and Burns, M. (eds) (2000) *Eager to Learn: Educating our Preschoolers*. Washington, DC. National Academies Press.

Broadhead, P. (2004) *Early Years Play and Learning: Developing Social Skills and Cooperation*. London: RoutledgeFalmer.

Broadhead, P. (2006) 'Developing an understanding of young children's learning through play: the place of observation, interaction and reflection', *British Educational Research Journal* 32(2): 191–207.

Department for Education and Skills (DfES) (2007) *The Early Years Foundation Stage.* Nottingham: DfES.

Elkind, D. (2007) *The Power of Play: Learning What Comes Naturally.* Cambridge, MA: De Capo Press.

Howard, J. (2002) 'Eliciting young children's perceptions of play, work and learning using the activity apperception story procedure', *Early Child Development and Care* 127: 489–502.

Howard, J. (2009) 'Play, learning and development in the early years', in T. Maynard and N. Thomas (eds) *An Introduction to Early Childhood Studies.* London: Sage.

Howard, J., Jenvey, V. and Hill, C. (2006) 'Children's categorisations of play and learning based on social context', *Early Child Development and Care* 176(3/4): 379–93.

Moyles, J. (2008) 'Empowering children and adults: play and child-initiated learning', in S. Featherstone and P. Featherstone (eds) *Like Bees Not Butterflies.* London: A & C Black.

Rogers, S. and Evans, J. (2008) *Inside Role-Play in Early Childhood Education: Researching Young Children's Perspectives.* London: Routledge.

Sutton-Smith, B. (2005) *Play: An Interdisciplinary Synthesis.* Lanham, MD: University Press of America.

Wood, E. (2007) 'New directions in play: consensus or collision?', *Education 3–13* 35(4): 309–20.

Wood, E. and Attfield, J. (2005) *Play, Learning and the Early Childhood Curriculum.* London: Sage.

Worthington, M. (2010) '"This is a *different* calculator – with computer games on": reflecting on children's symbolic play in the digital age', in J. Moyles (ed.) *Thinking About Play: Developing a Reflective Approach.* Maidenhead: Open University Press.

Introduction

Elizabeth Wood, Pat Broadhead and Justine Howard

This book arose from an invited research colloquium held at Leeds Metropolitan University in April 2008, which was jointly organised by Professor Pat Broadhead on behalf of TACTYC, and Professor Elizabeth Wood on behalf of the Early Childhood Special Interest Group of the British Educational Research Association. The colloquium was supported by a grant from the Vicky Hurst Trust, to whom we owe our thanks. Nine researchers, all established scholars in the field of early childhood education, came together to present and discuss their research relating to play, learning and pedagogy in educational settings, along with invited early childhood specialists. The colloquium had two main aims: to explore contemporary research on children as playful learners and adults as playful pedagogues, and to set an agenda for future research into play and learning. Whilst the research studies were varied in terms of their theoretical and methodological orientations, a further aim was to consider their findings in relation to their potential for informing (and sometimes challenging) policy and practice. In addition to this book, the colloquium led to a number of outcomes, including an invitation to present the research evidence to the Independent Review of the Primary Curriculum, led by Sir Jim Rose (DCSF, 2009); a seminar at the House of Commons, where some of the colloquium's original participants disseminated the research on play; and invited meetings with key policy makers in the Department for Children, Schools and Families, and the Qualifications and Curriculum Authority. Thus, the research reported in this book has already been influential in these different contexts. However, our aim (and hope) is that it will become even more influential as it is read, considered and acted on by practitioners at all stages of their professional development.

The book is well-timed, for different reasons. First, early childhood educators have fought long and hard for a curriculum that recognises the value of play to young children's learning and development. Those efforts have been productive, as evidenced in the attention given to play across the four UK countries and in international contexts. Although there are similarities in the ways in which play is valued in international early childhood curricula, there are differences in the age range that is encompassed within the term 'early childhood'. Whilst the English Foundation Stage involves children from birth to age five, the Wales Foundation Phase encompasses birth to age seven, which aligns

1

it more closely with that of other European countries. Second, in addition to developing policy frameworks for early childhood education, UK governments are investing in play from birth to 18, as evidenced in the policies of the national Play Councils (Play England, Play Wales, Play Scotland and Playboard Northern Ireland), and the growing field of Playwork. Third, children's rights to play are being aligned with improving the range and quality of provision for play in education and community settings. However, the policy agendas for early childhood education, and for Playwork, are driven by the expectations that play will have specific impacts such as improving children's educational outcomes; contributing to young people's health and well-being; and advancing the social justice agenda by improving access to and inclusion in play, games and sports, particularly for young people with special educational needs, those from minority ethnic communities including refugee and migrant families, travellers and gypsy communities, and socially disadvantaged groups such as homeless families (DCMS, 2004, 2006; DCSF/DCMS, 2008).

This leads to the fourth (and perhaps most important) reason for the timely publication of this book, namely that play cannot and should not be subordinated wholly to educational policy agendas that privilege narrow constructs of effectiveness and defined outcomes. Instead, the authors agree that play needs to be considered from the perspectives of the players – their motivations, meanings, intentions, imaginings and inventions, and in terms of the distinctive qualities and characteristics which mark out play from other activities, and especially from work. To achieve these aspirations, the authors have drawn on three theoretical perspectives: socio-cultural, bio-cultural and psychological, each of which provides a distinctive lens for understanding different aspects of play. Their choices reflect the ways in which contemporary play scholars have developed contrasting theoretical perspectives to conceptualise play, learning and pedagogy in early childhood, including post-colonial theories (Cannella and Viruru, 2004), post-developmental theories (Edwards and Brooker, 2010) and post-structural theories (MacNaughton, 2005)

The authors have also used contrasting methodological orientations and research designs, with a bias towards the interpretivist paradigm for eliciting the perspectives and interpretations of children, practitioners and family members. In terms of research ethics, the studies encompass contemporary concerns with respectful methods, which involve people not as 'donors of data', but as participants and as knowledgeable reporters of their social and cultural realities. This is evident in the range of research methods used, including experimental designs; photo elicitation techniques; stimulated recall via videos, diaries and artefacts;

participant and non-participant observations; and co-constructive dialogue with children and adults.

A further distinctive contribution of this book is that the authors do not shy away from critical examination of some of the truth claims that have been, and continue to be made, about play. This involves challenging universal assumptions about the efficacy of play, contesting the ways in which play is positioned in policy documents, and questioning long-established truths about 'free choice' and 'child-centredness' in light of social diversity and complexity. The authors demonstrate that, whilst the field of play scholarship remains theoretically and methodologically eclectic, these contrasting perspectives create new mosaics of knowledge and understanding about play, and the ways in which research can inform policy and practice. Thus, the claims that are being made *for play*, the pressures that are exerted *on play*, and the expectations that different stakeholders (parents, practitioners, policy makers) have *of play*, are considered critically in light of research evidence.

In Chapter 1, Wood explores the reasons for continuing tensions between the rhetoric and reality of play in educational settings. In part, this problem can be attributed to the long-established ideological claims that have been made about the primacy of free play, free choice, autonomy, control and ownership, all of which are characteristics of children's self-initiated activities. Although many of the claims that are made for play are supported by research evidence, practitioners continue to have problems in implementing good quality play experiences, and in demonstrating to parents and other professionals that children are learning when they are playing, and that their learning meets (or exceeds) the minimum standards laid down by the Early Years Foundation Stage (DCSF, 2007). Wood proposes a model of integrated pedagogical approaches, which includes child-initiated and adult-directed activities, and reflects socio-cultural theories of learning, with practitioners playing important roles in leading and responding to children's repertoires of choice, interests and activities. These arguments are consistent with wider international trends towards re-conceptualising adults' roles in play (Clark, 2009; Wood, 2009).

In Chapter 2, Brooker reports her research on 4–5-year-old children in English reception classes, and provides detailed consideration of the influence of cultural diversity on children's orientations to pre-school and school. This chapter provokes the question of whether play has been over-estimated as *the* way in which children learn. Brooker describes the mismatch of expectations that can arise between educators and ethnic minority parents about learning, and about play as a medium for learning. The research evidence challenges assumptions about the universal efficacy of play in relation to diversity, social justice and inclusion. Cultural diversity is not simply a matter of providing positive images, or clothes and artefacts in the role play areas, or of families sharing cultural artefacts between home and school. Researchers concerned with equity and social justice problematise the celebration of superficial differences, and argue that educators need to dig deeper to discover the funds of knowledge needed to support children's learning in culturally authentic ways (Goodwin et al., 2008: 7). Brooker's research demonstrates that the concept of integrated pedagogies should involve integration of families' cultural beliefs and childrearing practices, and the effect these have on children's repertoires of choice and participation in play.

The theme of choice and participation is continued in Chapter 3, where Broadhead reports her ongoing research into the links between play and learning in children's social and cooperative play, with children aged three to six years. Using an empirically driven observation tool, the Social Play Continuum, Broadhead demonstrates·the value of joint observations with practitioners for critiquing and informing practice. Her research reveals the ways in which children link the worlds of home, pre-school and school, through their use of tools and artefacts, and develop their thematic interests for stimulating high level, cognitively challenging play. This research raises a key issue about progression and continuity: with experience, children's play becomes more complex, more varied and more skilled, but this is typically the point at which play in educational settings is curtailed. Given the policy commitments to play (as described at the beginning of this chapter), it would seem timely to address this discontinuity, and to consider how complexity and challenge can be enhanced beyond early childhood.

In the following two chapters, Jarvis and Tovey address aspects of play provision that continue to provoke controversy, and to challenge practitioners' beliefs and practices. In Chapter 4, Jarvis reports her research into rough and tumble play, and its function as a basis from which children create pretend play and games with rules. Taking a bio-cultural theoretical perspective, Jarvis explores the gendered nature of rough and tumble play within both single and mixed gender episodes, and, in common with Broadhead, reveals the social complexity within the children's narratives and experiences. This study challenges practitioners to deconstruct the prevalent 'zero-tolerance' approach to rough and tumble play, to consider the ways in which players teach each other the rules and routines of their own play cultures, and to pay more attention to the ways in which gender differences in play are manifest in their settings.

One of the reasons for the zero-tolerance approach to rough and tumble play is, of course, the concern for children's safety and minimisation of risk. However, as Tovey argues in Chapter 5, there are tensions between perceptions of risk and danger in outdoor play, and the learning potential of risk-taking and adventurous play. Rarely are these tensions examined critically, particularly in relation to children's motivations and purposes. Tovey captures some of the paradoxes of risky play when she describes how players simultaneously experience joy and fear, feelings of being in control and out of control, and the ways in which these risky experiences contribute to their sense of mastery and control of their bodies, emotions and material worlds. Tovey reports contrasting perceptions amongst the practitioners she interviewed, and, like Jarvis, challenges practitioners to understand that risky, adventurous play activities can be vital for children's well-being and for developing positive learning dispositions.

The following three chapters focus on different ways of understanding children's meaning-making through multi-modal activities, and provide insights into the ways in which children create and sustain their own subjective possibilities through play. Combining socio-cultural and post-structural perspectives, Hall, in Chapter 6, uses visual and participatory research methods to explore the communicative potential of young children's drawings. The research findings show that children use drawings to make sense of the world around them, to create their own worlds and cultures, and to create playful authoring spaces in which their identities become visible. Hall explores the themes of power, agency, control and transformation through the children's explanations of their drawings, which reveal their imaginative capabilities, social relationships and ways of interpreting their social and cultural worlds. In common with the work of Jarvis and Broadhead, gender emerges as a dimension of diversity in what children choose to draw, and the narratives they construct in and about their drawings.

In Chapter 7, Ring focuses on an action research project with early years teachers, using visual images, observations and narrative accounts to explore their thinking and practices about drawing. The project demonstrates the importance of practice-based action research collaborations, in which practitioners have the time and support to challenge their taken-for-granted assumptions about drawing as 'mark-making' rather than as a powerful way of making meaning. The findings have clear implications for practice: Ring argues that practitioners should make continuous provision for playful drawing; and develop their pedagogical skills in supporting playful drawing.

Similar perspectives are reported by Worthington in Chapter 8, drawing on her ongoing research into children's mathematical graphics from their emergence in imaginative play. Taking a socio-cultural theoretical focus, the main focus is on young children's semiotic practices – the ways in which they explore, make and communicate meanings through complex signs or mental tools within their play, and the significance of signs as precursors of symbolic languages such as writing. As in the previous two chapters, Worthington describes the ways in which children's imaginative capabilities and internal representations become evident through their multi-modal communicative capabilities, including language, models, gestures, arrangements of artefacts and graphical representations. A direct relationship exists between children's ability to make meanings in play and to use marks and symbols to signify meanings. Thus, semiotic activities have social and relational significance for children as mediators of their internal and external worlds. In common with other authors in the book, Worthington argues for the pedagogical value of making and analysing observations of child-initiated play episodes, and of critical reflection in deepening professional knowledge and developing practice.

Howard in Chapter 9, and Whitebread in Chapter 10, draw on developmental psychology to research different aspects of play using experimental methods. Both authors report findings that attest to the fundamental power of play as a mechanism for learning and development, and to the role of adults in maximising this through their provision and cooperative engagement in play. Like Broadhead and Worthington, they describe how their research has developed cumulatively and over time, demonstrating the ways in which play scholars can become deeply immersed in the challenges and complexities of play. Howard continues a key theme in this book, namely the importance of understanding children's meanings and perspectives on playfulness as a mode of action, and especially what distinguishes play from other modes of action. Such a distinction could potentially prevent play being used as an umbrella category for all child-initiated activities. Using pictorial research methods enabled Howard to identify the cues that children use to signal play, and to control the experimental conditions in order to measure the impact of children perceiving a task as play. Howard makes important theory–practice links from her research: understanding children's views about their play can be formative and diagnostic, by informing the ways in which practitioners plan learning environments and opportunities where children adopt a playful mode of action that has a positive impact on task performance.

Whitebread goes on to synthesise the impact of socio-cultural theories on developmental psychology, in the context of understanding children's metacognitive and self-regulatory behaviours in play. He explains the significance of metacognitive or self-regulatory processes when cognitive tasks involve effortful attempts to learn intentionally. This is an important concept for researchers and practitioners: the apparent spontaneity and fluidity of play sometimes masks the effortful components of children's activities and behaviours, especially in problem-solving, perspective-taking and emotional self-regulation. Thus, it can be argued that children's motivations to play are intrinsically enmeshed with their motivations to learn, which enables them to behave, in Vygotsky's metaphor, 'a head taller than themselves'. The observational study reported by Whitebread showed that the richest opportunities for self-regulatory behaviour were predominantly within playful contexts (especially open-ended pretend or symbolic play), and that these contexts were particularly powerful for developing problem-solving capabilities and creativity. Whitebread identifies the pedagogical practices that support the development of young children's self-regulatory capacities as learners, and the potential role of playful activity within this. These include providing children with emotional warmth and security, with feelings of control, with cognitive challenge and with opportunities to talk about their play and learning.

In the final chapter, the editors summarise some of the key issues that have arisen from these studies, and consider how the findings can be used to inform professional knowledge and practice, particularly in relation to developing playful learning and playful pedagogies. An important concept is highlighted by the authors in this book, namely that *what play means* for children is just as important as *what play does* for children. This book makes a key contribution to understanding children's meanings and purposes, and to reconceptualising pedagogy in ways that will enhance the potential for learning through play, within and beyond early childhood.

References

Cannella, G.S. and Viruru, R. (2004) *Childhood and Postcolonisation: Power, Education and Contemporary Practice.* London: Routledge.

Clark, C.D. (2009) *Transactions at Play: Play and Culture Studies, Vol. 9.* Lanham, MD: University Press of America.

Department for Children, Schools and Families (DCSF) (2009) *Independent Review of the Primary Curriculum.* Available at: www.dcsf.gov.uk [Accessed June 2009]

Department for Children, Schools and Families (DCSF) and Department for Culture, Media and Sport (DCMS) (2008) *Fair Play: A Consultation on the Play Strategy.* London: DCSF. Available at: www.dcsf.gov.uk

Department for Culture, Media and Sport (DCMS) (2004) *Getting Serious About Play.* Available at: www.dcms.gov.uk

Department for Culture, Media and Sport (DCMS) (2006) *Time for Play.* Available at: www.dcms.gov.uk

Department for Education and Skills (DfES) (2007) *Practice Guidance for the Early Years Foundation Stage.* London: DfES Publications.

Edwards, S. and Brooker, E. (eds) (2010) *Challenging Play*. Maidenhead: Open University Press.

Goodwin, A.L., Cheruvu, R. and Genishi, C. (2008) 'Responding to multiple diversities in early childhood education', in C. Genishi and A.L. Goodwin (eds) *Diversities in Early Childhood Education: Rethinking and Doing*. New York: Routledge.

MacNaughton, G. (2005) *Doing Foucault in Early Childhood Studies: Applying Poststructural Ideas*. London: Routledge.

Wood, E. (2009) 'Conceptualising a pedagogy of play: international perspectives from theory, policy and practice', in D. Kuschner (ed.) *From Children to Red Hatters®, Diverse Images and Issues of Play: Play and Culture Studies, Vol. 8*, pp. 166–89. Lanham, MD: University Press of America.

1

Developing Integrated Pedagogical Approaches to Play and Learning

Elizabeth Wood

The aims of this chapter are to:

- consider the tensions between different pedagogical frameworks for supporting play and learning, in theory and practice
- enable practitioners to look critically at pedagogies of play, and how these are influenced by policy, theory and research
- describe the intrinsic qualities, characteristics and purposes of play and playfulness, and how these can inform integrated pedagogies.

Current policy frameworks and policy-oriented research in England provide positive validations for play as a key characteristic of effective practice in early childhood education. Similar validations can be found in many countries, reflecting a wealth of research findings regarding the benefits of different forms of play to learning and development. These benefits have been identified in the subject areas of the curriculum, and more broadly in children's social competence, well-being, positive orientations to learning and overall progression (Edwards and Brooker, 2010; Fromberg and Bergen, 2006; Kuschner, 2009). In addition, playful orientations to teaching and learning are characteristic of high-quality provision. Being playful can encompass personality traits and modes of interaction, flexible approaches to tasks and the ability to infuse different activities with the mood or spirit of play. Playful ways of interacting with others include humour, teasing, jokes, mimicry, riddles and rhymes, singing and chanting, and clapping games. Playful approaches to tasks include behavioural fluency, and using materials and resources in flexible and imaginative ways. Playful moods range from boisterous, wild and dizzy play to quiet, focused contemplation. So play and playfulness can be seen as integral to the ways in which humans learn, relate and interact across generations, cultures and contexts.

Although play scholars and practitioners endorse the many benefits of play, practitioners continue to struggle with their provision and, in particular, with their roles (Wood, 2009). Reflecting on my previous research which examined the continuities and discontinuities in teachers' theories of play and their classroom practice (Bennett et al., 1997), I have come to see this not just as a rhetoric–reality problem (as described in the Introduction), but as a fundamental tension between different pedagogical orientations and traditions in early childhood education, ambiguous policy recommendations, and the ways in which policies are implemented in practice.

I have been researching play and working with teachers on initial and continuing professional development programmes for over 20 years. I know that there are different ways of organising and managing play, and different beliefs and practices, even amongst those who have strong commitments to good quality play provision. These variations are evident in the following quotations which were provided by PGCE students when I asked them to write short summaries of the play provision they had experienced during their placements:

> **Ellie:** 'My placement was in a reception/yr1/yr2 class. There was no scheduled free play for any of the children. They had a role play area, which was well equipped for their topic, but they were only allowed in there if they had finished their work (which was rare). With the recent bad weather we were very low on numbers and the reaction I got when I said we shouldn't stick to the plans because of limited numbers was this: "but we can't just let them play?" I felt like saying "why not?" The children were trying to sneak in at lunchtimes to play in the role play area'!!

> **Ruth:** 'Play, what play? Oh that thing they did for about 30 minutes on a Friday afternoon if they had finished everything else off, but they had to earn those minutes. No raised voices, and not too much stuff out and definitely no fun allowed. Five weeks in the military style classroom, oh what fun we did not have'.

> **Jo:** 'Absolutely amazing!!! Everything we've been learning about on the course was there for us to see. Great provision indoors and outdoors (including a small Forest School area) with free flow activities from about 10 am every day. We were able to plan activities that we were responsible for, like creative arts, cooking and small group time for the adult-led input. So we were able to do our intentional teaching. But we had a great time setting up the role play area with the children – their ideas were much better than ours and they made lots of the resources from scrap materials. It took us a while to learn how to be good players but we realised how much assessment we could do when we were with the children, being the patient or the bad robber who had to be locked up and punished (this seemed to occur quite a lot with the boys'!!).

What underlies the students' experiences is not just contrasting beliefs and practices, but different orientations to education in general and to play in particular. Ellie and Ruth experienced the work–play dichotomy (as described by Howard in Chapter 9), where teacher-directed activities dominated provision, and play had little relevance. Jo experienced a more sophisticated approach, where adult- and child-initiated activities were integrated through curriculum planning, assessment and feedback. These orientations are defined here as the *cultural transmission/directive* approach, and the *emergent/responsive* approach. Whilst these orientations are not mutually exclusive, a critical consideration of their distinctions is used to examine why play provision remains such a challenge. I will argue that the focus on *what play* **does** *for children*, can be seen as an 'outside-in' perspective, which derives from the cultural transmission/directive approach, and privileges adults' plans for play, and their interpretations of play and educational outcomes. In contrast, *what play* **means** *for children* can be seen as an 'inside-out' perspective, which derives from the emergent/responsive approach, and privileges children's cultural practices, meanings and purposes. Both perspectives are important for understanding play in education settings, but problems arise when the former dominates the latter. I will argue that practitioners need to develop integrated pedagogies, which are informed by 'inside-out' perspectives: understanding the inherent qualities and characteristics of play, the importance of what play means for children and the complexity of adults' roles.

The first section examines play, pedagogy and learning, focusing on the tensions between these two orientations, and their underpinning theories. The second section considers these two orientations in light of some of the ambiguous messages about play and pedagogy in the Early Years Foundation Stage (EYFS) (DfES, 2007). The third section takes an 'inside-out' perspective, by looking at the intrinsic characteristics and qualities of play that are evident in much play research, but are often overlooked in policy discourses. The final section explores implications for developing integrated pedagogical approaches, so that provision is informed by knowledge about play, and not just by policy-centred versions of educational play.

Play, pedagogy and learning

The field of play scholarship draws on many contrasting disciplinary, theoretical and methodological perspectives, as evidenced in each of the chapters in this book. What play is, what play means and what play does for the players is conceptualised in different ways according to the particular lenses through which researchers view play (Fromberg and Bergen, 2006; Wood, 2009). However, making the journey from research to practice remains problematic for a number of reasons. First, as Howard argues in Chapter 9, it is difficult to isolate the benefits of play from the wider repertoire of children's activities, because play activities enable children to make connections with many areas of learning and experience. Second, any benefits need to be seen within the wider dynamic processes that occur within play, because of the unique ways in which play creates imaginative, relational and interactive spaces, and enables children to develop and express their cultures and identities. Third, findings from research studies have been interpreted in different ways in policy guidance documents. Whilst many studies have been influential in identifying the benefits of play, making links between play and learning, and play and pedagogy, has always been problematic (Rogers and Evans, 2008; Wood and Attfield, 2005). What tends to happen, particularly in reception classes (for four- and five-year-old children in UK primary schools), is that practitioners either see play and work as a dichotomy (as in Ellie and Ruth's accounts), or use *mixed* rather than *integrated* pedagogical approaches. In *mixed* approaches, adult-directed activities take centre stage in planning, assessment and feedback, and child-initiated activities, including play, are left at the margins of practice. In *integrated* approaches, adults are involved with children in planning for play and child-initiated activities, based on their observations and interactions. Planning and pedagogical decision-making are informed by children's choices, interests, capabilities and knowledge, which feed forward into further curriculum planning. Teaching and learning, therefore, become co-constructive processes, where the focus is on dynamic interactions between the people, resources and activities in the setting, with the curriculum being used as a framework rather than a straitjacket. Of course, different pedagogical strategies are appropriate for different educational goals, and this is the point at which the cultural transmission/directive and the emergent/responsive approaches collide, firstly because they embody contrasting orientations to learning and teaching, and secondly because national policy frameworks in England give more status to the former against the latter.

The cultural transmission/directive approach

Contemporary policy frameworks in England (and in many other countries) focus on *what play* **does** *for children*. This is conceptualised here as an 'outside-in' perspective, which can be linked to the cultural transmission/directive approach in which education is seen as a process of enculturation. The dominant cultural values, beliefs and aspirations of society determine what education is, what education is good for, and how education should be carried out. These positions are expressed through socially approved forms of knowledge that are organised sequentially and hierarchically in national curriculum policies (such as the six areas of learning in the EYFS). The role of educators is to transmit the knowledge, skills and understanding that are deemed valuable to children in the immediate and long terms. In relation to play, the main emphasis is on play as educational practice – a means of learning, progress and achievement, including preparatory skills training (for example, playing with manipulative materials improves fine-motor skills and leads to the coordination needed for pencil control and writing). In terms of power relationships, practitioners control what forms of play are allowed, and how much ownership and control children have, but with limitations on time, resources and space. This approach privileges adults' provision for and interpretations of play in line with defined educational outcomes, because they have to provide evidence of the benefits of play for the purposes of assessment, evaluation and accountability. Children are expected to acquire ways of being a pupil, and to learn in specific ways.

Drawing on the metaphors for learning used by Sfard (1998) and James and Pollard (2008), the cultural transmission/directive approach incorporates learning as acquisition, because learning is seen as the individual's gradual accumulation of knowledge and understanding, which become increasingly refined and organised into coherent conceptual structures. The contexts for learning are more likely to be controlled by practitioners, with specific aims and intentions that reflect socially approved goals and outcomes. Cultural transmission can also happen in subtle ways, for example through the types of play that are allowed or banned, the rules and culture of the setting, and the judgements that adults make about the value of child-initiated activities. This approach tends to homogenise and normalise children to the extent that difference and diversity may be seen as deviations from desirable norms and trajectories, rather than expressions of children's cultures, identities and life experiences. This is not to argue simplistically against the cultural transmission/directive approach, because in home and community settings, play is used to transmit important cultural information (Genishi and Goodwin, 2008; Pramling-Samuelson and Fleer, 2009). There is evidence to support the view that adults can have creative and flexible roles in designing play/learning environments, acting as co-players, and inspiring play for children who need assistance (Wood and Attfield, 2005). However, where practitioners create a dichotomy between work and play, it is more likely that adult-initiated activities will dominate provision, or that play activities will reflects adults' plans and purposes.

The emergent/responsive approach

The emergent/responsive approach is more closely associated with play provision, because the focus is on practitioners responding to children's choices and interests and to their emerging knowledge, skills and understanding. This approach takes an 'inside-out' perspective on *what play means for children*, which derives from children's socio-cultural practices. The contrasting metaphor is learning as participation (James and Pollard, 2008; Sfard, 1998). Knowledge is co-constructed with others as children participate in their social and cultural worlds as active agents who play decisive roles in determining the dynamics of social life and in shaping individual activities (Sfard and Prusak, 2005). Ways of knowing and participating emerge in different socio-cultural practices, which embody the beliefs, rules, patterns of behaviour, language and interaction, routines and expectations within communities. For example, children do not just learn isolated skills (such as decoding words, practising handwriting or recognising numerals); they become, for example, readers, writers, communicators and mathematicians through sustained engagement in repertoires of practice, which can be adult- or child-initiated.

Socio-cultural theories have shifted the focus from individual development to the social characteristics of play, and have provoked critical consideration of the sub-texts of agency, power and control in adult- and child-initiated activities (Edwards and Brooker, 2010). Agency, power and control have different meanings within play because of shared imagination and pretence, negotiated rules and meanings, and the joint understanding that 'this is play'. It is here that the cultural transmission/directive and emergent/responsive approaches are fundamentally in opposition. Play enables children to contest and deconstruct established power structures and the subjectivities they are assigned by adults (who holds power, where power is privileged, what rules and sanctions must be followed). The improvisational and spontaneous nature of play makes particular demands on children's imaginative and relational capabilities. Any play activity (particularly role play) is not one event, but many different multi-layered events, as shown by Broadhead in Chapter 3 and Jarvis in Chapter 4. Therefore, analyses of play need to capture the ways in which children's funds of knowledge are connected, how power relations operate, and what other possibilities and events are conjured into the mix.

In an emergent/responsive approach, the knowledge that children bring to the setting emerges and becomes visible through patterns of interests, motivations, choices and activities, and through multi-modal representations, as shown by Hall (Chapter 6), Ring (Chapter 7) and Worthington (Chapter 8). These processes lead to the transformation of participation – as learners become more skilful, competent and knowledgeable, they progress towards deeper engagement and responsibility for assuming active roles in the management and development of activities over time. However, as Brooker argues in Chapter 2, different cultural communities vary in their orientations to play, the ways in which they play, in the significance they attach to play at home and in educational settings (Pramling-Samuelson and Fleer, 2009). Culture not only frames and pervades children's ways of learning, it also powerfully influences their identities which, in turn, are constantly created and re-created in interactions between people (Sfard and Prusak, 2005). Where educators provide sufficient time and support for play activities to develop, children gradually extend their repertoires of participation, typically engaging in the more complex forms of play documented by Broadhead (Chapter 3), in which their everyday knowledge fuels the imaginative content and the purposes of their play.

Given that the emergent/responsive approach is valued by early childhood practitioners, why is it still so difficult to develop the integrated pedagogical approaches that support play and learning? The following section proposes that the ambiguous messages in policy frameworks, and in government-funded research, provide some explanations for these ongoing tensions.

Policy–practice tensions

The Early Years Foundation Stage (EYFS) (DfES, 2007) in England sets out the legal requirements and statutory guidance for children's learning, development and welfare. There are ambiguous messages in the EYFS about how children learn, alongside tensions between the transmissive/directive and emergent/responsive pedagogical approaches. A 'high-quality' setting provides 'challenging and appropriate play-based content reflecting individual needs' (DfES, 2007: 8). However, the quality of play is defined in relation to 'learning as acquisition', that is, the extent to which provision:

> improves children's outcomes (which can be measured by children's progression and achievement at the end of the reception year, as measured by the EYFS Profile), [and] builds foundations for future attainment in Key Stage 1 and beyond. (DfES, 2007: 8)

The emphasis on individual needs and individual progress conflicts with the social and co-constructive nature of learning, especially as children often act more competently in their play activities when they are with people who are more (or differently) knowledgeable (Wood and Attfield, 2005).

The EYFS is informed by findings from a government-funded study on the Effective Provision of Pre-school Education (EPPE), which has located play within a discourse of educational effectiveness:

> ... effective pedagogy in the early years involves both the kind of interaction traditionally associated with the term 'teaching', and also the provision of instructive learning play environments and routines.

> The 'excellent' settings provided both teacher-initiated group work and freely chosen yet potentially instructive play activities. (DfES, 2004: 38)

Practitioners are expected to use different pedagogical approaches, which include adult-led and child-initiated activities, as well as 'free' and structured play. Adult-led activities include structured approaches with defined learning intentions that are applicable to the whole class or to groups. However, there are varying degrees of flexibility for children in how tasks are presented, and what responses are expected. Whilst the EPPE findings regarding 'potentially instructive' and 'planned and purposeful play' indicate pro-active roles for practitioners, these are open to misinterpretation in practice, and raise questions about whose notions of instruction and whose plans are privileged. If it is those of the adults, then the activity will not really be play (though it may retain some playful elements such as positive affect, imagination and flexibility). Children do not always accept adults as co-players if they are unused to this, or if they make their own demarcations between work (adult-directed/controlled) and play (as shown by Howard in Chapter 9). Research on role play in early childhood settings has documented inappropriate interventions, which have served the purpose of providing adult instruction or control, but have undermined or interrupted the play (Rogers and Evans, 2008; Wood and Cook, 2009). In contrast, studies have documented the positive ways in which play tutoring has enabled children to access play activities, or has facilitated more equal roles across diverse groups and cultures (Berthelsen et al., 2009; Genishi and Goodwin, 2008). A key distinction is that the more frequently adults observe and engage in play where children control the activity, the easier it becomes for them to encourage playfulness in activities that are more structured. However, this requires integrated rather than mixed or dichotomised pedagogical approaches.

Where adults utilise *integrated* pedagogical approaches (including flexible planning, observation, documentation and reflective dialogue about children's learning), the potential for co-constructing knowledge between adults and children is enhanced, as educational goals are formulated around children's patterns of interests, motivations and activities. This does not imply *either* that these patterns are the leading influence on planning, *or* that the goals defined in national curriculum documents are irrelevant or undesirable. It is more the case that educators need to be subtle, creative and skilful in order to use integrated pedagogical approaches in ways that connect children's emergent knowledge and understanding (which will involve gaps and misconceptions) with more formally organised conceptual frameworks (as represented in the curriculum). For example, Plowman and Stephen (2007) describe the ways in which adults supported children's interactions with computers and other forms of ICT through guided interaction, which included direct teaching of specific skills and operational competences, demonstration and modelling, and orchestrating learning, all of which supported children's progress towards self-directed activity. Their model of guided interaction was co-constructive, where the focus was on a common activity, the pursuit of shared goals and the maintenance of mutual understanding, with opportunities for open-ended exploration to develop skills and knowledge.

The concept of integrated pedagogical approaches is consistent with a third metaphor for learning which has been proposed by James and Pollard (2008). They argue for a 'knowledge creation' metaphor, which involves learners making sense of the world, testing new experiences against existing ways of thinking and doing things, and creating new knowledge. These processes involve joint activity, co-construction and production of new ideas, and flexible ways of thinking and learning. Conceptualising learning as participation and knowledge creation reflects the processes involved in children's play, with the added dimension of imaginative engagement with their social and cultural worlds. Thus, different forms of play provide the conditions that help children to become flexible and creative learners, as argued by Whitebread in Chapter 10. This conceptualisation also raises questions about the ways in which early childhood educators can manage the tensions between policy-centred discourses, and the flexibility and creativity needed to implement integrated pedagogical approaches. One of the key problems here is that attempts to define the quality of play in relation to individual learning and developmental outcomes (as is the case in the EYFS) are limited, because these outcomes do not reflect the social nature of learning, and the distinctive qualities and characteristics of play.

The qualities and characteristics of play

By taking an inside-out perspective on children's play, a complex picture emerges of how children become successful players. They have to learn how to play – how to imagine and convey pretence, negotiate entry, sustain and develop a role, and defer gratification in order to maintain inclusion and flow. By mastering the rules and discourses of play, children develop the skills to create shared repertoires of activities. Developing the capacity to play, and being in a state of play, determines what players do, and enables them to be open to the spontaneous development of ideas and opportunities. They let play happen, by becoming immersed in the mood or spirit of play. Children can enter into a changed state of consciousness: when they are deeply engrossed, the focus of their consciousness is the play. They see the world from the perspective of play, creating their own playful meanings, symbols and practices, which are imbued with cultural significance (Wood, 2010). Play involves collective, relational activity, which is always culturally, socially and historically situated: children can act more knowledgeably and more competently through shared activity in different contexts (home/school, indoors/outdoors, virtual/'real' worlds), and with different resources (human and material).

Children use multi-modal ways of communicating, for example through symbols, tools, drawings, sculptures, constructions, artefacts and actions (including body language) in ways that are agreed and understood by co-players (see Hall in Chapter 6). Each act of communication requires an act of interpretation and leads to further negotiation of meanings and intentions, which may involve children in knowledge creation. Thus, successful communication requires deep levels of inter-subjectivity as the players must stay tuned to the sometimes rapid flow of information and directions that sustain play episodes. This is because play is continually undergoing creation, within individual episodes, and over time.

The capacity to play incorporates some sophisticated cognitive and meta-cognitive processes. These include:

- creating imaginary worlds and events (which are informed by existing knowledge)

- exploring the potential of objects, tools and symbols, and transforming these in imaginative ways

- communicating and understanding symbolic activities, meanings and transformations

- defining roles (imaginary/real)

- organising events and scripts

- sustaining the flow or narrative of the play – modifying actions in light of ongoing events

- expressing and negotiating personal knowledge and meaning

- remaining fluid and flexible when play changes direction.

In order to promote deeper engagement with integrated pedagogies, practitioners need a sound understanding of the qualities and characteristics of play:

- Personal attentiveness: watchfulness, observation, imitation, reciprocal engagement, curiosity, reflection, making conscious decisions and actions, developing flow and complexity in play.

- Personal involvement and motivation: taking risks, combining/offering ways of knowing and constructing the world, having the disposition to be playful and to act playfully (in 'what if' and 'as if' modes).

- Emotional engagement: playing in and with mood and feeling states (which also involves risk-taking), spontaneity, resilience and responsiveness. Being a skilled player demands considerable resilience: as new friendships develop, children may be included or excluded according to an individual play leader, or the whims of the group. Play can be seen as a form of 'emotional hyperventilation', where playing with emotions such as fear, anxiety and abandonment can lead to exuberant physical activity such as screaming, shouting, running, chasing/being chased, hiding/finding, being captured/released, being dead/coming alive.

- Imaginative potential: using everyday knowledge to inform and sustain play episodes, transforming ideas in the mind (making one thing stand for something else), dramatic exaggeration, evoking magical and superhero powers.

- Communicative potential and capability: attending, listening, co-constructing meanings, openness to multi-modal forms of representation, creating shared meanings and representations, using resources and materials – transforming their uses and meanings in imaginative ways, being multi-literate.

- Relational potential: trust, freedom to act differently in 'what if' and 'as if' modes, sense-making capacities – negotiating real–imaginary contexts, managing fluency, uncertainty and risk.

- Problem-creating and problem-solving potential: children have sufficient choice, freedom and control to develop strategic and flexible thinking skills.

- Evoking the spirit of play: going beyond known boundaries, negotiating ideas, meanings and possibilities, experiencing transcendental and spiritual qualities. Playfulness, laughter, gleefulness, zaniness, wildness, dizzy play, clowning, fooling around, inventing rules and rituals are used to begin, maintain and end play.

- A sense of humour: wit, cognitive flexibility and spontaneity, telling and laughing at jokes and funny stories, teasing.

By considering the qualities of play and playfulness, practitioners can understand some of the complex cognitive processes and dispositions that are involved in becoming a skilled player, and the ways in which play activities impact on learning and development.

Towards integrated pedagogies

It is argued here that practitioners can harness the qualities of play by developing integrated pedagogical approaches, which combine the benefits of adult-directed and child-initiated activities. The following model (Figure 1.1) represents this integration, and allows for elements of playfulness in child-initiated and teacher-directed activities. The model adopts the pragmatic perspective that play in early childhood settings is always structured to varying degrees by the indoor and outdoor environment, the curriculum, the adult:child ratio, the resources available, the rules, and the values, beliefs and practices of the adults.

The overarching pedagogical orientation uses the recursive cycle of planning the play/learning environment, interacting with children in a range of activities, observing, reflecting, evaluating and returning to further planning. The aim is to ensure a flow of information about children's play and learning from two pedagogical zones – adult- and child-initiated activities, both of which have contrasting but complementary forms of adult and child involvement, co-constructive engagement, and pedagogical strategies. In the child-initiated zone, freely chosen play activities are closest to 'pure play', because they will reflect the qualities and characteristics of play outlined above. The players will exercise choice, control and imagination, with little direct intervention from adults, and no pressure for products or outcomes. Children are free to choose an adult as co-player, refer to an adult for help, and set their own

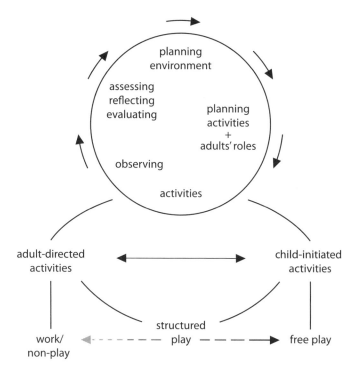

Figure 1.1 A model of integrated pedagogical approaches

goals or outcomes. They may choose structured play activities, such as playing a game with rules, or more 'work-like' activities, such as reading a story, carrying out an investigation, writing or doing a numeracy programme on the computer. All of these choices may have *elements* of playfulness, and should be seen along a continuum of activities in order to avoid the work/play dichotomy.

In the structured play zone, adult-directed activities may engage children in playful ways with curriculum content: there may be some elements of imagination, but with limited choice and control for children. For example, a practitioner may ask children to act out a story with puppets, or solve mathematical problems in the context of imaginary situations. Adult-directed activities can be a precursor to play, for example taking children on a trip, introducing new resources, or demonstrating technical skills. Practitioners can respond to their observations of child-initiated play by providing enrichment activities, making props for play, or extending challenge. Adult-directed activities are defined as 'work' when they are tightly controlled, with focused instructional strategies, no choice or flexibility for the children, and defined outcomes.

This integrated pedagogical model encompasses flexibility within a progressive cycle. Practitioners can move across zones in order to respond to children's interests and activities, and to make connections between curriculum goals and the children's own goals. Adults can be inspired by the play that they observe, and use feedback to inform further planning and provision. Equally, they can inspire play by connecting children with new skills, knowledge and ideas. Accordingly, the concept of 'balance' between adult-led and child-initiated activities depends on the child and the context. The balance of activities may change on a day-to-day basis, and will certainly change over time as children's friendships, play skills and preferences develop. The practical implications of this model are explored in the following vignettes. Each vignette includes reflective questions regarding pedagogical choices and actions.

Foundation Stage role play

This vignette describes integrated pedagogical approaches in an English Foundation Stage setting (age three to five years). The topic was 'People who help us', and the children visited a police station, a fire station, a health clinic and a veterinary surgery, with follow-up visits by people in these professions. The visits were recorded by the children using still and video digital cameras, which they loaded onto the computer.

Case study

Some pictures were printed out to show the everyday practices – a police officer completing a form, a nurse giving an injection, a vet writing a prescription. The teacher used these images in directed group time to stimulate discussion about what the children had learnt, what else they wanted to know, and how they might find out more information. With the teaching assistant, the children made props and resources from junk materials, including beds for sick pets, walkie talkies, and a large cardboard fire engine. In the role play area, they had dressing-up clothes and various props from their visits.

As the children developed their knowledge, they began to integrate different roles: a fire officer ringing the vet to come with a stretcher for a rescued cat; a police officer ringing for an ambulance: 'quick, quick, there's blood all over'. The props were used in imaginative ways: the fluorescent cuffs given by the police community liaison officer became handcuffs for the criminals, 'laser beamers' for stunning criminals, walkie-talkies, bandages and signifiers for the play leaders: 'who has the yellow band can be the chief'. The children took the props outdoors, where the wheeled toys afforded further imaginative potential, and they raced between emergencies, variously loading animals, patients and criminals into the trailers.

As a result of non-participant observations, the team noted the following details about children's choices and patterns. Jamie, Simeon, Khalid and Liam (all among the oldest children in the setting) engaged in a lot of 'adventure play' which involved some rough and tumble and much running and chasing around the themes of rescuing, capturing, kidnapping, killing and wrestling. Their play developed rhythms and patterns that were repeated and extended, and they rarely sought adult involvement except when they wanted to make new props for their play. Will (one of the youngest children in the setting) was keen to join in the boys' play, but was usually rejected because he was 'too little' or used the wrong strategies, such as pushing his way onto a bike or snatching props. Max sometimes hovered at the edges of the play, but was never invited to join, and did not attempt to gain entry. Instead, he played alone or with younger boys and girls, consistently choosing a caring role, typically focused on being the vet, nurse or doctor, looking after dolls or peers as patients. When girls were observed in the role-play area, they were often chatting to each other, writing or making food. They did not engage in the more boisterous play of the boys.

Reflection points 〰

Should an adult help Max and Will to join in the role play? If so, what strategies might be appropriate?

Should adults always respect children's choices? Or should they encourage children to take on different roles in play? How free are the children to make their own choices, when some children always dominate an area?

In free choice time, what are the patterns of participation for individuals or groups of children? To what extent are those patterns influenced by children's identities, preferences for play mates and play skills?

In what ways are children experiencing the provision? And how does this influence their learning?

What does balance look like for different children? And should adults be directive about ensuring that children experience all areas of provision?

Technological play in a reception/year 1 class

This vignette focuses on the pedagogical strategies that are used by adults and children, and the importance of observation in informing pedagogical decision-making.

Case study 📁

The children in this class use a range of information and communication technologies in adult-led and child-initiated activities. Many are very competent in using computer programs, programmable toys such as Roamers and Beebots, voice recorders, video recorders and digital cameras. Some of the older children can load videos and photos onto the computer, and do their own animations. Karl's family have moved from Poland, and he has recently joined the class, with no previous experience of using a computer. The children are working in pairs in the school's computer suite, using a paint and draw programme. Karl picks up the mouse and points it at the screen, clicking with his finger. When nothing happens, he shakes it and becomes frustrated. The adult realises that he is trying to use the mouse as if it is a television remote control. She shows Karl how to use the mouse correctly, using direct instruction and modelling. She covers his hand with hers, and helps him to feel the click of the mouse, then directs his attention to what happens on the screen. Karl fills the screen with black circles, laughing and jumping up and down with excitement.

Later that week, Karl is sitting alongside two children, observing them intently. They let him have a turn, reminding him how to use the mouse: 'point and click, Karl, point and click', and using similar strategies to the adults – covering his hand and directing his attention to what he does with the mouse, and what happens on the screen: 'See there, Karl, you did that'. Karl drags some shapes around the screen in an exploratory but random way. Later, Ruth says, 'Do you want us to teach you click and drag next time, Karl?'

Reflection points 〰️

What strategies do children use when they are teaching each other in play or playful activities?

What strategies can the adults use to support Karl's computer skills, and in what ways could adult-directed and child-initiated activities help?

Conclusion

This chapter has illustrated how policy documents might be interpreted as privileging a cultural transmission/directive approach, especially when these are aligned with assessment practices that are used to monitor children's outcomes and practitioners' effectiveness (Wood, 2009). In contrast, an emergent/responsive approach aligns more closely to contemporary metaphors of play and learning as participation and knowledge creation. In order to address some of the tensions outlined in this chapter, practitioners need to articulate the ways in which they interpret policy frameworks according to their own contexts and communities, and to their own knowledge of play, learning and pedagogy. This is a complex endeavour, which is often underestimated by those who expect play to align with a narrow outcome-focused agenda. However, it is an endeavour worth pursuing, particularly as the centralised 'command and control' model of educational policy-making is losing its power and credibility. Recent policy developments in England are placing more emphasis on developing flexible pedagogies from the Foundation Stage into Key Stages 1 and 2 (DCSF, 2009), with opportunities for children to plan some of their own activities, and to use and apply their knowledge and skills. The time has come to reverse the 'top-down' influence of the primary curriculum, and for early years practitioners to demonstrate the ways in which play and playfulness help to build strong foundations for children's learning and development.

Further reading

Edwards, S. and Brooker, E. (2010) (eds) *Rethinking Play*. Maidenhead: Open University Press.

Wood, E. and Attfield, J. (2005) *Play, Learning and the Early Childhood Curriculum*, 2nd edn. London: Paul Chapman Publishing.

References

Bennett, N., Wood, E. and Rogers, S. (1997) *Teaching through Play: Teachers' Thinking and Classroom Practice*. Buckingham: Open University Press.

Berthelsen, D., Brownlee, J. and Johannson, E. (2009) *Participatory Learning in the Early Years: Research and Pedagogy*. Abingdon: Routledge.

Department for Children, Schools and Families (DCSF) (2009) *The Independent Review of the Primary Curriculum*. Available at: http://publications.teachernet.gov.uk [Accessed 12 June 2009]

Department for Education and Skills (DfES) (2004) *The Effective Provision of Pre-school Education Project: Final Report. A Longitudinal Study Funded by the DfES 1997–2004*. Nottingham: DfES.

Department for Education and Skills (DfES) (2007) *Practice Guidance for the Early Years Foundation Stage*. Nottingham: DfES.

Edwards, S. and Brooker, E. (2010) (eds) *Rethinking Play*. Maidenhead: Open University Press.

Fromberg, D. and Bergen, D. (2006) *Play from Birth to Twelve – Contexts, Perspectives and Meanings*. New York: Routledge.

Genishi, C. and Goodwin, A.L. (2008) *Diversities in Early Childhood Education – Rethinking and Doing*. New York: Routledge.

James, M. and Pollard, A. (2008) *Learning and Teaching in Primary Schools: Insights from TLRP. The Primary Review: Research Survey 2/4*. Available at: www.primaryreview.org.uk [Accessed April 2009]

Kuschner, D. (2009) *From Children to Red Hatters®, Diverse Images and Issues of Play: Play and Culture Studies, Vol. 8*. Lanham, MD: University Press of America.

Plowman, L. and Stephen, C. (2007) 'Guided interaction in pre-school settings', *Journal of Computer Assisted Learning* 23(1): 14–21.

Pramling-Samuelson, I. and Fleer, M. (2009) *Play and Learning in Early Childhood Settings – International*

Perspectives. Milton Keynes: Springer.

Rogers, S. and Evans, J. (2008) *Inside Role Play in Early Childhood Education: Researching Young Children's Perspectives*. London: Routledge.

Sfard, A. (1998) 'On two metaphors for learning and the dangers of just choosing one', *Educational Researcher* 27(2): 4–13.

Sfard, A. and Prusak, A. (2005) 'Telling identities: in search of an analytic tool for investigating learning as a culturally shaped activity', *Educational Researcher* 43(4): 14–22.

Wood, E. (2009) 'Conceptualising a pedagogy of play: international perspectives from theory, policy and practice', in D. Kuschner (ed.) *From Children to Red Hatters®, Diverse Images and Issues of Play: Play and Culture Studies, Vol. 8*. pp. 166–89. Lanham, MD: University Press of America.

Wood, E. (2010) 'Reconceptualising the play–pedagogy relationship: from control to complexity', in S. Edwards and E. Brooker (eds) *Rethinking Play*. Maidenhead: Open University Press.

Wood, E. and Attfield, J. (2005) *Play, Learning and the Early Childhood Curriculum*, 2nd edn. London: Paul Chapman Publishing.

Wood, E. and Cook, J. (2009) 'Gendered discourses and practices in role play activities: a case study of young children in the English Foundation Stage', *Educational and Child Psychology* 26(2): 19–30.

2

Learning to Play in a Cultural Context

Liz Brooker

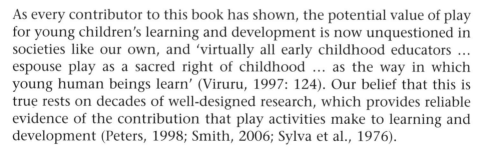

The aims of this chapter are to:

- explore the complex issues arising from parents' and practitioners' beliefs about 'learning through play'
- review research on play in global cultural contexts
- consider cultural explanations of the relationship between play and learning
- describe how effective communication with parents can construct understanding, and ultimately partnership, in supporting children's learning.

As every contributor to this book has shown, the potential value of play for young children's learning and development is now unquestioned in societies like our own, and 'virtually all early childhood educators … espouse play as a sacred right of childhood … as the way in which young human beings learn' (Viruru, 1997: 124). Our belief that this is true rests on decades of well-designed research, which provides reliable evidence of the contribution that play activities make to learning and development (Peters, 1998; Smith, 2006; Sylva et al., 1976).

As Wood describes in Chapter 1, practitioners continue to report that their efforts to provide playful learning opportunities are constrained by two powerful 'outside influences': the top-down pressure of the primary school curriculum, which continues to infiltrate into early years practice; and the continuing pressures from parents who, for a variety of reasons, are unconvinced that playful activities are as effective as didactic ones in supporting children's acquisition of the knowledge and skills they need to succeed in later stages of schooling, and in life. The former pressure has prompted collective action by groups (such as TACTYC and Early Education) who have taken positive arguments about play to politicians and policy makers, and are helping to shape the direction of early years policy. This debate is taking place both publicly, and on the centre stage of policy making. Whilst play is validated in the Early Years Foundation Stage for children from birth to five (DfES, 2008), providing good quality play experiences remains a challenge, especially in reception classes (ages 4–5) (Rogers and Evans, 2008). The latter pressures from parents are harder to resist, however, for at least two reasons. Firstly, they are experienced on a daily basis and by individuals: in numerous face-to-face relationships, in hundreds of settings and with thousands of parents. Secondly, those pressures are reinforced both by practitioners' own uncertainties, and by their professional conviction that they should respect, rather than reject, the views of the families who are their partners in caring for children. This is particularly the case when parents belong to immigrant or ethnic minority groups and have little previous experience of UK schooling.

This chapter aims to unravel these dilemmas by examining research about play in the lives of children growing up in different cultural contexts, and how practitioners can use this knowledge to promote children's playful learning in classrooms. The first section summarises research evidence about the similarities and differences in the ways that children play within their 'home cultures', and the ways that their play is shaped by parental beliefs and practices. It acknowledges the need to develop shared understandings about play and learning between practitioners and families, and concludes by exploring what we really mean when we refer to 'culture' or to the 'home cultures' of young children. The second section discusses the implications of cultural difference for pre-school practice, using one child's case study to explore three important aspects: the idea of partnership; the importance of play which reflects children's home interests; and the way that pedagogic practice can inform a genuine dialogue between educators and families.

The research evidence

Do all children play?

One myth that has circulated among early childhood educators in English-speaking societies is that children brought up in developing societies – including those who may be the parents of children in our own classrooms – don't play, or 'don't know how to play', and that for this reason these parents now discourage play for their own young children. Fortunately, cross-cultural studies have provided clear evidence to the contrary, along with explanations for the differences in children's play experiences within different cultures. Without doubt, as developmental psychologists have surmised, play is a universal characteristic, not only of children but of all humans (Göncü and Gaskins, 2006), but the ways that children play vary according to economic, social and cultural contexts (Göncü et al., 2006: 156). In consequence, 'theories of children's play should be situated in children's context, taking into account unique dimensions of children's specific communities' (Göncü et al., 2006: 175).

It is argued here that educators need to recognise both the universal and the local aspects of children's play. The universal elements are the biological components: the capacities, aptitudes and inclinations which accompany maturation and which may appear at surprisingly similar times in children's development in diverse contexts. As Bornstein reports (2006: 105), the evidence that children engage in symbolic play at similar ages in different cultures 'strongly suggests a neuropsychological timetable and a biological basis'. Furthermore, earlier studies confirm that: 'children's social and pretend play appear to be biologically based, sustained as an evolutionary contribution to human psychological growth and development' (Slaughter and Dombrowski, 1989: 290, cited in Bornstein, 2006: 115). These perspectives align with the research on play and gender by Jarvis in Chapter 4. Children growing up in different contexts are not *so* different, then, and research shows that pretend play really is a universal characteristic of young children. But within this broad truth, differentials do exist, and it is these differences which shape the identities and behaviours of the children in early years settings.

Why do some children play differently?

> Play is learnt behaviour, acquired as children interact with older members of the society in which they live. (Dao, 1999: 67)

One of the most important contributions of cross-cultural studies has been to show the mechanisms through which cultural differences in young children's development arise, as a consequence of early caregiving in families and communities. Many of these studies (e.g. Göncü et al., 2000; Rogoff, 1990) offer detailed descriptions of the ways in which caregivers (often mothers) interact with their infants and toddlers and support their play, directing them towards objects or towards people, and towards individual or collective goals, or towards dependence or independence. As might be expected, such studies find that children in the most affluent societies (in the USA, in particular) are more likely to be 'taught' by their caregivers that everything in life is a game, from pulling clothes over their heads to popping food in their mouths, while children in poorer economies (Guatemala, India and Mexico) may be played with less frequently. Nevertheless, one study of three communities (Göncü et al., 2006) compared European American, African American and Turkish families, and found that all the adults encouraged play and believed it to be beneficial for children's development and as preparation for adult life, although only the American children owned toys.

Although adults everywhere appear to take a benign view of children's play, they may not all approve of all kinds of play. Both James (1998) and Fleer (1999) have pointed out that the highly imaginative play which is encouraged in Western pre-schools may be regarded as fanciful and inappropriate in societies where adults are concerned for children to rehearse real-life roles in their pretend games. As a result, 'types of play activities in Western cultures differ from those in non-Western cultures' (Fleer, 1999: 74) and children's pretence may involve imitating adult behaviours rather than transforming them imaginatively. It is not surprising then that early studies of socio-dramatic play (such as Smilansky, 1968) reported that children from working-class and non-European backgrounds lacked the skills that were demonstrated by their more middle-class and European peers. In my own study (Brooker, 2002), four-year-olds from Bangladeshi families, with no pre-school experience, adapted easily to the home corner in their reception class; both boys and girls would spend all day sitting contentedly around the kitchen table or sharing pretend cooking and childcare. But subsequent efforts by the staff to engage them in imaginative, rather than imitative play, prompted a rapid exit from the role-play area, as the children resolutely refused to join in play involving monsters, witches or wild furry animals.

A failure to recognise the cultural origins of these differences in children's play repertoires may result in a deficit view of some children, and by implication of their families. But as Göncü et al. comment, 'cultural variations in children's play may be due to variations in adults' constraints imposed on children's activities rather than to differences in children's assumed inherent ability or motivation to play' (2006: 158). We have to remember that the 'constraints' imposed by adults are not mere cultural preferences but are inseparable from the social and economic circumstances of a community. In many societies in Asia and in sub-Saharan Africa, poverty is the largest contributor to children's way of life, to their place in the community, and to parental goals and values (Penn, 2005). A study of children in a Sudanese village (Katz, 2004) describes the daily lives of young children whose passionate engagement in play activity can only be observed *after* each of them has completed their morning chores of taking animals to pasture, collecting wood, running errands and so on. Once free from these tasks, the children retrieve their carefully stored collections of home-made props – dolls made of straw and fabric scraps, toy tractors fashioned from old tin cans – and resume the detailed pursuit of small-world scenarios involving housekeeping, storekeeping and farming. Their games are entirely rule-bound, and the rules are derived from the realities surrounding them. For the boys, they involve producing crops from dusty soil, repairing ancient farm equipment and storing and then bartering their harvests. For the girls, the tasks are caring for the old and young, finding food for the family and resolving relationships between adults and children.

The Sudanese children's play has clearly evolved as a preparation for life within their own culture, but as Katz shows, 'life' is changing even in such remote areas, as new agribusinesses and dam projects are introduced. In Western societies, the traditional housekeeping and family games played in home corners are also being changed, by children themselves, as they introduce new themes and artefacts, and construct new meanings from their own experiences of life outside the classroom. Through their play, children frequently reveal how life is lived in reconstituted families, or in homes where no one works. They demonstrate the coping strategies of hard-pressed adults, and the influence of new technologies and media cultures in their lives. It appears that young children are rather skilled in providing their own rehearsals for adult life. But is this all that play is good for?

What about learning?

It is when we move beyond the everyday realities of children's imitations of the adult world, which appear to occur in all cultures, that we may find ourselves disagreeing with parents about the purposes of play, and particularly of 'play in school' or 'educational play'. The value of 'preparation for life' is accepted in all cultures, as is the importance of preparation for school, which many parents would see as the main purpose of pre-school. Parents who want their children to be well prepared for school can see that when they play together in an environment filled with learning resources, they are being helped to acquire the knowledge and skills they will need for formal schooling – a familiarity with the uses of literacy and numeracy, a confidence in handling tools and technologies, and the ability to communicate successfully with English-speaking adults and children. The visible presence of numbers and letters, books and mathematical resources, computers and educational displays, are a reassurance for adults that children are 'learning' in their classrooms, and research has shown that this is a high priority for most ethnic minority groups (Gregory and Biarnès, 1994; Huss-Keeler, 1997). All parents take pride in their children's growing accomplishments, and bilingual parents are particularly alert to their child's acquisition of English. As my own year-long study showed (Brooker, 2002), after six months in reception, almost every parent could describe their child's progress in some detail, as did this mother:

> She learns some new words, reading ... she writes some times ABCD ... she teaches me, 'When you open the gate, say Scuse me' ... she tells me long, long words: 'Happy-mother's-day'. [Tuhura's mother, parent interview]

Often, however, parents made similar comments to Abdul's mother, who reported that 'if he brings something home then I know ... if I don't see something, a book, some writing, then I wonder if he is learning' [Abdul's mother, parent interview]. Once they are in school, even in an early years classroom, parents are likely to identify their children's progress by means of traditional evidence – principally, written letters and numbers – and such evidence is seen as a record of *work* rather than *play*. As Khiernssa's mother pleaded:

> She has to work harder, you have to stop her playing ... every day, play; 'what did you do?' – 'play', then after school – play; Monday, Tuesday, Wednesday – play ... she has to stop playing! [Khiernssa's mother, parent interview]

In other words, play may be seen as beneficial and natural for children in their free time, but from the start of reception class, it must be relegated to those times when the work has been satisfactorily completed. If this is not the case, parents may feel anxious and distressed, even if their limited English and lack of confidence make it difficult for them to discuss this with teachers. In Khiernssa's home, the children were only allowed to play each evening after they had read their school books, copied out spellings and memorised some verses in Bengali or Arabic: 'first study, then play' was her father's rule, and my suggestion that play might also contribute to his children's learning was regarded as foolish.

As many practitioners will recognise, this anxiety about the prevalence of play is not confined to ethnic minority parents (or even to parents). Research shows a persistent difficulty in accepting play-based learning among working-class families (e.g. in the UK, Newson and Newson, 1974; in the USA, Heath, 1983), and many teachers of children aged five to seven confine free play to a 'golden hour' when the week's work is finished. It is as if, despite the rhetoric, play and learning exist on the opposite sides of a deep ravine, rather than co-existing in children's participation in classroom activities. This work–play dichotomy continues to be seen in reception classes in primary schools, even though this age group falls within the remit of the Early Years Foundation Stage (DfES, 2008).

Most early years practitioners are familiar with the practical justifications for all kinds of play provision, and make genuine efforts to explain these to parents: the value of learning to discriminate shapes and sounds; the experience of volume and capacity; the sensory learning derived from malleable materials; the expressive value of imaginative play. All these are 'instrumental' reasons, since they attempt to demonstrate what play does for children in relation to imparting the knowledge and skills which form the foundations of subsequent school work. From this perspective, play becomes a means to achieving the learning objectives of the curriculum, as described by Wood in Chapter 1.

Reflective practitioners, however, will want to go further than this because they have a broader perspective on the value of play. They understand that play has been shown to be a leading source of development (Vygotsky, 1976), creating a zone of proximal development in which children's learning is assisted by companions and by the available cultural tools. They are aware of the importance of play in developing the 'higher mental processes' which enable children to move from concrete to abstract thought and to gain control of their own cognitive and metacognitive processes (Vygotsky, 1976), as evidenced by Whitebread in Chapter 10. As increasing numbers of early years educators undertake higher degrees and other forms of advanced training, there is a risk that their growing understanding of the profound importance of play in development will create an even deeper rift between their perspectives and those of parents. But how is this rather abstract perspective on play to be communicated to parents, for whom the sight of children scooping sand and filling jugs with water, dressing up as fire-fighters, or jointly constructing a giant junk model, is an affront to their core cultural beliefs about the value of education, and the role of 'hard work' in success?

Understanding culture

It is necessary to consider what is meant by the term 'culture', and the implications of the 'cultural backgrounds' that children have experienced before school. Michael Cole, drawing on the seminal work of the English sociologist Raymond Williams, explains that the word 'culture' means 'the tending of something, basically crops or animals' (Williams, 1976: 77) and that 'from earliest times, the notion of culture included a general theory for how to promote development', by providing 'optimal conditions for growth' (Cole, 1998: 15). This meaning is more commonly associated with terms like agriculture – the process of growing crops – but the same principles apply to the nurture of children. Human parents work hard, sometimes unconsciously, to create the 'optimal conditions for growth' for their children. After providing for their basic survival needs (the biological aspect of development), they turn to providing for their social, emotional, moral and intellectual needs (the cultural aspect). They provide instruction and stimulation, affection and discipline, and as children grow, they provide the tools for learning which will help them to achieve the parents' and the community's goals. These tools are infinitely various: they may include toys or workbooks; finger paints or pens and pencils; comics or prayer books. And along with the tools come the 'rules' for using them: exploring and discovering or listening and copying; inventing and improvising or memorising and repeating. The learning culture of each child's home provides children with more opportunities for learning than they will ever again encounter: by the time they enter the classroom, their minds are packed with knowledge (about how their particular world works) and skills (in speaking, mark-making, sorting and manipulating, ordering and problem-solving).

If all children are so knowledgeable when they move from their home culture to the school, why is it that some of them appear to experience difficulties in acquiring the knowledge and skills required in the school curriculum? The best explanation we have comes from understanding that the knowledge and skills acquired in the home are derived from that particular culture, which may bear little resemblance to the school culture, so that the 'cultural capital' children bring with them is invisible in the classroom (Brooker, 2002, 2003).

The Bangladeshi children described above were proficient in Sylheti and Bengali and some Arabic; they were skilled in childcare and assisted with cooking; they could recite the prayers and verses they were taught by their parents and the imam; and they played all kinds of games with their siblings and the neighbours' children, unobserved by adults. But when measured against the school's expectations and the 'baseline assessment' then in place, they appeared to know nothing, and achieved scores between zero and three on assessment items where their English classmates were scoring 11 and 12. They were even reluctant to engage in the play opportunities their kindly teachers provided for them, knowing full well that *this* was not what you came to school for. School, as they explained in interviews, was where you came to 'study', to 'sit still and listen'. This view, based on the cultural beliefs of their parents, could not have been more different from the perspectives of their teachers, who believed that children came to school to learn through active exploration, and principally through play. In the transition to school, such children are required to operate within an entirely alien environment, with different rules and tools.

The implications: partnership, play and pedagogy

The dilemma created by the conflicting cultural beliefs of homes and schools is fundamental and longstanding. The tension which exists, between educators' belief in the importance of play for children's development, and their desire to respect parents' wishes, is particularly evident at times of transition – home to pre-school, or pre-school to school – when all the adults involved are trying to ease the child's journey from a familiar to a new environment. In this section, we consider three intertwined aspects of this issue, which are exemplified in the case study of one Chinese girl's transition into nursery.

Case study: Yuk-Yue starts nursery

When two-year-old Yuk-Yue was starting nursery, her key worker Kerry knew that she needed to tune in both to the child's interests and wishes, and to those of her mother Joyce. Her discussions with Joyce revealed a strong expectation that Yuk-Yue would now be 'taught' things which would prepare her for school (Yuk-Yue had been taken away from another nursery where 'they didn't teach them anything'); and Kerry also learned that the children in this large family were brought up to be self-sufficient, and expected to contribute to the smooth running of the household. Kerry's observations of Yuk-Yue showed that she would spend all day in the home corner, 'cooking' with pots of sand and plastic food, without ever making eye contact with other children, or engaging with the nursery adults. While she appeared content, Kerry had concerns:

> I think because she does so much for herself, there's not quite as much interaction with her as you normally would. It's not like a child that needs to be changed, and comforted, where you're building that relationship all the time.

This reflection prompted her to plan a series of key-group activities based on Yuk-Yue's interests:

> I decided to do a week of cooking activity, to try and support that interest in the home corner, and it really worked, not just for her, it worked for other children's needs as well, and it created that bond with her ... and the week after that I extended it to malleable; she was quite skilled at those things, she uses a knife and fork to eat her food ...

(Continued)

(Continued)

In the process, Yuk-Yue became engaged for the first time with her peer group:

> For the cooking activity, and the malleable activity, they were sitting together, and they needed to pass things to one another, and that brought her in with the group and that tied her in with me as well.

Joyce was quite easily persuaded of the value of the nursery's approach when it was discussed with her, as she explained to me:

> Kerry is very professional teacher …

> Here because they have the policies, they have the procedure, they have the planning sheet and they have the policy to work together so either way I'm feeling security. I can say I see what you're doing, you have planning sheet, this is your target, I quite understand … And they organise activities a lot for that age, to encourage their imagination, because they have environment here, even cooking on the planning sheet.

Not long after this, Joyce proudly informed me that Yuk-Yue knew the names of all the children in her key group, and was able to point out their photos and pegs when she arrived at nursery. For Joyce, this was evidence of her daughter's cognitive development, while for Kerry it showed that the little girl had learned to make relationships and value the presence of other children. Her social and cognitive learning could now proceed hand in hand with her mother's support and approval.

Partners in learning

Since 2008, a statutory requirement has existed for teachers to work in partnership with the parents of young children (DCSF, 2008), which further reinforces practitioners' sense of their responsibilities towards parents. 'Partnership' of course is easier to recommend than to put into practice. The term was defined, by Pugh and De'Ath (1989: 33), as 'a working relationship that is characterized by a shared sense of purpose, mutual respect and the willingness to negotiate'. The 'shared sense of purpose' is not a problem since both parents and educators are committed to children's learning and well-being; but 'mutual respect and a willingness to negotiate' imply that both groups are prepared, not only to listen to the other's point of view, but to recognise that those with wholly different views on the way to achieve these goals may actually have reason on their side. As Pugh and De'Ath go on to say: 'This implies a sharing of information, responsibility, skills and decision making and accountability' (1989: 33). In the case of Yuk-Yue, the time taken by her key worker to explain the reasons for her approach, and the carefully planned strategies that this approach involved, were suffi-cient to assure her mother that Yuk-Yue's learning was safe in the hands of a skilled professional, whom she could trust.

The dilemma for many teachers is underpinned by the fact that they have succeeded in their own education by means of precisely the meth-ods that parents like Joyce are keen to see – by copying, memorising, repeating and regurgitating the knowledge their own teachers provided. As a result, they 'know' from their professional training that active and playful learning is effective, but they also 'know', through their own experience, that formal instruction, rote learning and even cramming for exams, has helped them to succeed. Perhaps if teachers reflected on the contradictions in their own personal, professional and cultural beliefs, they would find it easier to understand the perspectives of par-ents whose school experience – in China or the Caribbean, in Africa or Asia – has been entirely formal.

Providing proper play

Recent research into early years provision (The EPPE Project: Sylva et al., 2004) suggests that an approach which combines adult-led and child-led activities can produce the best outcomes for children; that 'effective' settings offer children both direct teaching, and oppor-tunities for 'potentially instructive' play activities; and that children's learning is supported by playing with peers as well as by extended conversations with adults. The risk in following this 'recipe' for effect-iveness, however, is that practitioners will offer children a watered-down curriculum in which short spells of activities which *look* like play, but are really adult-led, are interspersed with short bursts of explicitly adult-led instruction. The challenge for practitioners is to ensure that they provide play opportunities that enable children to continue to explore the paths they have constructed from their earliest learning in the home, at the same time as extending and challenging their thinking along new pathways.

Kerry did not attempt to 'distract' Yuk-Yue from her chosen activity of stirring sand in saucepans, although she was concerned by the child's isolation from the children and adults in the key group. Instead, she provided an activity which built on Yuk-Yue's interests (as Joyce acknowledged) but helped to create bonds between her and the other children. In free-play activities in subsequent weeks, Yuk-Yue's 'cooking' always involved offering food and drinks to others in the room, and her use of English became far more frequent and spontaneous. Rather than working in silence, she now made constant overtures to others: 'That your one', 'It sticky', 'Like it?', 'Want more?'.

We know that children learn well when their play enables them to act on their own ideas, and when they know that these ideas are valued and taken seriously. This was evident in Yuk-Yue's case, as was the fact that in developing her play she was also exploring and maintaining her own personal and cultural identity.

Practising pedagogy

Allowing children to make their own meanings through play does not of course mean abandoning a responsibility to teach, and this is where other findings from the EPPE project are relevant (Sylva et al., 2004). Observations of children's knowledge, skills and interests displayed in free play can enable practitioners to tailor their explicit teaching so that it finds a place in the Zones of Proximal Development (ZPD) of different individuals or groups. 'Teaching' may include direct instruction, but in Vygotsky's terms, it also includes all the ways in which knowledge and skills are acquired through the support of others: this includes playing 'games with rules' (an effective route to literacy and numeracy knowledge: Peters, 1998), and scaffolding learning by helping children to focus on the directions and destinations that are slightly in advance of their current thinking, through asking questions or directing their attention to what is salient (Wood, 1998). Jordan (2004) adds co-constructing knowledge to this repertoire, describing adults' endeavours to think *with* children towards new meanings, rather than lead them into discovering what is in the adult's mind. This approach has been further exemplified by Georgeson (2008) and Payler (2008) in their work with English three- and four-year-olds. Both these authors demonstrated, through close observation in settings which were more focused on either 'academic' or social and emotional outcomes, that children who were offered a more explicitly academic environment had fewer opportunities to develop their own meanings and construct knowledge independently. As Georgeson concludes (2008: 109), 'settings that prioritised care and socialisation fostered an interactive micro-climate which was more favourable to co-construction than those which emphasised educational outcomes'. By contrast, Payler (2008: 120) observed that a strong focus on educational outcomes permitted the 'negative positioning' of some children, with adverse consequences for their identities as learners. Respect for children's individual perspectives and meaning-making, and concern for the nature of adult–child relationships, are shown to promote the 'positive learning dispositions' which have been described as the most important outcome of early education (Ball, 1994).

If teaching is grounded in children's current levels of understanding, and targeted to enable them to construct new meanings in advance of their existing competence, it can be far more effective in producing the outcomes that parents wish to see than a poor-quality play experience. Role-play areas designed to promote basic skills can rapidly deteriorate into unconvincing and time-wasting play in which the shopkeeper starts to pay the customers, the waitress fails to write down the order, and the doctor climbs into bed with the patient. Do we really know how much children learn from such activities, repeated over a period of weeks? Do we always have the time, and skills, to challenge and extend their thinking as they play? Above all, does such 'play' really meet our definitions of an activity that is entered into voluntarily by children, if it is simply part of a carousel of directed learning experiences?

High-quality instruction, like high-quality play, needs to be fine-tuned to children's interests and capabilities, which will be identified through observing, listening and talking with children. Both observing and listening are difficult when educators are trying to monitor a range of 'potentially instructive' play activities at the same time as working thoughtfully on a problem alongside an individual or small group. If practitioners trust children to make their own meanings, individually and collectively, through their freely chosen play activities, then they should find time to observe and understand what their play reveals, and to act on this knowledge in planning meaningful instructional activities. Kerry's observations of Yuk-Yue, as she settled in to nursery, showed her where a simple intervention – in the form of a daily, ten-minute key-group activity for three or four children – could transform Yuk-Yue's satisfying but limited play into an experience which could bridge the cultures of her home and school environments, and integrate her into the new cultural identity the nursery offered – as a member of a boisterous and entertaining peer group (rather than simply the youngest of a line of capable older siblings!).

Conclusion: bridging cultures through dialogue

One of the chief obstacles to developing shared understandings with parents, and particularly with ethnic minority or bilingual parents, has been poor communication. Epstein (2002: 527), whose work on home–school links and partnerships has produced rich knowledge over many years, cites communication between home and school as a key to enabling parents to continue to be involved in their children's learning after the children have started school. But even if parents and teachers are 'talking to each other' (and many are not able to do so), contentious topics such as the pedagogy of play may cause the communication between them to break down. Studies in the UK show that ethnic minority parents like and trust teachers, and are grateful for the genuine warmth, interest and affection that is shown towards their children, which they often contrast with the more distant or negligent professional stance taken in their home countries. Yet, on the subject of play, their unwillingness to reject their own cultural knowledge in favour of the 'professional' knowledge offered by teachers, can lead to mistrust and misunderstandings (Brooker, 2003; Gregory and Biarnès, 1994). Creating a dialogue, as Kerry has with Joyce, is not difficult while children are in pre-school; sustaining the dialogue as children move into school, and then into Key Stage 1, is more of a challenge. However, this challenge needs to be taken on, as current policies recommend the extension of flexible pedagogical approaches into Key Stage 1, as noted by Wood in Chapter 1.

This chapter has presented research which shows how children are enculturated, within different cultural contexts, into the different forms and purposes of play. It has argued that it is important to be aware of the variation in children's play repertoires and behaviours which arise from their early family experiences, and also of the reasons why parents may find it hard to share practitioners' understandings of the value of play for children's development. The challenge this presents is useful, however, if it forces us to look critically at the quality of play, and the quality of other forms of teaching and learning that are provided in our classrooms. Reflection of this kind may lead us to offer children greater freedom in developing their play repertoires, at the same time as demanding greater clarity and explicitness of ourselves as teachers.

Persuading parents of the developmental and educational value of play will not be accomplished all at once. But the chapter concludes by suggesting that we prioritise the kinds of dialogue which can support practitioners and parents in working together on their common purpose of promoting children's well-being and their learning.

Further reading

Brooker, L. (2003) 'Learning how to learn: parental ethnotheories and children's preparation for school', *International Journal of Early Years Education* 11(2): 117–28.

Brooker, L. (2006) 'From home to the home corner: observing children's identity-maintenance in early childhood settings', *Children and Society* 20(2): 116–27.

Göncü, A., Jain, J. and Tuermer, U. (2006) 'Children's play as cultural interpretation', in A. Göncü and S. Gaskins (eds) *Play and Development: Evolutionary, Sociocultural and Functional Perspectives*. Mahwah, NJ: Lawrence Erlbaum Associates. pp. 155–78.

References

Ball, C. (1994) *The Start Right Report*. London: Royal Society of Arts.

Bornstein, M. (2006) 'On the significance of social relationships in the development of children's earliest symbolic play: an ecological perspective', in A. Göncü and S. Gaskins (eds) *Play and Development: Evolutionary, Sociocultural and Functional Perspectives*. Mahwah, NJ: Lawrence Erlbaum Associates. pp. 101–29.

Brooker, L. (2002) *Starting School: Young Children Learning Cultures*. Buckingham: Open University Press.

Brooker, L. (2003) 'Learning how to learn: parental ethnotheories and children's preparation for school', *International Journal of Early Years Education* 11(2): 117–28.

Cole, M. (1998) 'Culture in development', in M. Woodhead, D. Faulkner and K. Littleton (eds) *Cultural Worlds of Early Childhood*. London: Routledge/Open University Press. pp. 11–33.

Dao, E. (ed.) (1999) *Child's Play: Revisiting Play in Early Childhood Settings*. Sydney: Maclennan and Petty.

Department for Children, Schools and Families (DCSF) (2008) *Statutory Framework for the Early Years Foundation Stage*. Nottingham: DCSF Publications.

Department for Education and Skills (DfES) (2008) *The Early Years Foundation Stage*. Nottingham: DfES.

Epstein, J. (2002) 'School, family and community partnerships', in D. Levinson, P. Cookson and A. Sadovnik (eds) *Education and Sociology*. London: Taylor & Francis.

Fleer, M. (1999) 'Universal fantasy: the domination of Western theories of play', in E. Dao (ed.) *Child's Play: Revisiting Play in Early Childhood Settings*. Sydney: Maclennan and Petty. pp. 67–80.

Georgeson, J. (2008) 'Co-constructing meaning: differences in the interactional microclimate', in T. Papatheodourou and J. Moyles (eds) *Learning Together in the Early Years: Exploring Relational Pedagogy*. London: Routledge. pp. 109–19.

Göncü, A, and Gaskins, S. (eds) (2006) *Play and Development: Evolutionary, Sociocultural and Functional Perspectives*. Mahwah, NJ: Lawrence Erlbaum Associates.

Göncü, A., Jain, J. and Tuermer, U. (2006) 'Children's play as cultural interpretation', in A. Göncü and S. Gaskins (eds) *Play and Development: Evolutionary, Sociocultural and Functional Perspectives*. Mahwah, NJ: Lawrence Erlbaum Associates. pp. 155–78.

Göncü, A., Mistry, J. and Mosier, C. (2000) 'Cultural variations in the play of toddlers', *International Journal of Behavioural Development* 24(3): 321–9.

Gregory, E. and Biarnès, J. (1994) 'Tony and Jean-Francois: looking for sense in the strangeness of school', in H. Dombey and M. Meek (eds) *First Steps Together*. Stoke on Trent: Trentham Books. pp. 17–29.

Heath, S.B. (1983) *Ways With Words: Language, Life and Work in Communities and Classrooms*. Cambridge: Cambridge University Press.

Huss-Keeler, R. (1997) 'Teacher perceptions of ethnic and linguistic minority parental involvement and its relationships to children's language and literacy learning: a case study', *Teaching and Teacher Education* 13(2): 171–82.

James, A. (1998) 'Play in childhood: an anthropological perspective', *Child Psychological and Psychiatric Review* 3(3): 104–9.

Jordan, B. (2004) 'Scaffolding learning and co-constructing understanding', in A. Anning, J. Cullen and M. Fleer (eds) *Education: Society and Culture*. Maidenhead: Open University Press. pp. 69–79.

Katz, C. (2004) *Growing Up Global: Economic Restructuring and Children's Everyday Lives*. Minneapolis, MN: University of Minnesota Press.

Newson, E. and Newson, J. (1974) 'Cultural aspects of child-rearing in the English-speaking world', in M. Richards (ed.) *The Integration of a Child into a Social World*. London: Cambridge University Press. pp. 53–82.

Payler, J. (2008) 'Co-constructing meaning: ways of supporting learning', in T. Papatheodourou and J. Moyles (eds) *Learning Together in the Early Years: Exploring Relational Pedagogy*. London: Routledge. pp. 120–38.

Penn, H. (2005) *Unequal Childhoods: Young Children's Lives in Poor Countries*. London: Routledge.

Peters, S. (1998) 'Playing games and learning mathematics: the results of two intervention studies', *IJEYE International Journal of Early Years Education* 6(1): 49–58.

Pugh, G. and De'Ath, E. (1989) *Working Towards Partnership in the Early Years*. London: National Children's Bureau.

Rogers, S. and Evans, J. (2008) *Inside Role Play in Early Childhood Education: Researching Young Children's Perspectives*. Abingdon: Routledge.

Rogoff, B. (1990) *Apprenticeship in Thinking: Cognitive Development in Social Context*. Oxford: Oxford University Press.

Smilansky, S. (1968) *The Effects of Sociodramatic Play on Disadvantaged Preschool Children*. New York: Wiley.

Smith, P. (2006) 'Evolutionary foundations and functions of play: an overview', in A. Göncü and S. Gaskins (eds) *Play and Development: Evolutionary, Sociocultural and Functional Perspectives*. Mahwah, NJ: Lawrence Erlbaum Associates. pp. 21–49.

Sylva, K., Bruner, J. and Genova, P. (1976) 'The role of play in the problem-solving of children 3–5 years old', in J. Bruner, A. Jolly and K. Sylva (eds) *Play: Its Role in Development and Evolution*. Harmondsworth: Penguin. pp. 244–57.

Sylva, K., Melhuish, E., Sammons, P., Siraj-Blatchford, I. and Taggart, B. (2004) *Final Report: Effective Provision of Preschool Education (EPPE) Project*. London: Institute of Education.

Viruru, R. (1997) 'Privileging child-centred, play-based instruction', in G. Cannella (ed.) *Deconstructing Early Childhood Education*. New York: Peter Lang. pp. 117–36.

Vygotsky, L. (1976) 'Play and its role in the mental development of the child', in J. Bruner, A. Jolly and K. Sylva (eds) *Play: Its Role in Development and Evolution*. Harmondsworth: Penguin. pp. 537–54.

Williams, R. (1976) *Key Words*. London: Fontana.

Wood, D. (1998) *How Children Think and Learn*. Oxford: Blackwell.

3

Cooperative Play and Learning from Nursery to Year One

Pat Broadhead

The aims of this chapter are to:

- identify the links between play and learning in children's social and cooperative play across the 3–6 age range
- exemplify the development of a new area of play provision that has high impact on children's cooperative play and opportunities for learning: *the whatever you want it to be place*
- consider the pedagogical challenges and benefits of this new area.

The continuing research reported in this chapter began in the mid-1980s to investigate how children become sociable and cooperative through their play in early years educational settings. Studies have been undertaken in a range of settings with children aged 3–6 years. The research illustrates links between cooperative play with peers and high levels of intellectual challenge for children, acknowledging that where high levels of challenge exist, the potential for learning to occur may also be high (Broadhead, 1986, 1997, 2001, 2004, 2006, 2007, 2009; Broadhead and English, 2005; English and Broadhead, 2004). Data analysis has developed and refined an observational tool, The Social Play Continuum (SPC) (Appendix 3.1) with four domains of play, each characterised by increasingly complex language and action. The SPC has been used in joint observations of play by the author (as an 'outside' researcher – from outside the early years setting and knowledgeable about research processes) and by practitioners (teachers and nursery nurses/teaching assistants as 'insiders' who know the children and the setting). Insiders and outsiders bring their perspectives together in post-observation reflections, to consider how children learn through cooperative play and how adults might create and sustain effective pedagogies in support of playful learning opportunities.

The research approach was informed by Eikeland (2006: 45) who suggests:

> establishing communities of enquiry while being more relaxed – less 'ideological' – about specific ways of organising and doing things and let open enquiry and collaborative experimentation reveal what works and what doesn't.

This perspective informed my own work as I considered the extent to which practitioner reflections had informed the development of the research alongside my own analysis of the SPC and observational notes. Our discussions, always undertaken after joint observations using the SPC, impacted on the theoretical development and direction of the research. From these discussions emerged pedagogical insights into how and what children learn as they playfully engage with peers in their own learning communities.

The next section describes the research and details the development of the *whatever you want it to be place* as a potentially new area of provision in early years settings. The research is described fully in Broadhead (2004), and is summarised here as a lead into the final section where the *whatever you want it to be place* is illustrated through three vignettes from a nursery (ages 3–4), a reception class (ages 4–5) and a year 1 class (ages 5–6). The vignettes illustrate pedagogical challenges for educators in making this provision and in developing their understanding of the complexity and potential of open-ended play in relation to children's learning across the Foundation Stage and Key Stage 1.

The research

My research is concerned with developing knowledge around sociability and cooperation in ways that advance theory and inform practice. Research evidence shows that there is an increase in group play as children become older and as they develop their expertise as players (Blurton-Jones, 1972; Eifermann, 1971). In the right conditions, children can develop an expanding repertoire of behaviours to sustain their sociability (Verba, 1994), to resolve conflicts (Butovskaya et al., 2000) and to build friendships (Rubin, 1980; Verbeek et al., 2000). The SPC developed from a simple set of play descriptors (Charlesworth and Hartup, 1967) to study playful interactions with peers as they played together with materials that are typically available in early years settings – sand, water, large and small construction, role play and small world.

The relationship between play and learning in educational settings has always been elusive (Pramling-Samuelsson and Asplund-Carlsson, 2008). However, studies show that there is real potential for play and playful activity to support the maturation of knowledge, skills and understanding in young children (Moyles and Adams, 2001) and that children create knowledge when they play (Dau, 1999; Levin, 1996). In my own research, I came to acknowledge how playful learning might be 'illuminated' through the study of peer interactions in playful contexts, and that these interactions might make the playful potential of the children's engagements more evident and open for analysis and study.

Using the SPC

The SPC has developed as a tool for research and for professional development. Observations are undertaken with practitioners, with both the 'insider' and 'outsider' observers using the SPC and supplementing it with their own notes to record further details of play and language. At an early stage of development, the SPC was organised into four domains: the Associative Domain, the Social Domain, the Highly Social Domain and the Cooperative Domain (Broadhead, 1997). These domains have remained as the SPC has developed but the behaviours and language use of the SPC (Side 1) and the characteristics (Side 2) have been refined through subsequent iterations (Broadhead, 2004, forthcoming) as research has continued and as we have learned more about the differences between being sociable and being cooperative in play as manifest in children's behaviours and interactions. The Cooperative Domain on the SPC is characterised by reciprocal action and reciprocal language. It was hypothesised that instances of reciprocity, if they could be understood within the broader context of the whole play activity, might reveal the links with learning that are embedded in playful activity (Sutton-Smith, 1997) but somehow cannot be captured and articulated by practitioners other than at general levels. The research also aimed to identify which areas of provision and play activities might be most/least likely to stimulate play in the Cooperative Domain where the intellectual challenge is strongest.

Observations focus only on play with peers and last as long as the play. Using Side 1 (of the SPC), the observer records the instances of play numerically (1, 2, etc.) against the categories. Post-observation, each observer uses the characteristics of Side 2 to make a judgement about the overall play domain. This is undertaken individually prior to post-observation discussions and becomes a means of validating the SPC as a tool – whether the observers select the same domain – and a basis for related discussion of what has been observed/decided. Across the research overall, the corroboration rate of joint observations in the independent selection of the dominant play domain has been above 90%, which suggests that the SPC does have validity in capturing the dominant play domain of interacting peers from both 'insider' and 'outsider' perspectives.

The research is embedded in socio-constructivist frames of reference with an alignment between the SPC, Zones of Proximal Development (ZPD) and the impact on play and development of 'expert others' (Vygotsky, 1976, 1978, 1986). Building on Vygotsky's work, Saxe (1989) emphasised the importance of conventions or artefacts in mediating children's learning with peers within particular contexts whereby prior understandings are shared through collaboration. We might also think of these 'artefacts' as the resources provided for children through the pedagogies of the early years setting. As the SPC has developed, it has exemplified children's use of objects and of language and action/inter-action with peers as a progression along the four domains. Objects can be bargaining tools for social interaction (Hay and Ross, 1982) and, for young children, they may also link the important worlds of home and home experiences, which provides the raw material for much of children's play (Pramling-Samuelsson and Asplund-Carlsson, 2008). Objects are most transformative when they are sufficiently open and flexible in connecting with the ideas, interests and experiences that come to mind for children as they play (Nutbrown, 1994).

The behaviours, language and characteristics of the Cooperative Domain reveal clear links with intellectually challenging play so that when play is located within the Cooperative Domain, observers also see the deep learning potential of the play as they watch the children create and solve problems together and engage in the more complex uses of resources and language that characterise this domain. The post-observation reflections have allowed a focus on pedagogical decision-making in relation to the active promotion of increased opportunities for play in the Cooperative Domain. A recent study (Broadhead, forthcoming) shows that the capacity for play in the Cooperative Domain is not necessarily related to age but is closely aligned to the children's access to resources and whether these resources can connect meaningfully with the play themes that children develop as they play. This study showed higher levels of cooperative play in nursery children (ages 3–4+) than in the older reception children (ages 4–5+), even though these reception children had experienced the same nursery provision in the previous year. Children were losing opportunities for deep learning through cooperative play with familiar peers because of lack of access to appropriate resources.

In one study (Broadhead, 2004), we noted that sand play stimulated the most play in the Cooperative Domain of the SPC. The five teacher-researchers and I agreed at a project meeting that this was because play was open-ended, that is children could engage with whatever themes were occupying them as they played with tools and objects in the sand. We translated this initial finding into an extension of the research project and each teacher-researcher introduced 'an open-ended play area' (as we termed it) into their classrooms with wooden clothes horses, large pieces of fabric, cardboard boxes and other 'open-ended items'. It took us some time to decide upon these items because ideologically the concept of an 'open-ended role-play area' was quite new to us. Our aim in exploring this new concept together was to create a place that was sufficiently flexible to allow children to determine their play themes together, to establish and play out their evolving goals and to use the resources in shaping their own activities through social interaction.

Having established the areas, to their own liking and in all cases in discussions with the children, we jointly undertook a further 12 observations across their five reception classrooms using the SPC. All 12 observations were in the Cooperative Domain and we were seeing some previously unobserved interactions around the extended and dramatic development of play scenarios. This surprised us; we had not anticipated that these resources and objects would have such evident potential to challenge and engage the children in this way and with such consistency. The teachers reported that the children loved to play in the area and often would draw up chairs in order to sit and watch the ongoing play even when they were not involved.

In one of the classes, a four-year-old girl named the area the *whatever you want it to be place* because, as she told her teacher, 'it can be whatever you want'. And this of course is the essence of play – it belongs to the player (Sutton-Smith, 1997); it is improvisation without a script (Sawyer, 1997). However, there are tensions for the educator. On the one hand, it would seem that play is not a 'site' or an 'activity' that should be harnessed for teaching purposes or for adult goals. Yet play can still have and should have a place in a learning environment and pedagogy can and should be a feature of its provision (Pramling-Samuelsson and Asplund-Carlsson, 2008; Siraj-Blatchford et al., 2002; Wood, 2004, 2009, 2010).

These findings relating to the *whatever you want it to be place* have formed the basis of subsequent joint research undertaken with practitioners across the 3–6 age range as they have established this provision in their settings. The following vignettes illustrate the potential for open-ended play to create learning opportunities for young children whilst also respecting their right to control and determine the direction and content of their play. We also gain insights into some of the pedagogical challenges as practitioners combine structure and flexibility in their provision, as recommended by Wood in Chapter 1.

Implications for pedagogy: three vignettes

Each vignette synthesises a joint observation of play in the *whatever you want it to be place*. This is followed by discussion points and ideas for practitioner research. The aim is to support educators in setting up a *whatever you want it to be place* in a nursery, reception or year 1 classroom and to be alert to some of the challenges and benefits that the teacher-researchers have gained for understanding children as learners and for themselves as pedagogues.

Case study: Nursery children – the January Christmas

This observation was in the Cooperative Domain. The nursery nurse (in charge of this nursery) and I had worked together over several months making joint observations using the SPC, undertaking post-observation reflections to consider the developments to practice that emerged. In the course of this work, Denise (pseudonym) had established the *whatever you want it to be place* on a carpet area using, in the first instance, two large cardboard boxes in which new school photocopiers had been delivered, pieces of fabric of different shapes, types and sizes, writing materials (clipboards, pencils, etc.) cardboard tubes, long foam cylinders and other materials, some of which the children transferred into this area from other parts of the nursery, such as dressing-up clothes or 'domestic' artefacts from the home corner. This observation happened in January. A four-year-old boy playing in the area noticed a small Christmas tree that had not been put away. He fetched it into the area, set it on a small table and invited other children to his 'party'. Denise later remarked that her initial reaction had been to take the tree away and store it with the other Christmas materials. However, she decided against this direct intervention because she had developed new understandings about how educators might observe and support children's interests. She allowed the play to unfold and, as the Christmas theme developed, she began to realise that these young children (aged just three or a young four) were perhaps experiencing their first full recollections of the 'Christmas experience' in their own homes. The memories seemed powerful and the play began to incorporate more children as they draped themselves with fabrics for a party and wrapped artefacts in paper or fabrics to place under the tree.

Denise asked the children if they wanted some more of the Christmas 'objects' that had been tidied away and they said 'yes'. She brought out baubles for decorating, tinsel and Christmas dressing-up clothes, and they also began finding boxes to wrap as presents. Some children began making Christmas cards. It became apparent from watching the children that they were both emotionally and intellectually engaging their recent memories of Christmas in and around their own homes; re-living and internalising some powerful events. The play went on for several days and gradually tapered as the children no longer selected the resources but moved on to other play themes in the *whatever you want it to be place*. The January Christmas was of no further interest to them.

This vignette illuminates Vygotsky's theories about how tools/artefacts/resources change us; they connect with our thought processes to refine our view of the world, how it functions and how we function within it. These resources had powerful emotional resonance for the children which Denise recognised. This recognition came from her past experiences of observing children's play, using the SPC, and from our joint discussions which were valuable for both of us in relation to making meaning from play. Denise saw the importance of allowing the tree to remain available and, by adding more resources, she extended the possibilities for the children to become cooperative players. They jointly engaged with intellectual challenge as they decided upon the directions of their play and used the resources to develop their play themes and to set and solve related problems. She also demonstrated to the children that she valued their ideas, and that she saw them as important in their day-to-day lives in the classroom. As Howard describes in Chapter 9, these positive messages are essential to children and adults valuing play.

Reflective task 〰

As you observe children's play, look out for the times when they transfer objects/resources (or tools) from one part of the room to another. Try and work out why they are doing this and how it adds to their play, either alone or with peers.

If you want to try out the *whatever you want it to be place*, talk to the children about what might be in the area. Denise took advantage of the delivery of the photocopier and the large boxes were also used for many purposes such as dens, a school and a hiding place from monsters. Children need access to places where they can create explanations and understandings of their lives that are logical and accessible for them (Paley, 1981), and are imbued with their own cultural meanings. In some ways, the space can mirror the opportunities of outdoor spaces for children in that it presents fewer constraints on play ideas. Tovey (2007: 23) discusses the tendency for the indoors to 'be more serious, where excitement can be seen as something to be dissipated and children urged to calm down'. Play in this indoor space may be very different from your usual practice, and it would be helpful to reflect with colleagues.

Case study: Reception children – the magical area

This observation was in the Cooperative Domain. The *whatever you want it to be place* was established on a large carpeted area. The staff in this large reception unit had worked together to establish the area, and pooled their ideas. As the area developed, they talked to the children about it being a place where they could follow their own play ideas. From one of these circle-time discussions, one child named it *The Magical Area*, which then 'stuck'. On this particular occasion, the children selected wooden blocks and planks; large, circular, plastic cushions; boxes large enough to sit in and fabrics. They also regularly brought materials from other parts of the classroom into the area as the nursery children above had done. In both classes, this transference of objects from one area of provision to another was permitted and enabled children to expand and develop their ideas. During one observation period, the children progressed through various domestic themes. Burglaries had prevailed for some time (a commonly observed theme) alongside the frequently observed cat, dog and baby play. Two children sat in their bed (a large box) 'putting DVDs into the DVD player at the side of the bed and discussing what they were watching' (achieved by pushing smaller bricks through slits in larger bricks to simulate the DVD entry). They also interconnected with the ongoing burglary theme by talking about how they could 'hear people moving around downstairs and should they fetch the police or get a gun'. From this play, two girls detached and began to make a large, flat construction using planks, boxes, bricks and the circular plastic cushions carefully located at intervals. They often worked individually but came together to discuss and plan. It was difficult to hear all they were saying but gradually the floor became covered with their design and one of them announced to the others that 'the gym is open' and 'you can come if you want to and be shown what to do'. Neither the class teacher nor I knew whether the girls who had designed the gym had visited a gym or seen one on television/DVDs but they had a clear idea of how different pieces of equipment were used to exercise different parts of the body. One girl stood on a circular cushion and swivelled from left to right and announced 'this is how you work your hips'.

Whilst there might be some concerns about over-emphasis of body image with young children, there is no doubt that 'the gym' is part of contemporary culture. These children were able to engage playfully with the prevailing ideas about exercise and health. We might also consider how far 'burglaries' are integral to children's home cultures. It may be something only viewed on television but it may be quite literally closer to home for some children. Think about the themed role-play areas that you regularly provide for children and be prepared to re-evaluate them in terms of whether they accurately reflect the home-cultural experiences that young children are engaging with, or do they in fact reflect your own cultural experiences? The garden centre is a common theme in early years settings but how relevant is it to young children? This is not to say you should not provide these themed areas but think also about the co-construction of the curriculum (Anning, 2009) where partners, in this case educators and children, work together to create the learning experiences that support children's learning opportunities and that connect with the children's daily lives as lived. Whilst educators may not know about this detail, we can see how these open-ended spaces allow the children's familiar, cultural norms to enter the classroom and find voice alongside the planned curriculum of the educator, as recommended by Brooker in Chapter 2.

Reflective task 〰️

Look at how children transfer objects within the classroom and consider what the purposes of transference might be. Try and observe full play episodes to see how children progress their play.

The transference of objects has been noted in both the above vignettes. Children select an object from a range of possibilities because they have a plan for it; they are using it to re-create some internal model or idea that is forming in their minds. The object represents an idea that is coming alive for them, it progresses that idea and possibly re-directs their inner vision or intention. If we observe children regularly in their settings, we can begin to understand the richness of the inter-connectedness of their thinking over time. These aspects of play are illustrated in the work of Arnold (2003) who provides theoretically informed reflections on Harry's development over a five-year period. Whilst we cannot replicate this longevity, regular observations that capture the whole of a play episode help to build knowledge and understanding of children's interests and how their repeated engagement with these preoccupations becomes their learning. We know there have been top-down pressures on reception teachers to overly emphasise formal literacy and numeracy activities (Adams et al., 2004; Wood, 1999). However, given the now positive validations for play in early years policy frameworks in the UK, practitioners can legitimately resist these pressures and plan activities that are more suited to young children's intellectual, physical, social and emotional capabilities, as well as their culturally diverse backgrounds.

Year 1 children: investigating new materials and playing at the literacy hour

The following vignettes are drawn from two observations – one undertaken at the beginning of the research period in year 1 (in the Social Domain) and one undertaken at the end of the period (in the Cooperative Domain). In this school, two year 1 teachers had introduced the *whatever you want it to be place* in a corner of a corridor and in an adjoining, enclosed outdoor area. Later in the year, as the weather deteriorated, they re-sited it in a corridor outside their adjoining class-rooms. They had borrowed some resources from the nursery where open-ended play materials were in greater supply. They provided crates, foam tubes, cable reels, large pieces of fabric, a large and some smaller cardboard boxes. When the area had first been introduced to the children, many of the observations recorded the play in the social or highly social domains on the SPC. Initially, it was surprising to see that these older children seemed less expert in their play than many younger children previously observed. Our continued observations revealed that these older children needed to re-discover their playful approaches, familiarise themselves with the resources and their potential, and understand what the teachers really meant when they said: '*You can do whatever you like in this area*'.

Case study

This first observation recorded high levels of excitement as the children moved into this new area, as the following dialogues reveal:

> I'm playing in that big box.
> I am.
> You can draw.
> I'm drawing.
> Is there any water?
> Yes.

One boy brings a box out:

> I'm standing on it.
> Look at my big strong arms.
> I know, let's put pegs on our ears.
> Put them on your hat.
> Put them on your nose.
> And your fingers.

(These latter discourses are all from boys in the area as the girls begin to develop domestic play elsewhere in the area.)

As the play progressed, the children often looked across at their teacher who was observing them, perhaps to check if she had really meant it when she said they could do as they pleased. Were there boundaries that might emerge? It seemed not, and the play continued. The boys began to participate in the domestic themes but the overall play themes seemed relatively under-developed and repetitive (characteristic of play in the Social Domain):

> I've found a den. Look at me. Look at me.
> I'm coming in.
> No, you can make another one.
> You can get in now if you want.
> I'm taking my computer (a long, flat box) in, into the den.

(Some children have pencil and paper and are drawing inside the box/den.)

Somebody's robbing my den.

(From a boy outside the box who seems to want to connect to the other players.)

The others chat as they draw:

I wish it would rain so I can do cartwheels in puddles in me wellies.

There is then further discussion of snow and snowmen.

Although this play seemed fragmented and exploratory, over time we came to see that the children often incorporated the writing and reading materials near the area into their play. These children were experiencing a daily literacy hour so this was an integral part of school culture. The conversations about their lives and interests as they sat around drawing and writing became a common feature of play in this area, which resonates with research by Anning and Ring (2004). They tuned into children's discourses as they drew in their own homes and at school and showed the extent of their meaning-making whilst using this medium. They illustrated how narrative links with cognitive development, and how the socio-cultural worlds of home and school are places where meanings must be made by the children in order to feel comfortable and to operate effectively, as described by Hall in Chapter 6. Towards the end of the research, we observed a group of children in the following episode.

Case study

The group of three boys and three girls went into the area and dressed up. They assigned roles and began to play out a familiar narrative. The reciprocity was evident, locating the play in the Highly Social Domain with a progression into the Cooperative Domain. The narrative included children reading storybooks to others 'in bed'. Other dialogue included: 'Pretend it's morning and I can't go to work because I'm not well'; 'Pretend that today I have to go to college and learn things'; 'Pretend I go to sleep and you can't wake me up'; 'You have to get the babysitter and tell her I have to go to bed early but I don't want to'. As play progressed, one boy went to a small table with pens and paper and said over his shoulder: 'Pretend I'm at work but I have to draw'. Another child came to sit with him and said: 'Pretend I am writing and need a password but what I do is scribble'. In my observational notes, I wrote: *Many of the themes are similar to nursery play but the descriptive language implies more detailed conceptual understanding of the intricacies of life.* This play continues for some time but gradually all the children drift over to

(Continued)

(Continued)

the 'writing table' and get paper and pencils and begin to make 'storybooks' (they fold the paper, write sentences and draw pictures). One makes a 'spelling book' and asks other children to write the words she doesn't know. They all spell out the words phonetically as they write them, in much the same way as the teacher later admitted she did. They share their narratives and give one another ideas for their stories. One girl had not joined in the play. She continued with the domestic play alone, although she occasionally stops, watches and listens. After a while, she gets some paper and says to the seated group: 'I'm going to make a story but it's a secret' and she moves off to work away from the others, beginning to draw and make marks.

In our post-observation discussion, the teacher remarked how pleased she was with this girl's response to story writing. She was a very reluctant writer in formal literacy times and this was the first time the teacher had seen her 'take up her pencil' voluntarily. Subsequently, she noted the girl's gradually increasing willingness to participate in the more formal literacy activities in the classroom. The teacher also welcomed the children's sheer enjoyment of this literacy work and commented that it was seldom common to see that level of 'sheer fun and enthusiasm' in the teacher-directed literacy lessons.

Discussion

The vignettes/case studies show that when young children are allowed to bring their own thematic interests into the classroom, they base these around home as well as school experiences and memories. Accordingly, when play is thematically driven by the children, the opportunity to follow their own interests and preoccupations means that the play is more likely to be located within the Cooperative Domain with its characteristic, rich use of language, problem-solving and reciprocity. When children cooperate and collaborate in this way, a careful observer gains insight into the children's learning processes by attuning to their play across this community of learners. This is quite distinct from observing individual children but, of course, it also gives insight into the achievements and needs of individual children.

Research on classroom practice has revealed that play has been limited in frequency, duration and quality, particularly in reception and year 1 settings; adults have often adopted a predominantly non-interventionist approach (Bennett et al., 1997; Wood, 2009). More recently, educators have been encouraged to act strategically and see play as a tool for delivering the curriculum through brief observations of individual children (Broadhead, 2006, 2009) as a means to achieving outcomes pre-determined by policy and 'distant' adults – that is distant from the current preoccupations of the playing child. Both the non-interventionist and the strategic approaches do a disservice to the child's right to engage in playful ways with a given curriculum in an educational setting. This insider–outsider collaborative research based on the SPC has illustrated how open-ended provision and pedagogy might come together to allow for rich, playful learning experiences in educational settings, and how those experiences draw from the cultures of home and school in supporting learning.

The pedagogical responsibilities of the *whatever you want it to be place* relate to the provision of space and materials – or 'tools, objects and artefacts' as was discussed above. They relate to willingness by the adult to study and understand what is happening in the space and to be patient if the play of older children (the Y1s above) seems immature in their early engagement with the new space. It may mean engaging in discussions with children after play is finished to show that it is valued just as much as any teacher-initiated and teacher-directed activity. It does not necessarily mean joining in the play as, in the above cases, it is quite likely that any intervening adult might have tried to re-direct the themes emerging from the children's thinking. Whilst I don't want to leave the reader believing it is wrong to join in children's play in educational settings, I do think educators should be clear about the nature and intent in children's goals before they do participate. In addition, they should be conscious of whether their involvement subsequently stifles the creativity which clearly arises when children are able to pursue their own interests through their playful engagements with peers in their early years setting.

Appendix 3.1   The Social Play Continuum – a tool for the observation and understanding of playful learning and for the evaluation of areas of provision

Observation start time:

Area of provision:

Observation finish time:

Children entering play:

Children leaving play:

L = *Language*	A = *Action observed*	L/A = *Language and action combined*
RL = *Reciprocal language*	RA = *Reciprocal action*	Rl/RA = *Reciprocal language and reciprocal action combined*

Associative Domain	Social Domain	Highly Social Domain	Cooperative Domain
A: Looks towards peers	A: Smiling	RA: Offering/accepting of objects evident	RA: Offering/accepting objects sustains/extends play theme
A: Watches play	A: Laughter	RL: Comment on own action/described intent with acknowledgement leading to extended exchange	RL: Explanations/descriptions utilised
A: Imitates play	RA: Eye contact made		
A: Object offered, not accepted	L: Play noises, play voice	RL: Dialogue is a mix of activity-related and non-related but a theme is evident	RL: Sustained dialogue is activity-related and clear theme(s) emerge
L/A: Object taken, altercation	A: Object taken, no altercation	RL: Sporadic dialogue develops role play	RL/RA: New idea/material extends play and is sustained
A: Parallel play period	L/A: Object offered and received	RA/L: Eye contact/laughter (play noise) combined as behavioural cluster	RL/RA: Children display a shared understanding of goals
L: Self-talk	RA: Object offered and received	RA/RL: Brief reciprocal sequences, e.g. giving/following instructions seeking/giving approval offering/accepting objects asking/answering questions	RL: Offering and accepting verbal help
L/A: Comment on action directed at peer; peer does not respond	L/A: Consent sought and object accessed		RA: Offering and accepting physical help
	L: Approval sought, not given	RL/RA: New ideas or materials have some impact	RL/RA: Verbal and physical help combined
	RL: Approval sought and given		RL/RA: Problem identified and solved
	L: Instruction given, no response		RL/RA: Dramatic scenarios enacted linked to play theme(s)
	L/RA: Instruction given, positive response		
	L: Question asked, no response		
	RL: Question asked, response		
	L/RA: Comment on own action/described intent directed at peer, peer looks		
	RL: Comment on own action/described intent directed at peer, verbal response		

Emergent play themes noted:

Appendix 3.1   The Social Play Continuum – reflecting on and locating the observed play

THE SOCIAL PLAY CONTINUUM – REFLECTING ON AND LOCATING THE OBSERVED PLAY

Increasing levels of reciprocity and momentum →

Characteristics of associative play	Characteristics of social play	Characteristics of highly social play	Characteristics of cooperative play
Self-talk does not elicit a response	May involve much movement indoors or outdoors	May involve movement or one location	Players remain predominantly in one location
No/very little dialogue	Children leave and join the play at frequent intervals	Group relatively stable with some entering or leaving	Shared understanding of goal orientation
No/very little eye contact	Associative players often nearby	Suggestions emerge which begin to extend ongoing play	Players remain until goals achieved; new goals identified
Seemingly little regard for proximity of peers	Little development of play ideas, often repetitive	New objects/materials brought to play but may not become integral to play	A highly imaginative use of ideas and materials as play themes are taken on board and explored
Limited periods of peer interaction	Little shared understanding of goal achievement	Sporadic evidence of shared understandings of goal orientation	Players seek additional resources to extend their play themes
Overtures ignored	Dialogue does not always relate to activity	Role play may be evident with some combined dramatic intent	Role play has clear dramatic aspects
	Play punctuated by periods of associative play	Interruptions/altercations may be evident when play returns to social	A relative absence of play noises
	Altercations evident when play returns to social	Adult intervention seldom sought	Absorption in task with extended levels of concentration
	Adult intervention may often be sought		Altercations are resolved in play as problem-solving activity
			Play achieves a finished product (where design is involved)
			Adult intervention not sought until completion

Comments and records (e.g. information about individual children, ideas for developing area of provision in focus and associated resources, location, extensions, adult intervention, class/group discussions):

Identify play domain (including 'moving towards'): Associative   Social   Highly Social   Cooperative

Further reading 📖

Arnold, C. (2003) *Observing Harry: Child Development and Learning 0–5*. Maidenhead: Open University Press.

Broadhead, P. (2007) 'Working together to support playful learning and transition', in J. Moyles (ed.) *Early Years Foundations: Meeting the Challenge*. Maidenhead: Open University Press.

Wood, E. (2009) 'Developing a pedagogy of play', in A. Anning, J. Cullen and M. Fleer (eds) *Early Childhood Education, Society and Culture,* 2nd edn. London: Sage.

References

Adams, S., Alexander, E., Drummond, M.J. and Moyles, J. (2004) *Inside the Foundation Stage: Recreating the Reception Year. Final Report*. London: Association of Teachers and Lecturers.

Anning, A. (2009) 'The co-construction of an early childhood curriculum', in A. Anning, J. Cullen and M. Fleer (eds) *Early Childhood Education, Society and Culture*, 2nd edn. London: Sage.

Anning, A. and Ring, K. (2004) *Making Sense of Children's Drawings*. Berkshire: Open University Press.

Arnold, C. (2003) *Observing Harry: Child Development and Learning 0–5*. Berkshire: Open University Press.

Bennett, N., Wood, E. and Rogers, S. (1997) *Teaching through Play: Reception Teachers' Theories and Practice*. Buckingham: Open University Press.

Blurton-Jones, N.G. (1972) 'Categories of child–child interaction', in N.G. Blurton-Jones (ed.) *Ethological Studies of Child Behaviour*. Cambridge: Cambridge University Press. pp. 97–129.

Broadhead, P. (1986) 'A continuum of social play in the early years', *Sheffield Educational Research Current Highlights* 8, October.

Broadhead, P. (1997) 'Promoting sociability and cooperation in nursery settings', *British Educational Research Journal* 23(4): 513–31.

Broadhead, P. (2001) 'Investigating sociability and cooperation in four and five year olds in reception class settings', *International Journal of Early Years Education* 9(1): 23–35.

Broadhead, P. (2004) *Early Years Play and Learning: Developing Social Skills and Cooperation*. London: Routledge/Falmer.

Broadhead, P. (2006) 'Developing an understanding of young children's learning through play: the place of observation, interaction and reflection', *British Educational Research Journal* 32(2): 191–207.

Broadhead, P. (2007) 'Working together to support playful learning and transition', in J. Moyles (ed.) *Early Years Foundations: Meeting the Challenge*. Maidenhead: Open University Press. pp. 79–91.

Broadhead, P. (2009) 'Conflict resolution and children's behaviour: observing and understanding social and cooperative play in early years educational settings', *Early Years: An International Journal of Research and Development* 29(2): 105–118.

Broadhead, P. and English, C. (2005) 'Open ended role play: supporting creativity and developing identity', in J. Moyles (ed.) *The Excellence of Play*. London: Open University Books. pp. 72–85.

Butovskaya, M., Verbeek, P., Ljungberg, T. and Lunardini, A. (2000) 'A multicultural view of peacemaking among young children', in F. Aureli and F.B.M. de Waal (eds) *Natural Conflict Resolution*. Berkeley and Los Angeles, CA: University of California Press. pp. 243–58.

Charlesworth, R. and Hartup, W.W. (1967) 'Positive social reinforcement in the nursery social peer group', *Child Development* 38: 993–1002.

Dau, E. (1999) *Child's Play: Revisiting Play in Early Childhood Settings*. Sydney: MacLennan Petty.

Eifermann, R.R. (1971) 'Social play in childhood', in R.E. Herron and B. Sutton-Smith (eds) *Child's Play*. Chichester: Wiley and Sons. pp. 270–97.

Eikeland, O. (2006) 'Condescending ethics and action research: extended review article', *Action Research* 4(1): 37–47.

English, C. and Broadhead, P. (2004) 'Theatre and open-ended play in the early years – combining to promote opportunities for creativity', *TOPIC 32: Practical Applications of Research in Education*. Slough: NFER.

Hay, D.F. and Ross, M.S. (1982) 'The social nature of early conflict', *Child Development* 53: 105–13.

Levin, D. (1996) 'Endangered play; endangered development: a constructionist view of the role of play in development and learning', in A. Phillips (ed.) *Topics in Early Childhood Education 2: Playing for Keeps*. St. Paul, MI: Inter-Institutional Early Childhood Consortium, Redleaf Press. pp. 325–43.

Moyles, J. and Adams, S. (2001) *StEPS: Statements of Entitlement to Play*. Buckingham: Open University Press.

Nutbrown, C. (1994) *Threads of Thinking*. London: Paul Chapman Publishing.

Paley, V.G. (1981) *Wally's Stories: Conversations in the Kindergarten*. Cambridge, MA: Harvard University Press.

Pramling-Samuelsson, I. and Asplund-Carlsson, M. (2008) 'The playing learning child: towards a pedagogy of early childhood', *Scandinavian Journal of Educational Research* 52(6): 623–41.

Rubin, Z. (1980) *Children's Friendships*. Glasgow: Fontana.

Sawyer, R.K. (1997) *Pretend Play as Improvisation: Conversation in the Preschool Classroom*. Mahwah, NJ: Lawrence Erlbaum Associates.

Saxe, G.B. (1989) 'Transfer of learning across cultural practices', *Cognition and Instruction* 6(4): 325–30.

Siraj-Blatchford, I., Sylva, K., Muttock S., Gilden, R. and Bell, D. (2002) *Researching Effective Pedagogy in the Early Years (REPEY)*. Oxford: Department of Educational Studies, University of Oxford.

Sutton-Smith, B. (1997) *The Ambiguity of Play*. London: Harvard University Press.

Tovey, H. (2007) *Playing Outdoors: Spaces and Places, Risks and Challenges*. Berkshire: Open University Press.

Verba, M. (1994) 'The beginnings of collaboration in peer interaction', *Human Development* 37: 125–39.

Verbeek, P., Hartup, W.W. and Collins, W.A. (2000) 'Conflict management in children and adolescents', in F. Aureli and F.B.M. de Waal (eds) *Natural Conflict Resolution*. Berkeley and Los Angeles, CA: University of California Press. pp. 34–52.

Vygotsky, L.S. (1976) 'Play and its role in the mental development of the child', in J. Bruner, A. Jolly and K. Sylva (eds) *Play: Its Role in Development and Evolution*, pp. 537–54. New York: Basic Books.

Vygotsky, L.S. (1978) *Mind in Society: The Development of Higher Psychological Processes*. London: Harvard University Press.

Vygotsky, L.S. (1986) *Thought and Language* (trans. and ed. by A. Kozulin). Cambridge, MA: MIT Press.

Wood, E. (1999) 'The impact of the National Curriculum on play in reception classes', *Educational Research* 41(1): 11–22.

Wood, E. (2004) 'Developing a pedagogy of play', in A. Anning, J. Cullen and M. Fleer (eds) *Early Childhood Education*. London: Sage. pp. 19–30.

Wood, E. (2009) 'Conceptualising a pedagogy of play: international perspectives from theory, policy and practice', in D. Kuschner (ed.) *From Children to Red Hatters®: Diverse Images and Issues of Play. Play and Culture Studies, Vol 8*. Lanham, MD: University Press of America. pp.166–89.

Wood, E. (2010) 'Reconceptualising the play–pedagogy relationship: from control to complexity', in S. Edwards and L. Brooker (eds) *Rethinking Play*. Maidenhead: Open University Press.

'Born to Play': The Biocultural Roots of Rough and Tumble Play, and its Impact Upon Young Children's Learning and Development

Pam Jarvis

The aims of this chapter are to:

- describe recent research into young children's rough and tumble' play in the early years and to inform practice
- consider the importance of children's narratives in understanding their rough and tumble activities
- consider the development and learning that takes place through rough and tumble play, and how this process may be studied by practitioners.

The research: theoretical perspectives on rough and tumble play (R&T)

R&T consists of physically active behaviours (e.g. running, chasing, jumping, play fighting) that create positive emotional engagement amongst players. It is frequently observed between children who are friends, and very rarely observed between children who would not otherwise choose to associate with each other. This clearly differentiates R&T from the behaviour that it might seem to mimic such as aggression. Whilst aggression involves a serious contest of physical strength, in R&T, children voluntarily manage their physical contact and often swap roles, for example from chasing to being chased.

Studies of childhood sociability have found that young children who are popular amongst their peers deal skilfully with the culture of the school playground, recognising teasing and R&T signals from other children as invitations to play. In contrast, children who are rejected by their peers are far more likely to mistake such interactions for real aggression and respond in kind; this is particularly prevalent in boys. Pellegrini and Blatchford (2000) found that, for five-and-a-half-year-old boys, the amount of time spent in R&T with other boys directly predicted their level of success in social problem-solving one year later. An observational study of children's playground behaviour concluded that engaging in R&T allows children to create complex social hierarchies which 'seem to reduce aggressive behaviour and help children develop socio-cognitive skills ... (for instance, social intelligence)' (Braza et al., 2007: 209).

Recent research suggests that young mammals engaged in R&T are creating important neuronal connections within areas of the brain that deal with emotion and sociability (Gordon et al., 2003; Pellis and Pellis, 2007). R&T play would consequently seem to be a key topic for educational and developmental research, particularly in view of contemporary concerns about the anti-social behaviour and poor social skills of some children and young people.

Gender and language in R&T research

Findings from biological research have linked observed gender differences, including greater male engagement in R&T, to the effects of testosterone upon the developing male brain. A 'priming effect' is created by the release of a small amount of testosterone within the adrenal system of human males around the time of birth, instilling a basic gender setting. Studies of the priming effect in human beings are rare. However, a study by Hines et al. (2002) found that higher levels of maternal testosterone in pregnancy resulted in significantly higher rates of R&T amongst female children. Berenbaum and Snyder (1995) demonstrated that girls who have been accidentally exposed to male androgens before birth undertake significantly higher rates of R&T play and exhibit a preference for boys' toys during early/mid childhood. Such findings were recently extended by Hassett et al. (2008) who found that, despite not being subject to human socialisation processes, male and female rhesus monkeys showed similar toy preferences to human boys and girls at a similar point in their infant development, with the male monkeys showing significantly stronger preferences for wheeled toys. This suggests that a pre-disposition for R&T is linked to the presence of testosterone and may be a natural condition of human development that could differ across genders.

Studies of children's physical activities within R&T (e.g. Humphreys and Smith, 1987; Pellegrini and Smith, 1998) have reflected the gender difference observed in animal R&T described above. However, when studying human behaviour, the most distinguishing feature is language. This allows researchers to go beyond physical behaviour, and provides a 'window' into the *meaning* that action has to actor(s). Like adults, children understand the world through the symbols that they carry within their minds, which are shared with peers and elaborated through different forms of communication, including spoken language. The human ability to use language internally/individually and outwardly/collectively to problem-solve, hypothesise and reflect upon our own and others' behaviour sets us apart from other species, and creates unique capacities to collectively understand, plan, create and construct.

With regard to 'gendered' language in general play activity, Jordan (1995) identified a 'warrior discourse' amongst boys, proposing that research evidence suggests that male fascination with physical competition has been present for many generations, represented in the discourse of both historical and contemporary human cultures. Kyratzis (2000) proposed that both genders vie for position in the peer group, boys seeking to be the most dominant, and girls the nicest, on the basis of her finding that girls tell stories to indicate and consolidate alliances, while boys' stories are designed to emphasise to one another how naughty (authority-flouting/dominant) they can be. Marsh (2000) correspondingly found that when both genders were explicitly invited to engage in superhero fantasy play by an adult, while both boys and girls enthusiastically engaged in the activity, the narratives created to underpin the resulting play showed gendered orientations. Boys engaged in justice mediation, chasing, catching and dealing with 'bad guys', while girls used their imaginary powers to help more vulnerable people, small animals and each other. This continues to suggest gendered preferences in play.

Taking a combined approach to researching R&T – bioculturalism

Human beings are clearly a complex mixture of evolved and culturally mediated behaviours. Given that, previously, much of the R&T

literature had been rooted in the comparison of species, I felt that a new investigation of R&T should take a theoretically holistic perspective. I wanted to incorporate a biological/evolutionary focus with a socio-cultural approach. This led me towards 'bioculturalism'. Mallon and Stich (2000: 143) state that the 'biocultural model [of the human being] … reflects a confluence between innate and learned influences'. The more complex and flexible the adult society, the longer animals spend in their juvenile, pre-adult period, and the more complex and flexible the play activities in which they engage. Hence, like all young creatures, children are effectively 'born to play'. Such play activities provide essential practice experience to develop skills that adults of that species require to survive in their evolutionary 'niche': 'the play of children (and of animals) has an essential functional value … preliminary training for the future activities of the individual' (Piaget and Inhelder, 1969: 60). The most socially and technologically sophisticated societies on earth are those created by human beings, underpinned by our capacity to collaborate and compete, rooted within our ability to communicate highly abstract thoughts through the medium of language. An adult human being is simultaneously an evolved organism and the product of a long developmental period within a language-based culture; it is proposed that a biocultural perspective provides a productive way of exploring human developmental behaviour in which language plays such an important role.

As such an inherently flexible species, it follows that although boys and girls may exhibit different play *styles*, they often play in essentially similar *ways*, for example equally seeking dominance, but approaching this from subtly different perspectives (e.g. see Kyratzis, 2000 and Marsh, 2000 above). It can be proposed that the differences can be revealed within play narratives both in relation to children's intentions and adult's interpretations. Consider this play that unfolded within a classroom visited by Yinka Olusoga, and her account of the different effects that gendered narratives had upon the adult practitioner:

> … The teacher was constantly telling boys off for play fighting. They'd use some of the wooden blocks as guns and pretend to shoot each other. They were giggling all the time and never actually touched each other but she had a 'no guns' policy and always noticed and stopped this kind of play. On the other hand, some of the girls developed a game whilst playing Sleeping Beauty where they would all be fairies with wands. One girl, Natalie, always liked to be in charge, and she'd use her wand almost as a weapon, threatening to turn other girls into horrible creatures unless they did as she wanted … Like the gun play, it was all pretend and no contact was made, but I felt that sometimes there was real aggression behind it as each one tried to dominate the play. However, the teacher never stopped this … [she] said that the girls were being creative and developing language skills when engaged in this sort of fantasy play. To me it seemed like a double standard. (Olusoga, 2008: 61)

Holland (2003: 67) proposes 'a common theme of magic powers and of experiencing power in a fantasy realm [which] can be traced across gendered play forms'. It is further suggested that simple, evolved R&T physical actions such as chasing, catching and grappling provide an underpinning frame for human children to independently undertake early peer-shared integration of physical activity and language. My own research would locate the narratives underpinning R&T play as the principal focus of data collection and analysis, in order to create an integrated picture of narrative and action within human R&T. The findings are outlined here to help practitioners to consider how to deconstruct and facilitate this complex behaviour in their own educational settings.

The research

My study was framed within the following research questions:

- What narratives can be found within R&T, and how can we use these to understand what the play means to children?

- Do the narratives that children use in R&T differ with respect to gender?

- What might such narratives tell us about complex social learning and skill development taking place within R&T?

The research used an ethnographic, longitudinal design over an 18-month period. It was undertaken in a medium-sized primary school located amongst the suburbs of a city in northern England. The sample comprised 18 children: the eldest nine of each gender within their year group. The research focused on their outdoor free play from their final term in nursery and into their first term in year 1 (aged 4.5–6 years). The research used non-participant observation in which I endeavoured to ensure that the children would act as naturally as possible during observations. For example, I spent time with them, modelling my role on that of a parent-helper who did not engage in any type of interaction relating to behaviour issues. I spent time talking to the children about their play (including asking for their permission to observe, which was also formally requested from their parents in writing). During their last term in nursery, the children became used to me walking around their outdoor play area, speaking quietly into a dictophone. This method was chosen because more data could be gathered in real time in speech than by note-taking, and it was not as intrusive or technologically demanding as videotaping. The principal technique used for the observations was that of 'focal child' when each participant was observed for one hour in total, across different play periods.

Identifying R&T narratives in observational data

Each observation audiotape was fully transcribed; the transcript was then summarised onto an observational data sheet (Appendices 4.1 and 4.2 provide examples with pseudonyms). The summarised data were organised into gender-based groupings with subsets for girls' play, boys' play and mixed-gender play. Using these references, I returned to the full set of fieldnotes and collated all the information relating to the children's 'scripting' of their R&T under the headings of girls, boys and mixed-gender play. Scripts could be divided into over-arching themes (for example, a key theme emerged relating to boys chasing/girls fleeing) with more detailed narratives being attached to specific episodes of play, which varied from play session to play session. These had a certain pragmatic quality in that the specific narrative tended to be tailored to the available play environment at the time, including variations for different weather conditions. Most of the R&T observed had *some* aspect of narrative that engaged the children and directed their play, in the sense that the moment-to-moment activity had a specific meaning for the child or children concerned, and that they were able to articulate such meanings while they were involved in the activity, or if asked about it directly afterwards. Understanding children's narratives is fundamental to understanding their meanings and intentions in play, as evidenced by Broadhead in Chapter 3, Hall in Chapter 6 and Worthington in Chapter 8.

Single-gender R&T

The rarity of girls-only R&T is the first aspect to note; only two games were observed. One was a chasing and catching game which involved fantasy roles for the players, one pretending to be a 'magic rabbit', while another was a witch who wanted to turn her into wood with the third player pretending to be a prince who saves the rabbit from the witch. The other 'all girl' R&T game was played on a hot summer day. It was spontaneous and lively, involving a large amount of physical contact, with the girls chasing one another around a signpost and then very gently grappling within a lazy 'pile-on' on the grass, rolling around, snuggling close together and laying on top of one another, giggling and hugging. The underlying narrative was 'putting baby to bed', in that baby gets up, goes and plays (spins around the post) and then gets tired and fractious so has to go to bed again. The girls played at temper tantrums, yelling 'give me my teddy', followed by one shouting 'alarm clocks, ring, ring', causing most of the players to jump up and run around frantically again. A few remained lying down, one announcing, 'No, I'm going to sleep for a hundred years'. This element of spontaneous fast-moving narrative with competing 'threads' was quite typical of the girls' play in general (not only that associated with R&T).

The boys' R&T play was in some ways less fluid as individual episodes tended to rely upon media-derived narratives. R&T was a common male play style, appearing in the majority of observations undertaken with male participants. Beyblades, a Japanese fantasy cartoon about spinning warriors, was popular and I observed several boys' spinning activities where they pretended to be the 'Beyblades', sometimes taking on the names of the characters. The game involved spinning whilst karate-chopping at one's opponents, the aim being to knock the other player out of a 'ring'. They perceived the boundaries of the 'ring' in the same manner in which they constructed their football play boundaries (see below), and when a player was knocked 'out', he generally collected himself and went straight back into play; there did not seem to be any concept of being 'out' for any length of time. It was this sustained level of energy in boys-only play that separated the genders most distinctly. A typical example emerged from a chasing and catching game that the boys underpinned with a 'Robot Wars' narrative, based on a factual television programme featuring fighting robots. From a superficial perspective, the theme (chasing, catching and conflict) was no different from the 'witch and magic rabbit' all-girls game. However, the pace, roughness and nature of the contact between the boys and the 'protection' concept that existed within the girls' narrative but not the boys', indicated subtly different gender orientations, as indicated by the comparison in the following observation notes:

> **Boys' game:** James is play-punching Andy with sound effects ('pow, pow'), Andy is chopping at James. Later they tell me that the chopping motion is Mr Psycho's hammer.

> **Girls' game:** Vicky has her hands up by the side of her head (rabbit ears). She runs away and then back to Emily. Emily puts her hands around Vicky and then Marina comes and puts her arms around them both ... the game also seems to involve Vicky and Marina getting just so close that Emily can nearly touch them, then they laugh and pull back.

There was more physical confrontation in the boys' game, and less coherent vocalisation. Male claims of 'toughness' were also routinely made. I noticed that when boys took on roles in fantasy play based on current television programmes, the largest and 'toughest' characters were most popular; for example, two boys chose the role of 'Mr Psycho' in the Robot Wars chasing game that I observed, and the only footballer's name I heard invoked in football play was that of David Beckham, at that time the England team captain. I also sometimes heard competing claims for toughness. Danny proposed that he was 'one boy but I can tackle a thousand men', to which a much smaller boy, Rory, answered rather falteringly, 'I can tackle lots of men'. During football play, Andy proposed on scoring a goal that he was 'like Beckham'. A few minutes later, when the bell rang, he tapped Rory on the shoulder and commented, 'winners, we the winners, 85–0. We won, 85–100'. Rory smiled broadly and nodded. By contrast, the girls seemed more concerned to appear caring. In the witch and magic rabbit narrative, the youngest player, Emily, was allocated to the most powerful but most villainous role, that of the witch, by the two other players who were several months older and recognised 'best' friends. The male narratives of 'war' and physical contest, and the female narratives of fairy tale and protection described in the literature outlined above (e.g. Holland, 2003; Jordan, 1995; Kyratzis, 2000; Marsh, 2000; Olusoga, 2008), were therefore also observed within these play interactions.

Mixed-gender R&T

Mixed-gender R&T inevitably seemed to involve chasing and catching games in which a clear ongoing theme emerged, that of girls offering a 'tag and run' invitation to boys, after which boys acted as chasers while the girls were chased. This evokes the 'preference and competition' gender theme described by Buss (1994). The narratives varied, and were frequently matched to the available environment, particularly in terms of the weather. In winter 'chase and catch' games, the chaser would frequently pretend to be some kind of 'monster', indicated by a grimace and a lumbering walk or run with the hands held up in a 'claw' shape. These games were typically undertaken in a mixed-gender cohort, with a boy 'monster' in pursuit of a small group of girls; I only observed a girl acting as 'the monster' once, in an all-girl play cohort. After a very short time, a girl went to invite a boy to play:

> Kayleigh just made a monster gesture at Imogen. Imogen runs away, and pats James on the chest. Imogen and Kayleigh run away from him, screaming; he runs after them, immediately assuming the 'monster' role.

I subsequently observed essentially the same game scripted by several different narratives. I described one as 'The Drop Dead Tag Game', which was played on a hot summer day on the grass. Two further games were played on a damp tarmac playground on sultry summer days, scripted by two further narratives, 'capturers and captives' and 'dodge and catch'. In 'the drop dead tag game', Corey was the 'catcher' and Rosalind and three of her friends were chased. When the girls were caught and 'tagged' by Corey, they fell down and lay still with their eyes closed; if another girl subsequently touched the girl 'playing dead', she could get up and rejoin the game. When Corey tired of the game and laid down on the grass, the girls took it in turns to 'tag' him until he joined in again. At this lull in the proceedings, I asked the girls what they were playing and they told me rather shyly that it was kiss-catch. I did not see any kissing taking place in this game or in any other, however. The 'capturers and captives' game was again initiated by Rosalind, who 'tagged' Nathan while he was playing with a group of boys; thereafter, this group attempted to drag individual girls from Rosalind's play cohort to a wall. When they got them to the wall, they used an imaginary rope to tie them there. In practice, the girls seemed to run away as soon as the boy concerned ran off, although there were also some sporadic 'rescue' attempts by girls upon one another, accompanied by an action that implied untying imaginary ropes. The 'dodge and catch' game was rather more simplistic in nature; the girls and boys lined up facing each other, the girls with their backs to the wall and the boys approximately five yards in front of them; the girls then ran past the line of boys who tried to catch them as they ran. '… Children involved in mixed gender chasing were practising complex social skills, simultaneously competing and colluding within a highly gendered, independently directed activity' (Jarvis, 2007: 184).

Supervision or mentoring? The role of older children and adults

The children's play narratives were not always located in pure fantasy; they were equally likely to be rooted in quite complex rule construction and negotiation, in which older children frequently took a key mentoring role. This was most clearly demonstrated within the boys' emergent football play. Both Blurton-Jones, the originator of modern human R&T research (1967), and Pellegrini (1989) proposed that human beings use R&T as the platform from which to build games with rules, and within the boys' football play, this set of observations captured some examples of this emergent process 'in action'. The reception/year 1 (Y1) boys' football play (children aged between four and six years) was underpinned by rule negotiation, the reception boys frequently appearing to orient to this by working within their Zones of Proximal Development (ZPD) (Vygotsky, 1978), scaffolded by the Y1 boys' slightly more conceptually mature understanding. In general, the game involved agreeing then marking (often with a pile of sweaters on either side) where the goal would be and who would be goal-keeper; the 'players' would then simply put the ball into play. The resulting game involved generally good-natured R&T style scuffling for possession of the ball, the odd pass to another player, and ongoing nego-tiations occurring relating to who should pass (or should have passed) to whom, 'time wasting', 'hand ball' and whether a goal should be 'allowed' or not. While much of the logic underpinning these debates was incon-sistent, five-year-old children sometimes showed surprisingly sophisticated negotiating skills. For example, early in their reception year, two small groups of boys carried out a negotiation relating to how a foot-ball should be shared between two separate 'games', which were principally a mixture of R&T scuffling and sporadic 'kick about' as (probably due to the lack of Y1 involvement) neither group had desig-nated a goal area or goalkeeper. Nevertheless, the interaction between the groups occurred on and off across most of a 20-minute play period, and did not result in aggression or appeal to an adult at any point. My interpretation was that the negotiation process progressively became far more important to the children involved than the actual possession of the football. As Swain (2000: 103) suggests, 'it was the performance, rather than the result that counted: the taking part'.

The boys were also aware of the boundaries of their imagined football 'pitch'. On warm, dry days, when the children were allowed to play on the large grassed area, there were always several football games going on, but the players from one game seldom intruded into another. These bound-aries were not formally defined by adults; the territories for children from different age groups and 'fair play' relating to the use of these areas by dif-ferent ongoing games appeared to be part of the playground customs that were culturally communicated from older to younger players. Older chil-dren, boys in particular, seemed to have an important role to undertake in the development of much of their younger peers' play, principally as men-tors and instructors in the physical and social skills needed to negotiate the playground environment successfully. Some older siblings were inclined to act as mentors for the younger sibling's whole play cohort, particularly in the case of older and younger brothers. For example, when Ben and some of his friends sat down to watch his older brother (Y2, aged 6–7 years) play football, the older boys engaged in the game got them all to stand up and showed them how to make a 'wall' in front of the goal, while another boy (whose gesticulation indicated that he was not at all pleased by this turn of events) prepared to take a 'free kick'.

There were also several brief, casual interventions from older boys in the younger boys' emergent football play, usually from Y2 players taking 'time out' from their own game for a few minutes, with occasional participation from male Y6 'playground monitors', demonstrating how to tackle and shoot at goal. While reception/Y1 boys were inclined to show passive resistance to the interventions of adult females in their play, they clearly paid great attention to these interventions from older boys. Throughout my observations, I noted that, while walking around with the adult supervising the playground was a privilege for which the girls competed, reluctant boys were sometimes instructed by the adult to do this for a few minutes as a 'time out' punishment! Maccoby (1998: 52) correspondingly reported: 'as early as toddlerhood, boys ... have been seen to be less responsive [than girls] to the reactions of their teachers to their behaviour; they are sensitive, however, to the reactions of other boys'.

The interventions of older children tended to be briefer than those undertaken by adults, and, particularly amongst the boys, generally resulted in a type of casual mentoring that led to an enhanced continuation of the original game that the younger children were playing. In contrast, adult interventions tended to consist of 'supervisions' that changed the activity altogether, with a risk of introducing ideas that were conceptually beyond the child players, as shown in the following observation notes:

> After Rory took a heavy fall during one Reception/Y1 football game, a lunchtime supervisor intervened and told the boys that she was going to help them to 'play properly'. This initially involved picking teams ... however the concept of 'teams' did not exist within these children's shared narrative of football play ... The game quickly became chaotic as boys left and joined the game at will in their usual haphazard way ... it halted for the best part of twenty minutes and restarted five minutes before the end of the lunch break with mainly Y1 participants.

> After stopping a group of boys running after Rory, who was dragging a skipping rope, the teacher on playground duty showed Nick how to turn the rope, and said to Ashley 'we turn, you jump'. He tried but he fell over ... Rory also had no idea of when to jump, nor did Nathan ... They gradually wandered off, got small 'push wheels' and began to chase one another again. When the bell rang, I asked Rory what they were playing at playtime. 'Fire engines', he said. I wondered if that was also the game ongoing with the skipping rope. If so, the play narratives used by the boys and the adult were not at all compatible.

Conclusion

These children created an outdoor, socially complex, gendered society underpinned by their R&T activity, in which they were sometimes casually but congruently mentored by slightly older children. Where adults became involved, they tended to supervise rather than mentor, appearing to struggle to tune into the players' meanings and intentions. Children engaged in complex negotiations and collaborative rule-making activity, enacting the 'R&T to rule-based play' transformation described by Blurton-Jones (1967) and Pellegrini (1989); however, this tended to be curtailed when adults attempted to accelerate the process. When asked open questions by a familiar adult at a suitable time (usually directly after an activity had concluded or in a lull in proceedings), the children were able to provide explanations and insights into their R&T narratives and it was clear the play had meaning for them.

These observational research findings, added to the evidence from the literature, indicate that much social and gender role development appears to be mediated through R&T. R&T activities create a basis for independent and shared physical and linguistic experiences, allowing children to create simple, rule-based and gendered interactions in which shifting, gendered patterns of competition and collaboration begin to emerge. By closely studying and striving to 'tune into' children's play narratives as they chased and grappled with one another in their outdoor play areas, I began to understand that they constructed their own, sometimes surprisingly sophisticated, social worlds within their activity and associated play narratives, from which their independent identities began to emerge, often in quite gender-specific ways.

Implications of findings for practice: What developmental learning may occur within R&T?

What implications does this study have for practitioners? If we consider R&T from the biocultural perspective, we can begin to contemplate how and why 'play ... is what children are "intended" to do. Remembering this may cause us to think twice before modifying children's environments to achieve ... more focused learning opportunities ... at the expense of play' (Bjorklund and Pellegrini, 2001: 331). Correspondingly, it was observed that these children's narratives were prone to crumble when adult modifications were introduced; such 'modification' can also be currently viewed in the decision taken by some early years and primary school settings in Britain and the USA to ban or actively curtail activities such as 'kiss-chase' and superhero play in free play periods, a measure which Holland (2003: 99) proposes 'relies upon the use of adult power in the real world to enforce a moral and behavioural imperative against powerless children operating in a fantasy world'. It is suggested that children's opportunities to collectively build such original constructions give them an important forum in which they learn how to independently and flexibly problem-solve within natural, fluid, social situations: 'the natural school [and] ... self teacher' (Luria and Vygotsky, 1992: 3). This standpoint is also supported by Tovey in Chapter 6, in relation to allowing children the time, space and freedom to explore risk and challenge in their play. It can be posited that children who have regular opportunities to independently test and recalibrate their interaction skills, using the feedback provided by playmates to self-correct and 'stay in the game', engage in the social neuronal pathway building described by biological researchers.

> Playground-based social events ... are highly developmental experiences for the child concerned. These form a set of ongoing learning experiences relating to the human social world, which are both relevant to the child's independent management of his/her day-to-day life and underpin his/her eventual adult potential to deal competently with the vast range of complex social situations, including misunderstandings, that one meets in the adult world. (Jarvis, 2008: 12)

While it is important to recognise the evolutionary and biological factors underlying R&T which have been studied over many years by biological researchers, it is also equally necessary to recognise that the human version of R&T pivotally includes associated language that creates an underpinning narrative to 'script' the meanings and understandings that children share within their play. These narratives (with the children's permission) can consequently become valuable data that help practitioners and researchers to explore the potential value of children's R&T activities for learning and development. This potential for a multidisciplinary perspective makes R&T unique within the field of play research. Its inter-species occurrence has inspired generations of researchers within the biological sciences to gather information relating to its evolutionary and physiological origins, and in the study of the human version of the activity, social scientists are now beginning to investigate the narratives that children create to underpin R&T, and how gendered identities and rule-based play may emerge from such early social experiences. This is a more recent venture, and there is consequently potential for further practitioner research in this area.

Reflection points 〰

- What narratives do the children in your setting create when they engage in R&T? Undertaking some non-participant observations could help you to investigate these activities.

- What similarities and differences appear between the narratives used by boys, girls and mixed-gender groups? You could extend your observation focus to the consideration of 'gendered' narratives.

- How does your setting decide what is 'acceptable' behaviour in active free play? Has this chapter changed your perspective on this point?

- How does your setting manage free play between different age groups? Has this chapter given you 'food for thought' on this topic, in terms of highlighting some potential roles for older children in the development and learning of their younger peers?

Appendix 4.1   Observation data sheet: Example 1

Name (initials/pseudonym) Rosalind	Time Period Lunchtime
Date Xxx	**Weather** Hot/sunny

Activity Log	Comments
Hands on Corey's shoulders rocking him from side to side With Suzanne, Briony, Charlotte and Joanne. Briony leaves Zac hits Suzanne with his cap. Rosalind 'tells' Joanne leaves, Anastasia joins 'Drop dead' kiss catch with Corey as 'he'. The other boys join in. Zac, Rory, then Andy and Sam. Then the rules get confused and the children stop 'sleeping'. Game gets rougher and Charlotte gets bumped in the mouth and cries.	This was one of the clearest R&T narratives which also had clear gender roles attached. At the end of it, got rather confused when the boys joined in en masse. I don't see that girls 'don't play complicated games' (or vice versa when you look at the football). Complexity is not the issue, specific roles based on gender are.

Contact with/Played with

Corey, Suzanne, Briony, Charlotte, Joanne, Anastasia, Zac, Rory, Andy, Sam.

Role of Language/Narrative

Clear narrative with clear male/female roles, male touch causes the 'sleep' and female touch wakes the child up again.
'This is an interesting narrative, there are echoes of fairy tales in here with sleeping princesses'.

Overall Comments

'I ask them what they are playing. They tell me awkwardly that it is "kiss catch", but this is again clearly something that you don't talk to adults about'.
'This game again seems to be very much initiated by the girls'.
'Corey growls like an animal ... he is sort of guarding Joanne's "body", while the girls try to get past him to touch her'.

Appendix 4.2   Observation data sheet: Example 2

Name (initials/ pseudonym) 'Football'	Time Period Lunchtime
Date Xxx	**Weather** Warm/sunny

Activity Log	Comments
Game exactly where it was. Same rules, territories Boys keep leaving and coming back Rory asks Andy for permission to play Haroon in goal again – he is very agile both in goal and when he runs and kicks - @ Y1 standard (see below) Rory not attempting to form another goal this time. Debate between Ben and Andy about whether a goal is a goal.	After Rory falls a dinner lady intervenes Five minutes later she stops the game - too much pushing. Y1 puts ball under his arm R boys start R&T on 'pitch' while Y1's debate about teams Dinner lady organises team picking - R's wander off, she calls them back. (Y1's are 'captains' because they answered a maths Q quickest) Game becomes chaotic as non-team members join Stops - teams now seem to be Y1s Vs R, and R1 says his team is 'England'. R boys debate about who they are (confused!) R's R&T (Jon and Rob join) while the Y1 tries to get his team back together. Game re-starts - R boys v. Peripheral - but not Andy who is treated as equal by Y1's. Only 10 minutes of play before bell.

Contact with/Played with (R boys)
Rory, Andy, Haroon, Ben, 13 @ start, some Y1's. Y1's noticeably more accurate @ kicking etc. Jon and Rob join in.

Role of Language/Narrative
Ben just got the ball and Rory got a hefty shove in the back from one of the other boys. He fell quite heavily. He gets up and runs back into the crowd, smiling ... another Y1 boy runs past and gently pats him on the back.

Overall Comments
Every time (Rory) gets near the goal he seems to get heavily pushed by one of the older boys.
?? question of a hierarchy here? Would being in goal raise his status?
Dinner lady tells me 'we split them into equal teams'.
'There has been no football since the team picking'.

Further reading 📖

Bjorklund, D. and Pellegrini, A. (2001) *The Origins of Human Nature.* Washington, DC: American Psychological Association.

Bruner, J. (1986) *Actual Minds, Possible Worlds.* Cambridge, MA: Harvard University Press.

Maccoby, E.E. (1998) *The Two Sexes: Growing Up Apart, Coming Together.* Cambridge, MA: Harvard University Press.

Smith, P. (2009) *Children and Play (Understanding Children's Worlds).* London: Wiley-Blackwell.

References

Berenbaum, S. and Snyder, E. (1995) 'Early hormonal influences on childhood sex-typed activity and play-mate preferences', *Developmental Psychology* 31: 31–42.

Bjorklund, D. and Pellegrini, A. (2001) *The Origins of Human Nature.* Washington, DC: American Psychological Association.

Blurton-Jones, N. (1967) 'An ethological study of some aspects of social behaviour of children in nursery school', in D.R. Morris (ed.) *Primate Ethology,* pp. 347–68. London: Weidenfeld & Nicolson.

Braza, F., Braza, P. Carreras, M., Munoz, J., Sanchez-Martin, J., Azurmendi, A., Sorozaba, A., Garcìa, A. and Cardas, J. (2007) 'Behavioral profiles of different types of social status in preschool children: an observational approach', *Social Behaviour and Personality* 35(2): 195–212.

Buss, D. (1994) *The Evolution of Desire.* New York: Basic Books.

Gordon, N., Burke, S., Akil, H., Watson, S. and Panksepp, J. (2003) 'Socially-induced brain "fertilization" play promotes brain derived neurotrophic factor transcription in the amygdala and dorsolateral frontal cortex in juvenile rats', *Neuroscience Letters* 341: 17–30.

Hassett, J., Siebert, E. and Wallen, K. (2008) 'Sex differences in rhesus monkey toy preferences parallel those of children', *Hormones and Behaviour* 54: 359–64.

Hines, M., Golombok, S., Rust, J., Johnston, K. and Golding, J. (2002) 'Testosterone during pregnancy and gender role behavior of pre-school children: a longitudinal population study', *Child Development* 73(6): 1678–87.

Holland, P. (2003) *We Don't Play with Guns Here.* Maidenhead: Open University Press.

Humphreys, A. and Smith, P.K. (1987) 'Rough and tumble, friendship and dominance in schoolchildren: evidence for continuity and change with age', *Child Development* 58: 201–12.

Jarvis, P. (2007) 'Monsters, magic and Mr Psycho: rough and tumble play in the early years of primary school – a biocultural approach', *Early Years: An International Journal* of Research and Development 27(2): 171–88.

Jarvis, P. (2008) 'The usefulness of play', in A. Brock, S. Dodds, P. Jarvis and Y. Olusoga (eds) *Perspectives on Play,* pp. 11–19. Harlow: Pearson.

Jordan, E. (1995) 'Fighting boys and fantasy play: the construction of masculinity in the early years of school', *Gender and Education* 7(1): 69–87.

Kyratzis, A. (2000) 'Tactical uses of narratives in nursery school in same sex groups', *Discourse Processes* 29(3): 269–99.

Luria, A. and Vygotsky, L. (1992) *Ape, Primitive Man and Child: Essays in the History of Behaviour.* Hemel Hempstead: Harvester/Wheatsheaf.

Maccoby, E.E. (1998) *The Two Sexes: Growing Up Apart, Coming Together.* Cambridge, MA: Harvard University Press.

Mallon, R. and Stich, S. (2000) 'The odd couple: the compatibility of social constructionism and evolutionary psychology', *Philosophy of Science* 67: 133–54.

Marsh, J. (2000) 'But I want to fly too: girls and superhero play in the infant classroom', *Gender and Education* 12(2): 209–20.

Olusoga, Y. (2008) 'We don't play like that here', in A. Brock, S. Dodds, P. Jarvis and Y. Olusoga (eds) *Perspectives on Play,* pp. 40–64. Harlow: Pearson.

Pellegrini, A. (1989) 'Categorising children's rough and tumble play', *Play and Culture* 2: 48–51.

Pellegrini, A. and Blatchford, P. (2000) *The Child at School.* London: Arnold.

Pellegrini, A. and Smith, P.K. (1998) 'Physical activity play: the nature and function of a neglected aspect of play', *Child Development* 69: 557–98.

Pellis, S. and Pellis, V. (2007) 'Rough and tumble play and the development of the social brain', *Current Directions in Psychological Science* 16(2): 95–8.

Piaget, J. and Inhelder, B. (1969) *The Psychology of the Child.* London: Routledge and Kegan Paul.

Swain, J. (2000) 'The money's good, the fame's good, the girls are good: the role of playground football in the construction of young boys' masculinity in a junior school', *British Journal of Sociology of Education* 21(1): 95–109.

Vygotsky, L. (1978) *Mind in Society.* Cambridge, MA: Harvard University Press.

5

Playing on the Edge: Perceptions of Risk and Danger in Outdoor Play

Helen Tovey

The aims of this chapter are to:

- **identify the characteristics and value of 'risky' adventurous outdoor play in young children's learning**
- **consider contrasting perspectives on issues of risk and safety in early years settings and their possible impact on children's learning**
- **promote pedagogical approaches that can enrich children's learning through opportunities for challenging play outdoors.**

Many children are drawn to activities such as climbing high, sliding fast and balancing precariously, and show delight in physical risk-taking such as jumping from heights, hanging upside down and so on. Margaret McMillan, a pioneer of early childhood education, argued that children should be able to play 'bravely and adventurously' in a provocative challenging environment (McMillan, 1930: 78). She created opportunities for children to climb trees, ladders and steps, swing on ropes, and slide down steep slopes in a richly resourced outdoor play environment. However, there is evidence that opportunities for such adventurous play for children today are limited by a culture of risk aversion, risk anxiety, restrictions on children's freedoms to play outdoors and increased regulation (Beck, 1993; Furedi, 2002; Gill, 2007). How do early years practitioners view risky, adventurous play and how do they make provision for it within the requirements for keeping children safe? This chapter considers the nature and benefits of play outdoors. It reports findings from my research that examines early years practitioners' perspectives on children's risk-taking in play outdoors and considers the possible implications of these findings for policy, provision and practice.

Risky, adventurous play

Stephenson, researching outdoor play in New Zealand kindergartens, observed children's deliberate attempts to search out 'scary' situations. She concluded that the significant elements which made an experience seem 'scary' to a four-year-old were attempting something never done before, feeling on the borderlines of 'out of control', often because of height or speed, and overcoming fear (Stephenson, 2003). Sandseter (2007) identified similar features in her research on play in nature kindergartens in Norway and included play with great heights and play with speed in her attempts to categorise what she termed 'risky play'. Both noted that children typically increase the challenge or level of risk as they repeat their play, suggesting that it is not just the feelings of joy that motivate children but the desire to experience the borderlines of fear and exhilaration. Such play has similarities to Hughes' (2003) notion of 'deep play' and Lyng's (2005) notion of 'edgework'.

Caillois captures the joy of such adventurous play. He identified an aspect of play he called *ilynx* or 'dizzy play' (Kalliala, 2006), which is characterised by 'an attempt to momentarily destroy the stability of perception and inflict a kind of voluptuous panic upon an otherwise lucid mind' (Caillois, 2001: 23). *Ilynx* is the Greek word for whirling water and dizzy play often has this freewheeling, exhilarating, excited quality such as when children spin round a post, hang upside down, pump high on a swing, or roll down a steep bank. Deliberately seeking out situations of precariousness and uncertainty and inverting or distorting normal posture, perception and balance is a source of fun. Danger and fear are often exaggerated with displays of mock terror, or what Corsaro refers to as feigned fear (2003). Such play is characterised by positive affect and is very different from the body tension and cautious trepidation which might characterise real fear (Sandseter, 2009). Players simultaneously experience joy and fear, feelings of being in control and out of control, risk and mastery.

Risk-taking is not just a feature of adventurous play outdoors. Rather, risk could be considered a characteristic of play itself as children seek to push boundaries, try things out, toy with ideas and explore the unknown. Nevertheless, the focus here is on play where an element of risk and possible danger, whether real or imagined, is central. Such play can thrive in the more open, flexible, diverse and indeterminate nature of the outdoor environment where children have greater space, freedom of movement, choice and control (Tovey, 2007). In this environment, children, rather than adults, choose the place, pace and duration of the play and the degree of risk and challenge.

Discourses on risk

While risk appears to be an attractive feature of children's challenging play outdoors, the word risk carries ambiguities. Douglas (1992) argues that notions of risk have little to do with mathematical probabilities and that to most people risk means danger. High risk means high danger. Risk has become something to be regulated, assessed, managed, controlled and in many cases avoided and removed.

However, other discourses view risk more positively. Little (2006), for example, defines a risk as any behaviour in which there is uncertainty about the outcomes. It involves a consideration of the benefits against the possible undesirable consequences of the behaviour as well as the probability of success or failure. Similarly, Madge and Barker (2007: 10) define risk as 'perceptions of dangers and uncertainties that may have negative outcomes but which may also be undertaken with positive consequences'. Risks are not absolutes and perceptions of risk and danger are individually and socially constructed (Lupton, 2006). What is acceptable in one context or in one culture may be unacceptable in another (as evidenced by Brooker in Chapter 2), and what is an acceptable risk for one child may be a hazard to another. Gender, for example, can shape perceptions of risk, with research suggesting that parents perceive risk-taking and possible injury to be more acceptable for boys than for girls (Morrongiello and Hogg, 2004). Risk, then, is embedded with cultural values about what is considered appropriate or inappropriate for children.

The problem with the risk discourse is that it is too often focused on risk as a negative concept with little emphasis on the benefits of risk-taking in play. Risks can be calculated and accident rates measured but the benefits of play are less easily quantified. The following section examines some of the evidence of the value of risk-taking in outdoor play.

The value of risky and adventurous play

First, risk-taking is part of life. Being able to assess and manage risk is a life skill: as adults, we weigh up the risks and benefits of particular activities and make decisions about our actions. Bumps, bruises, tumbles and falls are part of children learning to crawl, stand, run, ride bikes and find out about their bodies in relation to the world. Assessing and managing risk is a skill which needs to be developed, practised and refined, and, as Moss and Petrie (2002) argue, for children not to engage with risk is for them to be cut off from an important part of life.

Second, risk-taking allows children to push out boundaries and extend limits. The boundaries are limited by the child's own competence and confidence, allowing children to learn at the very edge of their capabilities. Assessing whether or not to attempt a difficult manoeuvre requires considerable self-awareness. Can I do this? Is it safe? Success or failure provides important sensory feedback and often the motivation to try again. Kloep and Hendry (2007) draw on Rutter's notion of steeling experiences to argue that mistakes, providing they are not overly disastrous, can offer protection against the negative effects of future failure.

As in other aspects of play, risk-taking allows children to vary the familiar, to try out new ideas or ways of doing things, and to be innovative in their thinking, for example by finding different ways of coming down a slide. As Bruner (1976) has argued, such play can contribute to greater flexibility in thinking and new combinations of behaviour can be tried. Such flexibility can be an important element in innovative and creative thinking (Claxton, 1999; Sutton-Smith, 2001). Adventurous play outdoors can offer rich opportunities for children to combine materials and ideas in original ways and to pursue seemingly irrational ideas, such as rolling down a slope inside a barrel or transforming an unsteady plank into a 'bucking bronco'.

Evidence on the links between movement and cognition suggest that whole body experiences of a varied terrain outdoors are highly important in developing key mathematical and scientific concepts such as balance, height, gradient, gravity, speed, distance and energy (Athey, 1990). For example, swinging on a rope or racing wheeled toys can provide experience of momentum, energy, forces, weight, gravity, speed, distance, time, cause and effect. This suggests that taking risks in play outdoors can enrich and extend the range of experiences which support children's conceptual development.

Recent research on movement play suggests that the sorts of activities which often feature in children's adventurous play, such as sliding, swinging, rolling, hanging and tumbling, are not just joyous physical activities but are important in stimulating the vestibular and proprioceptive senses which are central to spatial and body awareness, balance, coordination and posture (Greenland, 2006). Goddard Blythe (2004) argues that the absence of such physically challenging play can contribute to clumsiness, attention problems and later learning difficulties, for example in reading, telling the time, riding a bike and so on, all of which require an awareness of balance, coordination, space and direction.

Dweck (2000) suggests that a sense of 'mastery', an 'I can do it' attitude, a willingness to try things out and to take risks, are important characteristics of effective learners. She contrasts what she terms 'mastery' children who have a strong sense of self-efficacy and who see challenges to be relished rather than avoided with those she terms 'helpless' who tend to lack persistence and give up easily. Her research suggests that positive dispositions of mastery are key to successful learning. Significantly, Dweck found that dispositions in children were shaped by the environment and the attitudes of those around them. Environments where children are discouraged from taking risks, where adults themselves are anxious and fearful, are less likely to develop the disposition to persist, to see challenges as problems to enjoy rather than things to fear. 'It doesn't help a child to tackle a difficult task if they succeed constantly on an easy one. It doesn't teach them to persist in the face of obstacles if obstacles are always eliminated' (Dweck, cited in Claxton, 1999: 35).

To be broad and adventurous is the first of seven thinking dispositions which Tishman et al. (1993) identify as characteristics of a good thinker. Similarly, Stephenson (2003: 41) suggests that 'there may be a fundamental link between a young child's developing confidence in confronting physical challenges, and her confidence to undertake risks of quite different kinds in other learning contexts'.

Finally, risk-taking in play appears to be positively associated with emotional well-being, resilience and mental health. Such active, exhilarating play can help children feel powerful and competent and can contribute to group camaraderie, friendship and social cohesion (Caillois, 2001). Fear and danger are themes which often underpin children's imaginative play, as described by Jarvis in Chapter 4. For example, Corsaro (2003) observed tidal waves, earthquakes, falls from cliffs, fires, quicksand and poison as frequent themes in children's play. He argues that, through such play, children are trying to gain control over their lives and share that sense of control with each other. In a similar way, children can begin to exert control over and master fear in their adventurous play outdoors. Sutton-Smith (2001) argues that, in play, a strong emotion such as fear is evoked without being fully experienced. Such an emotion is then met with a secondary emotion such as daring, or resilience, allowing children to gain a sense of mastery over the primary emotion. 'The player is able to be in control of being out of control and so enjoy a sense of both risk and mastery simultaneously' (Gordon and Esbjörn-Hargens, 2007: 216).

Managing fear, uncertainty and holding your nerve could be considered of vital importance to emotional well-being. However, a study by the UK Mental Health Foundation raised concerns that the lack of risk in play outdoors is damaging children's well-being and resilience and contributing to increased numbers of children with mental health problems (Mental Health Foundation, 1999: 36).

Despite this evidence of the value of risky adventurous play, research by Maynard and Waters (2007) found that teachers' concerns about safety were a limiting factor in their provision of challenging outdoor experiences. Stephenson (2003) also found that opportunities for physically risky experiences in the outdoors, in general, were more dependent on the teachers' attitudes than on the physical environment. These findings raise two important questions that are explored in the following section: how do early years practitioners perceive risk and risk-taking in outdoor play, and how do these perceptions influence provision and practice?

The research

The research was carried out as part of a larger project focusing on perception of risk and play outdoors in four early years settings in two south London boroughs: a reception class, a nursery school, a children's centre and a private nursery. One-to-one semi-structured interviews were undertaken with 20 early years practitioners including teachers, nursery nurses and staff working towards qualifications.

The research used photo elicitation interviews to gain practitioners' perspectives. This involved the use of eight A4-sized colour photographs of children involved in challenging play outdoors as prompts for discussion. The images were selected according to the criteria of risky play identified earlier in this chapter. They included images of children balancing along a narrow beam, moving head first down a slide, hanging upside down from a climbing bar, playing on a moveable ladder propped against a wall, riding wheeled toys at speed down a slope, climbing a tree, and so on. Practitioners were also invited to bring their own photographic examples of adventurous, challenging play outdoors.

The established technique of photo elicitation is useful in establishing rapport, sharing experiences and probing meanings associated with the photographs and the experiences (Loeffler, 2004). It was chosen because of my experience of using photographic images as successful prompts for discussion with students and practitioners on in-service courses. An image can capture and communicate a situation more powerfully than words alone and can therefore elicit a response, stimulate imagination and recall and act as a provocation for discussion (as shown by Howard in Chapter 9). It can also facilitate shared understandings and allow a more equal partnership in that participants in the research can bring their own images to contribute to the discussion. As Prosser and Schwartz (1998) have argued, an image is ambiguous in nature and purposefully provocative and disruptive so it can elicit people's values, attitudes and beliefs as well as match people's visual thinking.

Key research findings

Interviews were taped and transcribed and a summary of the interview, with irrelevancies deleted, was returned to each participant for accuracy checking. The data were sorted according to key themes which related to the research questions, with responses coded according to the practitioner and the early years setting. Three organising themes were then identified from the data as capturing the perspectives of the respondents. These themes are: risk aversion and anxiety, autonomy in risk-related decision-making and risk promotion.

Risk aversion and anxiety

The majority of those interviewed showed a reluctance to allow risk-taking in play and demonstrated anxiety about possible adverse outcomes. Aspects of play which were considered too risky included climbing high, hanging upside down on bars, jumping off equipment, speeding on wheeled toys and using apparatus in a way for which it was not designed. Most of these involve height, speed or motion and are precisely those aspects of play outdoors that were most valued by children in research by Stephenson (2003) and Sandseter (2007) discussed earlier in the chapter. Additional photographs contributed by practitioners showed features such as a wall which children liked to balance along, the roof of a wooden hut children liked to climb on and an area of long grass where they wanted to play. All of these were considered as potentially dangerous places for play and therefore not permitted.

A frequent response to the photographic images was the phrase: 'that wouldn't be allowed'. For example, a photograph of a girl sliding head-first down a slide prompted the following response:

> That wouldn't be allowed ... our children have to sit on the slide to go down ... I think it's a shame because it's not very exciting for them

> *Why wouldn't it be allowed?*
> It's just always been like that – I suppose someone might hurt their hands.

Photographs prompted considerable 'what if' speculation, revealing a tendency to focus on what might go wrong. For example, one practitioner looked at an image of children balancing on top of a frame with their hands in the air and said 'but where's the rail? What if they fell back?' Similarly, another looked at an image of a child hanging upside down from a bar and said, 'Oh, is there a safety surface underneath? What if she lost her grip?'.

Rather than discuss issues or weigh up possible risks, a small number of practitioners, such as this manager, preferred to err on the side of safety:

> Children must be safe ... I tell my staff – if in doubt – don't. I know it's sad and the children miss out but we can't take any risks with children's safety.

Significantly, staff in the same setting interpreted children's challenging play as challenging behaviour and reported that the more restrictions they imposed, the more attractive the play became to children, 'so we ended in regular conflict with a particular group of boys who wanted to climb on the roof of the wooden hut'.

A pervasive sense of anxiety emerged from the interviews and many practitioners described how they felt permanently on high alert outside and anxious about what might happen. Some practitioners tried to make provision for more challenging play but lack of support from other team members or from those in higher authority caused them to feel vulnerable and potentially liable for blame in the event of an accident:

> We kept the milk crates though they're banned in other nurseries ... but I'm always thinking what if ... what would happen if a child hurt themselves and I would get the blame.

Autonomy in risk-related decision-making

Although most practitioners were reluctant to allow physical risk-taking in the outdoor area, it would be wrong to suggest that they were necessarily risk-averse. For some, there was a tension between what they believed to be right for children and what they were told to do by a higher authority. A sense of powerlessness emerged with some practitioners following decisions made by others, even though they believed them to be wrong as these examples illustrate: (my emphasis)

> **We were told** ... to get rid of the slide 'cos it was too high. Now we have a small plastic one which the children hardly use. It's so boring but **who am I to argue? We didn't have a choice.**

> **The head told us** to stand by the climbing frame all day but I don't agree with it because there's just as likely to be an accident on the brick wall [of the sand pit] but **I have to do it** and **I do get scared** that someone will have an accident and the parents will sue.

Other practitioners were more willing to ignore or subvert such restrictions in order to provide more challenging play opportunities:

> We really encourage children to be confident and take risks and touch wood we haven't had any accidents but I have a very supportive head. She tells us to hide the milk crates and take away the high planks when the health and safety man comes.

However, this willingness to subvert rules could also increase levels of anxiety as staff were left feeling unsupported and therefore vulnerable:

> Sometimes I do put the planks up high but I stand with them all the time and hope no one sees me. I just pray the Head doesn't walk in.

Despite their anxiety about risk, the majority of the practitioners responded in the affirmative to a question asking if children can be 'too safe'. They recognised the dangers of over-protecting children and frequently made reference to their own childhood experiences, expressing regret that these opportunities were diminishing:

> It's not about mollycoddling them. They need some freedom to play and do things for themselves. They learn from mistakes … We're wrapping them up in cotton wool these days and it's sad but the world's a different place now.

Nevertheless, eight of the 20 practitioners, nearly half of the participants in the study, considered that children could 'never be too safe' and that safety was the main consideration outside: 'You can never be too careful'; 'Keeping children safe is our main priority outside'. Safety was viewed as an absence, – for example, 'removing risk'; 'no accidents'; 'nothing dangerous'; 'safe from harm' – rather than as a positive feature of an enabling environment.

Risk promotion

One group of practitioners revealed a different approach to risk-taking in play. Risk was not something to be avoided and eliminated but instead something to be developed and celebrated. Photographs prompted such comments as: 'that's great', 'exciting', 'wow, confident child!' and images of children dropping down a fire-fighter pole and balancing along an unsteady rope bridge were provided as examples of challenging play. Links were made between physical risk-taking and other areas of children's learning:

> That looks great! We have those ladders and it's a bit wobbly and scary but they [the children] love it … and sometimes they push back with their feet just to enjoy that scary moment when it's nearly tipping over. It's all learning isn't it?

> *What sort of learning?*
> Well, about balance and stability. They learn the same things when they go on the

rope bridge and when they play with blocks and the blocks begin to wobble, when it's unstable, so they're making a link between what their bodies do and what the blocks do.

These practitioners reported that outdoor play involved adventure, challenge and confidence. Risk-taking was seen as a valuable part of play. Safety was still a concern but it was viewed not as an absence of risk or harm but as helping children achieve their intentions and learn safe ways of doing things. Issues of risk and safety were negotiated with children. For example, children's desire to run with sticks had been a difficult issue but 'in the end we showed children how to carry sticks safely and insisted that very long sticks were carried by two children'.

Rather than seeing parents as potential critics or sources of blame, practitioners in this setting saw parents as partners in the controversial debates on risk and safety. Practitioners shared their professional understanding with parents and listened to their concerns. Rather than promising a safe environment at all times, they decided to tell parents that absolute safety could not be guaranteed:

> We have a big poster with photos in the entrance hall which says 'Risky play is encouraged here'. We want children to feel safe to take risks – to be daring ... We tell parents we can't guarantee accidents won't happen ... but we explain all the things we do to promote safety.

A supportive team, knowledge about children's play, an ability to tune in to children's intentions in play, a willingness to discuss difficult issues with parents and an environment which offered sufficient space and time and opportunity for adventurous play were identified as significant issues in their approach to risk-taking in play outdoors.

Discussion

A number of issues emerge from this research. All practitioners acknowledged the widespread desire of young children to seek out potentially risky, challenging play experiences outdoors, confirming the findings of Stephenson (2003) and Sandseter (2007). However, their reported responses to such play in practice revealed different perceptions with *some* emphasising the benefits of such play over the risk but *many* emphasising the risks over the benefits.

Risk control measures that were designed to reduce uncertainty and anxiety appeared to have the paradoxical effect of increasing anxiety, perhaps because of the intensity of the focus on potential danger outdoors. It also appeared that restricting risk-taking actually increased children's attempts to take risks, resulting in potential conflict with practitioners. Pellegrini and Smith's (1998) reference to the 'rebound effect' following deprivation of physically active play could be relevant here. In the setting where practitioners reported fewer overt risk-control measures, and more opportunities for risk and challenge, adults reported comparatively little anxiety while still emphasising their responsibility for children's safety.

There has to be some concern for those practitioners who reported spending a considerable part of their working lives in a state of anxiety for their own personal and professional reputation and a state of fear that any accident could be viewed by others as a result of their own lack of care or judgement. Such anxiety can impede positive learning relationships outdoors. It can also lead to adults assuming predominately supervisory, monitorial roles outdoors, roles which were so strongly criticised by researchers such as Hutt et al. (1989).

However, given the evidence of the value of risk-taking in children's play outside discussed earlier, the impact of such a culture of risk aversion on young children's learning and their developing dispositions to be confident risk-takers is of considerable concern. Clearly, dispositions are not all positive. Children can learn to be fearful, to avoid risk and challenge and stick to the rules or they can learn to be reckless and gain some thrill and excitement from transgressing adult rules (Kloep and Hendry 2007; Waters and Begley, 2007). However, as Hall argues in Chapter 6, power, agency, control and transformation are essential characteristics of children's identities, and play provides valuable contexts in which these can be developed.

Are there any grounds for practitioners' fear? Statistically, serious injuries and fatalities in outdoor play areas are remarkably rare (Ball, 2002), as are incidents of litigation in the UK (Gill, 2007). However, such statistics are unlikely to persuade those who hold a view of risk as danger as, despite all probabilities, there is always a chance that, as one practitioner said, 'it might be me'.

Some practitioners in this research seemed to have little autonomy to make professional judgements for themselves and were constrained as much by the risk aversion of others as by their own views. In contrast, where there was a shared philosophy on the value of risk-taking and adventurous play and a supportive team which had discussed approaches to children's risk-taking, practitioners were more confident to support children in taking risks and to see risk not as a threat or danger but as a positive feature of children's play and learning.

This links with research by Douglas and Wildansky (1982), cited in Gladwin and Collins (2008), which suggested that risk management can be linked to levels of personal autonomy, the extent to which individuals feel able to make decisions about matters affecting them and their degree of group identification. When there is high group identification but low personal autonomy, individuals, they argue, are more likely to manage risk by adhering to official rules set by authority. There are implications here for the way teams work together, as well as for the degree of autonomy given to children in decisions about their play.

The research also highlights the different perspectives on children's play. Those practitioners who supported risky play did so because they saw the value in such play and could identify the potential learning within it. As Sandseter (2007) noted, when practitioners regard risky play as positive and necessary, they are willing to support children's reasonable risk-taking, even when this exceeds their own tolerance of risk.

Implications for pedagogy

This small-scale, exploratory research makes no claim that the findings are typical of practitioner perspectives in other early years settings, nor does it suggest that practitioners' practice is necessarily consistent with their reported views during the interview. Missing from this study are the children's and parents' perspectives on risk in play outdoors and analyses of these are ongoing. Nevertheless, the research presented here raises issues which readers may find sufficiently plausible to consider, question and resonate against their own experience. The findings also suggest possible implications for practice.

First, there is an urgent need for the issues of risk-taking and play to be debated within early years teams. Without a shared understanding of the value of adventurous play outdoors and without a shared sense of trust within the team, staff can be left feeling anxious, vulnerable and unsupported. Engaging parents in such a debate is essential if shared understandings are to be achieved and parents are to be seen as partners rather than critics or potential litigators.

A shared philosophy and associated ongoing discussions appeared to reduce anxiety and enabled practitioners to be adventurous themselves and to find ways of solving problems in the inevitable tension between risk and safety. Isolation, within a 'blame' culture, appeared to increase practitioners' anxiety and sense of vulnerability, leading to a pedagogy which restricted opportunity, experience and learning.

A characteristic of risky play is that players feel 'on the edge' between safe and unsafe and practitioners need to engage with this zone of uncertainty. This requires considerable knowledge of young children's play as well as of individual children's competence, a sense of trust and a concern to help children to avoid injury. If we want to develop confident children willing to embrace risk and challenge, then it is important to develop confident adults who have a deep understanding of the issues surrounding risk-taking in play which goes well beyond procedural risk assessments.

Second, the research identifies the need to reflect more critically on the meanings of familiar words such as risk, danger, safety and the values which underpin them. All of the early years settings in this research included in their statement of aims a phrase such as 'we aim to provide a safe, secure environment' yet this research has raised questions about the meanings attached to these words. Clearly, there can be many different interpretations of the word safety which can lead to ambiguities and misunderstandings in our pedagogical relationships.

If, as most practitioners in this research agreed, children can be *too safe*, then safety cannot be an ultimate objective. A safe outdoor play environment, I would argue, is one where safety is not seen as safety *from* all possible harm but offers safety *to* explore, imagine, try things out and take risks. Such an environment can never make claims to be safe because accidents are always possible, but should promote awareness and management of risk as part of its ethos. As the UK Health and Safety Executive has stated, 'we must not lose sight of the important developmental role of play for children in the pursuit of the unachievable goal of absolute safety' (cited in Ball et al., 2008: 117).

Third, if children's adventurous play is to thrive, then we need pedagogical approaches which recognise children as risk-seekers and risk-takers. This means moving away from a view of risk as something to be assessed, controlled, eliminated, to one which embraces risk-taking as an essential part of play with significant benefits to children's learning and well-being. A pedagogy which focuses on developing children's resilience and ability to assess risks for themselves, without exposing children to adverse effects, can be empowering for both children and adults, as Jarvis also argues in Chapter 4. This means looking critically at the environments we provide for children to ensure that children have sufficient time, space and opportunity to engage in experiences that they find satisfactorily risky but which do not expose them to unexpected hazard nor create undue anxiety for practitioners.

Fourth, practitioners need to recognise risk as an integral part of our pedagogical relationships with children (Smith, 1998). Engaging with children's intentions in play and supporting them to pursue these, without undue harm to themselves or to others, has to be embedded in integrated pedagogical approaches, so that play can be extended rather than curtailed (as recommended by Wood in Chapter 1). This would include communicating a positive attitude to challenge so that it is something to be relished rather than feared and celebrating achievements however small. Adults can also model a flexible, innovative approach to play contexts: 'that's a good idea, let's try it', rather than the more rigid and cautious: 'we can't, we're not allowed, it's not safe'. As some practitioners in this research suggested, we must see the potential learning in play not just the potential danger.

Lastly, if we deny children the opportunities to be risk-takers, we may paradoxically risk creating a generation of children who may be either reckless in their pursuit of thrills and excitement or risk-averse, lacking the confidence and skill to be safe but also lacking the disposition to take risks in other areas of their learning, to take metaphoric leaps in the dark and to be innovative and creative in their thinking. Over 70 years ago, Susan Isaacs, another pioneer of early years education, addressed a meeting of the UK National Safety Congress and argued that keeping children safe required opportunities for risk and challenge. It seems apt to give her the last word:

> If you are going to keep children safe … you must provide places in which they can get the thrills they need; there must be trees they can climb and ways in which they can safely get the experience of adventure and the sense of challenge that they crave. (Isaacs, 1938: 4)

Reflection points 〰

- What opportunities for adventurous play do you provide in your setting? Are there opportunities for play which children find enjoyably 'scary'?

- Why not ask the children in your care about which activities they particularly enjoy and why? Are some especially risky? How comfortable are you with their choices?

- What do you mean by keeping children safe? Is it as safe as possible or just as safe as necessary? Reflect on what restrictions you impose. Are they always necessary?

- To what extent can you empower children to keep themselves safe? How can you support children in this?

- Do you have a shared approach to risk and safety outdoors that has been discussed with colleagues? Discussing the document *Managing Risk in Play Provision: Implementation Guide* (see Further reading) could be a useful starting point for reflecting on your policy and practice.

Further reading 📖

Ball, D., Gill, T. and Spiegal, B. (2008) *Managing Risk in Play Provision: Implementation Guide.* London: Department for Children, Schools and Families.

Gill, T. (2007) *No Fear: Growing up in a Risk Averse Society.* London: Calouste Gulbenkian Foundation.

Tovey, H. (2007) *Playing Outdoors: Spaces and Places, Risk and Challenge.* Maidenhead: Open University Press.

References

Athey, C. (1990) *Extending Thought in Young Children.* London: Paul Chapman.

Ball, D. (2002) *Playgrounds, Risks, Benefits and Choices.* Norwich: Health and Safety Executive, HMSO.

Ball, D., Gill, T. and Spiegal, B. (2008) *Managing Risk in Play Provision: Implementation Guide.* London: Department for Children, Schools and Families.

Beck, U. (1993) *Risk Society: Towards a New Modernity.* London: Sage.

Bruner, J. (1976) 'Nature and uses of immaturity', in J. Bruner, A. Jolly, and K. Sylva (eds) *Play: Its Role in Development and Evolution.* Harmondsworth: Penguin.

Caillois, R. (2001) *Man, Play and Games* (trans. M. Barash) Urbana, IL: University of Illinois Press.

Claxton, G. (1999) *Wise Up: The Challenge of Life Long Learning.* London: Bloomsbury.

Corsaro, W. (2003) *We're Friends Right? Inside Kid's Culture.* Washington, DC: Joseph Henry Press.

Douglas, M. (1992) *Risk and Blame: Essays in Cultural Theory.* London: Routledge.

Dweck, C. (2000) *Self Theories: Their Role in Motivation, Personality and Development.* Hove: Psychology Press.

Furedi, F. (2002) *Culture of Fear: Risk Taking and the Morality of Low Expectations.* London: Continuum.

Gill, T. (2007) *No Fear: Growing Up in a Risk Averse Society.* London: Calouste Gulbenkian Foundation.

Gladwin, M. and Collins, J. (2008) 'Anxieties and risks', in J. Collins and P. Foley (eds) *Promoting Children's Wellbeing: Policy and Practice.* Bristol: The Policy Press and the Open University.

Goddard Blythe, S. (2004) *The Well-balanced Child: Movement and Early Learning.* Stroud: Hawthorn Press.

Gordon, G. and Esbjörn-Hargens, S. (2007) 'Are we having fun yet? An exploration of the transformative power of play', *Journal of Humanistic Psychology* 35(1): 198–222.

Greenland, P. (2006) 'Physical development', in T. Bruce (ed.) *Early Childhood: A Guide for Students.* London: Sage.

Hughes, B. (2003) *A Playworker's Taxonomy of Play Types.* London: Playlink.

Hutt, S., Tyler, S., Hutt, C. and Christoperson, C. (1989) *Play Exploration and Learning: A Natural History of the Pre-School.* London: Routledge.

Isaacs, S. (1938) 'Lecture to National Safety Congress', in *National Froebel Foundation Bulletin (1960)* no. 125. London: National Froebel Foundation.

Kalliala, M. (2006) *Play Culture in a Changing World.* Maidenhead: Open University Press.

Kloep, M. and Hendry, L. (2007) '"Over-protection, over-protection, over-protection!" Young people in modern Britain', *Psychology of Education Review* 31(2): 4–8.

Little, H. (2006) 'Children's risk-taking behaviour: implications for early childhood policy and practice', *International Journal of Early Years Education* 14(2): 141–54.

Loeffler, T. (2004) 'A photo elicitation study of the meanings of outdoor adventure experiences', *Journal of Leisure Research* 36: 536–56.

Lupton, D. (2006) *Risk.* London: Routledge.

Lyng, S. (2005) *Edgework: The Sociology of Risk Taking.* Abingdon: Routledge.

Madge, N. and Barker, J. (2007) *Risk and Childhood.* London: RSA.

Maynard, T. and Waters, J. (2007) 'Learning in the outdoor environment: a missed opportunity', *Early Years* 27(3): 255–65.

McMillan, M. (1930) *The Nursery School.* London: Dent.

Mental Health Foundation (1999) *Bright Futures: Promoting Children and Young People's Mental Health.* London: Mental Health Foundation.

Morrongiello, B. and Hogg, K. (2004) 'Mothers' responses to sons and daughters engaging in injury-risk behaviours on a playground: implications for sex differences in injury rates', *Journal of Experimental Psychology* 76: 89–103.

Moss, P. and Petrie, P. (2002) *From Children's Services to Children's Spaces.* London: Routledge.

Pellegrini, A. and Smith, P. (1998) 'Physical activity play: the nature and function of a neglected aspect of play', *Child Development* 69(3): 577–98.

Prosser, J. and Schwartz, D. (1998) 'Photographs within the sociological research process', in J. Prosser (ed.) *Image-based Research.* London: Falmer Press.

Sandseter, E. (2007) 'Categorising risky play: how can we identify risk taking in children's play?', *European Early Childhood Research* 15(2): 237–52.

Sandseter, E. (2009) 'Children's expressions of exhilaration and fear in risky play', *Contemporary Issues in Early Childhood* 10(2). Available at: www. wwwords.co.uk/ciec [Accessed 16 June 2009]

Smith, S. (1998) *Risk and Our Pedagogical Relation to Children.* New York: State University of New York Press.

Stephenson, A. (2003) 'Physical risk taking: dangerous or endangered?', *Early Years* 23(1): 35–43.

Sutton-Smith, B. (2001) *The Ambiguity of Play.* Cambridge, MA: Harvard University Press.

Tishman, S., Jay, E. and Perkins, D. (1993) 'Teaching thinking dispositions: from transmission to enculturation', *Theory into Practice* 32(3): 147–53.

Tovey, H. (2007) *Playing Outdoors: Spaces and Places, Risk and Challenge.* Maidenhead: Open University Press.

Waters, J. and Begley, S. (2007) 'Supporting the development of risk-taking behaviours in the early years: an exploratory study', *Education 3–13* 35(4): 365–77.

6

Identity and Young Children's Drawings: Power, Agency, Control and Transformation

Emese Hall

The aims of this chapter are to:

- highlight the potential of drawing as an 'authoring space' for self
- describe, via case studies, how two children use their drawings as a starting point for narratives that explore and make sense of their identities
- illustrate the potential of discussion around drawings in order to understand children's meaning-making.

In recent years, there has been a shift from a de-contextualised, psychological focus on children's drawings towards an increased interest in children's meaning-making through drawing, and a focus on the socio-cultural contexts of drawing activity (Anning, 2003). In my research, I am interested in the meanings that children attach to their drawings in discussion, what Wright (2007: 43) refers to as 'telling'. In addition, as a post-structural researcher, I support the view that identity and meaning are never fixed; rather they are dynamic and intertwined with the individual's 'social and material circumstances' (Hughes, 2001: 47). The first section of the chapter provides a discussion of identity in relation to play and drawing, followed by: an overview of my research; an introduction to the two focus children and their self-drawings; an analysis of the drawings, organised around the key themes of power, agency, control and transformation; and a conclusion, which offers some theoretical and practical implications. Finally, some tasks and reflection points are suggested, along with further reading.

Identity, play and drawing

Contemporary theorists define identity as a complex and changeable construct, influenced by socio-cultural factors. For example, De Ruyter and Conroy (2002) argue that changes in social contexts result in changes in social roles and perceptions of self. Consistent with this view is the multidimensional model of identity formation and identity maintenance proposed by Côté and Levine (2002). They suggest that identity is negotiated in social contexts in an iterative process; identities are affirmed or discredited by the individual as well as being either validated or challenged by others. Adults play a significant role in the formation of children's identities, particularly in terms of offering 'ideas and ideals' (De Ruyter and Conroy, 2002: 510). However, children are also actively involved in their own identity construction through their participation in the discourses and practices of their social worlds, and the ways in which meanings are negotiated in different contexts (Edmiston, 2008). This raises the question: where are children's explorations of these identities visible in early years settings, and what does this mean for educators?

In examining young children's spontaneous narratives in play and visual representation, Ahn and Filipenko (2007) identified engendering (i.e. identity construction) as a key theme. They found that children used narratives to explore roles and positions, constructing their identities as moral, social, cultural and gendered beings. These findings are closely related to those of Hawkins (2002: 216), who asserts that children's identities are 'called into being' through drawing, and Edmiston (2008), who highlights the significance of play as a vehicle for children's exploration of possible selves and identities. Interestingly, Edmiston (2008) notes that themes in his son's play were also present in his drawings, further highlighting the relationship between play and visual representation as observed by Ahn and Filipenko (2007).

Referring to the post-structural writings of Bakhtin, Edmiston (2008: 98) says that play events involve combining everyday experiences with imagination, and in between everyday space and imagined space, there is an 'authoring space' for self. He explains that the overlap of imagined space and everyday space is ever present, as imagined spaces have their roots in everyday spaces. However, young children find imaginative worlds more compelling than the everyday, adult world; therefore, in play, imagined spaces assume more importance than everyday spaces. In addition, he states that:

> Children, like adults, have agency in authoring selves and, over time, identities. They do so by improvising responses to affect their relative position. They opportunistically draw on their cultural resources in response to particular situations,

as mediated by their senses and sensitivities. They will co-author selves and identities when they improvise in a situation with an adult. Such improvisation
requires an aesthetic approach to life ... everyday authoring occurs in the same
aesthetic projective-evaluative space where pretend play is authored. (Edmiston,
2008: 98)

Cox (2005) shows how drawing is a cultural resource; the children in her
study used their drawings in a playful way to make jokes and share stories,
and meanings about the drawings were constructed and negotiated within
a social context. Adopting Moyles' (1989: 12) definition of drawing as a
type of 'intellectual play', involving aesthetics, imagination, fantasy, reality and innovation, I propose that drawing – when it combines everyday
experiences with imagination – also offers an authoring space for self.
Children not only use drawings to make sense of the world around them
(Matthews, 2003) but also to create their own worlds and cultures
(Thompson, 1999). These worlds and cultures create authoring spaces
where children can construct – and play with – identities. By examining
the communicative potential of children's drawings, my study provides
insights into children's identities, and the authoring spaces they created
through making and talking about their drawings.

The research

The study on which this chapter is based focuses on the communicative
potential of young children's drawings, as explored through case studies of children in an early years class (Hall, 2009). My research builds on
the work of researchers such as Anning and Ring (2004) and Brooks
(2005), who have used socio-cultural theory to explore the influence of
context on young children's drawing, meaning-making, and representation at home and in school. This theoretical stance on representation
and meaning-making is shared by Ring (Chapter 7) and Worthington
(Chapter 8). From a socio-cultural perspective, communication has a
key role in identity formation. As noted above, Edmiston (2008) suggests that children can co-author identities with adults. In my study,
meanings were co-constructed around the children's drawings; therefore, it can also be argued that co-authored identities were formed in
that context. It is acknowledged that alternative interpretations of
the children's identities – as presented below – are possible. Crucially,
the study does not seek to interpret meaning in the isolated content
of the children's drawings, rather in the retrospective discussion about
these drawings between the children and me. In addition, consistent
with a post-structuralist approach, the meaning the children attached
to their drawings is also open to change with time and shifts in thinking. For these reasons, the retrospective narratives offer a flexible and

unconstrained opportunity for children's exploration of meaning. According to Lenz-Taguchi (2006: 258), post-structural theory maintains that: 'anything we think we know about ourselves or the world is simply constructed and formulated meanings in different forms of human expressions and languaging'. As detailed below, my readings of the drawings are based on the inter-subjective understandings that were created through dialogue.

The school in which the case studies were undertaken was situated in a rural area of south-west England and the research involved 14 children in a mixed reception/year 1 class: eight girls and six boys aged between 4 years, 8 months and 5 years, 11 months, their parents and teacher. The main research questions were:

- What meanings do children attach to their drawings?

- How are these meanings communicated?

- What influences young children's communication through drawing?

Following ethical consent from all parties, data were collected over one school year, in three seven-week research phases (autumn, spring and summer). Before data collection began, I spent some time in the classroom as part of a familiarisation process, and the children seemed excited at the opportunity to share their drawings. As an experienced early years teacher, I ensured that the research was conducted *with* the children rather than *on* them (Mayall, 2000). For example, I made and shared a storyboard about the research and the children took a small version of this home. Each child was given home and school scrapbooks in which to collect their drawings, and these were discussed fortnightly (seven children in week A; seven children in week B) in individual, audio-recorded, research conversations where I sought to sensitively explore the children's ideas with them. The research conversations were naturalistic, i.e. unstructured, and usually took place in the school staffroom, which I think the children saw as a privilege. In discussing the drawings, I asked open questions, with the aim of eliciting the children's own interpretations. The length of the conversations was dependent on how many drawings the children had in their scrapbooks and how much they wanted to say about them; very rarely did they ask to end the conversations. The class teacher, Faye, was interviewed at the beginning and end of each phase (a total of six times), and the children's parents were interviewed once every phase (a total of three times). These interviews were partly semi-structured around the children's drawing practices at home and school and partly unstructured around a discussion about the children's drawings. Observations of the children drawing in class were also conducted and were recorded by running records. These methods were repeated for each phase. The children were asked to choose their own project names and throughout the research, in line with Wood's (2005) advice, the children were recognised as expert informers and witnesses regarding their own experiences and perspectives.

In total, 882 drawings were collected over the three phases, facilitating in-depth analyses and interpretation. The analytical framework was developed through an iterative process, drawing on previous studies and the nature of the data gathered in my study. As it is possible to misinterpret or over-interpret drawings (Lewis and Lindsay, 2000), internal validity was achieved through utilising multiple data sources: drawings produced at home and school, conversation and interview transcripts, observation notes, my research diary and other empirical research. Analysis was based on the children's own narratives about their drawings, which were triangulated with the data that I gained from the interviews with their parents and Faye to capture the 'shifting realities' of the participants (Greig et al., 2007: 88). In order to ensure reliability and consistency, expert colleagues were asked to interpret data samples by assigning coding. For example, in terms of drawing content, categories were identified to include all visible elements. The analysis was later expanded to include non-visible elements and the socio-cultural context of the drawing, in terms of where and when it was made and what influences were apparent. Matthews (1999: 30) argues that 'Drawing and emergent representations as a whole are concerned with the children's search for their own identities and structures of events and objects'. The analysis highlighted this theoretical stance.

Case study: Elizabeth and Red Dragon

Elizabeth (year 1) and Red Dragon (reception) were the most prolific drawers in the study, producing a total of 176 drawings between them in the autumn and spring research phases. In addition to being the most prolific drawers, they were both verbally articulate and as I spent longer talking to them than any of the other children in my study, I got to know them well.

Elizabeth was 5 years, 9 months at the start of the study. She had two older brothers, Lucas (13) and Harry (15). According to her mum, Elizabeth's interests were: writing, playing make-believe, playing in the garden, and having friends for tea. However, she also commented that 'whenever you look for Elizabeth she's drawing!' In the autumn, 68 drawings were collected from Elizabeth and she told me that 38 of these were self-drawings (56%). She drew herself alone in 23 drawings, with family members in 10 drawings, with friends in 4 drawings, and with her ballet teacher and a fantasy person in 1 drawing. In the spring, 40 drawings were collected from Elizabeth and she

(Continued)

(Continued)

told me that 12 of these were self-drawings (30%). She drew herself alone in 4 drawings, with family members in 5 drawings, and with a cousin in 3 drawings.

Red Dragon was 4 years, 8 months at the start of the study. He had one older brother, Lawrence (15). According to his mum, Red Dragon's interests were: playing in the garden, playing on the beach, drawing and writing, computers, playing with Duplo, Lego and Brio railway, music and singing, and doing jigsaw puzzles. In the autumn, 39 drawings were collected from Red Dragon and he told me that 6 of these were self-drawings (15%). He drew himself alone in 4 drawings, and with a fantasy person in 2 drawings. In addition, 2 drawings featured Red Dragon as an invisible entity (i.e. he referred to himself being in the drawing but had not drawn himself). In the spring, 29 drawings were collected from Red Dragon and he told me that 4 of these were self-drawings (14%). He drew himself alone in 1 drawing, with a family member in 1 drawing, with an animal in 1 drawing, and with friends and Faye – the class teacher – in 1 drawing. In addition, 1 drawing featured Red Dragon as an invisible entity.

A higher proportion of Elizabeth's drawings were self-drawings compared to Red Dragon, and this was the case in both phases, although there was a smaller difference in the spring. This finding supports evidence from previous studies (e.g. Anning and Ring, 2004) that girls are more likely to draw human figures than boys. Elizabeth's autumn self-drawings reflected her social world: she drew herself with family members, friends, her ballet teacher and her 'little sister'. In contrast, Red Dragon only drew himself with Tommy Zoom, a fantasy character. In the spring, Elizabeth moved away from drawing herself with immediate family members and friends and became more interested in her cousin, Daisy. However, Red Dragon *started* to draw himself with family members, and also had a drawing featuring his teacher and classmates. Interestingly, this suggests some kind of developmental progression. Over both phases, Red Dragon had fewer drawings featuring 'real' people, which seems to support the view that younger children have a closer interest in play worlds than everyday life (Edmiston, 2008). In addition to socio-cultural influences, gender might also account for this difference, particularly as there were other boys in the study who more frequently drew fantasy people than family members.

Despite the differences noted above in terms of *who* was drawn, all of Elizabeth and Red Dragon's self-drawings highlighted aspects of power, agency, control and transformation. These themes emerged from the analysis of the narratives about the drawings, but are also prevalent in the literature on identity and play (e.g. Kelly-Byrne, 1989). Below, each theme will be considered in relation to a selection of the children's drawings. In order to ensure anonymity, all names on the drawings have been obscured.

Power

In terms of power as physical strength or force, a significant difference between the children's self-drawings was that Elizabeth appeared to be more concerned with *being* and Red Dragon more concerned with *doing*. This evidence matches Millard and Marsh's (2001) observation that girls' drawings tend to be decorative and boys' drawings tend to depict action.

When Elizabeth described her drawings, she was interested in the power of beauty over ugliness, and maturity over immaturity (Kelly-Byrne, 1989). Many of her self-drawings included wigs, hats, dyed hair and detailed clothing. Her mum said that she was 'desperate to grow up' and this comment helped me to make sense of some of Elizabeth's drawings. For example, she sometimes talked about her mum having her hair dyed and so perhaps drawing herself with dyed hair signified maturity, and a wish to be like her mum. In three autumn self-drawings, Elizabeth was perched on her brother's shoulders to look taller and older. She also drew herself standing on tip-toes, 'growed up [sic] with a wig on', as a bride, and 'going to go out with my boyfriend'. In her spring self-drawings, she implied maturity by association with her teenage cousin, Daisy, who can be described as part of Elizabeth's 'ideal identity' (De Ruyter and Conroy, 2002). Figure 6.1 shows Elizabeth (right) with Daisy and it is interesting to note the similarity in their appearances. Daisy appeared in more of Elizabeth's spring self-drawings than any other person, taking the place of Elizabeth's (immature) friends. One drawing featured Elizabeth and Daisy talking about a fight that Elizabeth had with her brother, Lucas. The fight, shown in another drawing, was a rare example where Elizabeth seemed to be exhibiting power as physical strength or force, as the most common actions in her self-drawings were walking and waving.

In contrast to the relatively inert nature of Elizabeth's self-drawings, when Red Dragon talked about his drawings, the vast majority involved some sort of action (flying, climbing, running, etc.), either in the past, present or future. In the autumn, two of Red Dragon's self-drawings featured Tommy Zoom, a television superhero, who can be described as part of Red Dragon's 'ideal identity' (De Ruyter and Conroy, 2002). Red Dragon appeared interested in the power of technology and nature and

Figure 6.1 Elizabeth (6 years, 1 month)

his drawings often featured non-human action, such as machines with moving parts, erupting volcanoes and meteorites. In one Tommy Zoom drawing, he told me that a meteorite was going to hit the sun, but he could fly away from danger as he had *more* superpower than Tommy Zoom. Competition is a common feature of boys' drawings (Boyatzis and Albertini, 2000), and there was also a spring drawing with a competitive theme. In Figure 6.2, Red Dragon explained that he had run a race with a giraffe, which the giraffe won. However, he then altered the story's ending, saying 'We both won actually'. This comment could be interpreted as a desire for fairness but it might also be explained by a desire for physical strength, particularly as Red Dragon is tiny in comparison to the giraffe. However, it should be noted that this interpretation of the drawing content reflects my subjectivity; and others may read it differently.

Power as authority was also evident. Both children seemed aware of power structures/social hierarchies and could use narratives to play with this knowledge and make sense of it on their own terms (Ahn and Filipenko, 2007). In the spring, both Elizabeth and Red Dragon described secret identities that gave them authority over their mums. Red Dragon said he was an invisible bird in a drawing featuring his mum, but his mum was unaware of his presence. This transformation seems to fit with the interest in flying that he showed in the autumn. In Figure 6.3, Elizabeth (right), dressed as Superman, is pretending to rescue her mum. Commonly, more attention has been given to boys' interest in superhero characters, but girls also find superheroes appealing (Marsh, 2000). In this instance, Superman can be described as part of Elizabeth's 'ideal identity' (De Ruyter and Conroy, 2002). It is interesting to note that Elizabeth's Superman has dramatic eyelashes. This might be taken to suggest that Elizabeth is playing with the idea that this character can be both pretty and physically powerful.

Figure 6.2 Red Dragon (5 years exactly)

The children's explanations of their drawings showed that in playful contexts, they were more powerfully positioned than in their everyday lives. For example, one of Red Dragon's spring self-drawings featured him with his teacher, Faye, and some friends in their classroom. However, he did not want to discuss the drawing in any depth, possibly because it did not hold any special interest for him. In Ahn and Filipenko's (2007) study, they found that the children recognised the teacher as the 'power figure' in the classroom, which may have been the case with Red Dragon. Taking into account that children's identities vary between home and school due to 'interactive dynamics' (Mayall, 1994: 117), my interpretation is that the drawing shows an everyday space in which Red Dragon – as a pupil – is not powerful; instead Faye – as the teacher – has the ultimate and incontestable power in the classroom.

Figure 6.3. Elizabeth (6 years, 1 month)

A further aspect of power concerned power as ability and personal disposition. In the autumn Elizabeth drew herself doing the splits, in a 'statue' ballet position, drawing on the computer and singing. Red Dragon drew himself singing in two of his autumn self-drawings and in another drawing, he was singing as an invisible entity. He was also a pilot, and in another drawing (as an invisible entity), he was the lighthouse keeper on Katie Morag's island – implying that he could imagine himself as if he were more knowledgeable and more powerful. In the spring, Elizabeth did not exhibit any particular abilities in her self-drawings other than jumping to catch a balloon, and fighting her brother. In contrast, and in fewer drawings, Red Dragon had the ability to run, climb and fly (as the invisible bird). It can therefore be argued that Red Dragon presented himself as being more physically competent in his self-drawings compared to Elizabeth, who, as noted above, was mainly concerned with her appearance.

Agency

Power is related to agency, as one cannot be powerful without agency. Helwig (2006: 459) tells us that: 'As children develop skills and abilities related to psychological needs for self-expression and competence, they will claim areas of autonomy related to the exercise of these abilities, in accordance with the possibilities afforded by different cultural environments'. Drawing is one such area, and both Elizabeth and Red Dragon appeared to develop personal agendas through their self-drawings. In considering the significance of drawing as an area for the development of agency and autonomy, it is important to recognise that the drawings were mostly spontaneous. Produced through self-motivation, rather than being requested by another person, spontaneous drawings reflect children's interests and may also show things that the child is unable to express in words (Clement, 1992). For example, Elizabeth did not tell me 'I want to grow up' and Red Dragon did not say 'I want to fly', but they used their self-drawings to communicate to me in our conversations these wishes and imagined roles. Edmiston (2008) suggests that children have high agency in play because they can make their own choices. This is also the case with spontaneous drawing. It could be argued that, as a drawer, Elizabeth had (slightly) higher agency, as all of her drawings were self-motivated whereas Red Dragon's mum occasionally suggested to him that he make a drawing.

Control

Control was most evident in the children's behaviour as drawers. According to Whitehead (1999: 31–2), personal narratives 'help children deal with abstract ideas and difficult problems, and provide them with theories of life which can be modified and improved in the light of experience and new information'. In Elizabeth's autumn self-drawings, she appeared to control events that she would not typically control in her everyday life. For example, she drew herself as taller and older, and she drew herself with her pet cat that had been re-housed and which she desperately missed. Figure 6.4 features Elizabeth (left), her ballet teacher (centre) and her 'little sister' (right). Elizabeth did not have a little sister, but her mum explained that, in her head, she did. She also had a doll that she called her 'little sister' and this could have influenced the drawing. In addition to having a female sibling, perhaps imagining having a little sister made Elizabeth feel more mature, which would fit with her apparent interest in growing up. As a queen in the autumn and as Superman in the spring, she demonstrated control over others in playful contexts. In contrast, Red Dragon seemed more interested in technical control in his autumn self-drawings (e.g. flying the plane, and taking charge of the lighthouse on Katie Morag's island). In the spring, he took control in changing the ending of the giraffe story, which also made him more powerful in the story context.

Figure 6.4 Elizabeth (5 years, 10 months)

Transformation

On the understanding that identity is dynamic and multidimensional, it can be argued that all of Elizabeth and Red Dragon's self-drawings involved some sort of self-transformation. In the majority of Elizabeth's autumn self-drawings, she appeared to transform her identity on a superficial level (e.g. by varying her hair and clothing). However, she also altered her bodily appearance in terms of height, and explored the possibility of being a queen, a bride, a pirate, a pony and a scarecrow. In the spring, she pretended to be Superman, but the most radical transformation is shown in Figure 6.5 where she has drawn herself as a reindeer, with her mum and two brothers. Pollard (1996) writes about a little girl called Hazel who had a particular skill in drawing and would sometimes portray herself and her family as dragons. Hazel was a highly imaginative child and so too was Elizabeth: they could both picture themselves as animals. Although this is the only drawing featuring Elizabeth and her family as reindeer, it may nevertheless be significant in terms of her identity, particularly as an animal lover. At the time of making this drawing, Elizabeth showed a special interest in television wildlife documentaries and, according to her mum, was fascinated by the natural world.

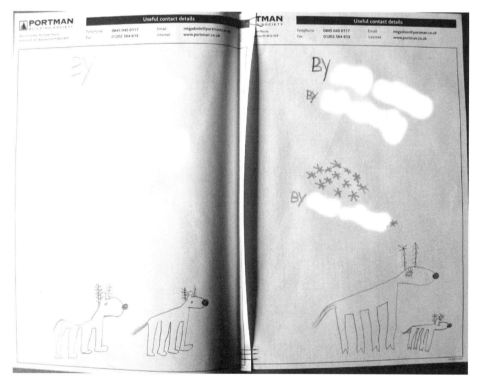

Figure 6.5 Elizabeth (6 years exactly)

In the autumn, Red Dragon transformed into a superhero, like Tommy Zoom, a pilot and a lighthouse keeper. In the spring, he was an invisible bird and he explained that he had pretended to be a computer printer when he had drawn the sky in that same drawing. In Figure 6.6, from the autumn, Red Dragon is in a flying house. Here, he could be described as an inventor, an engineer, a designer, a problem-solver, a traveller, an adventurer, and so on. My interpretation of this drawing shows the limitations of role theory, where the understanding of identity is restricted to definitions on the basis of pre-defined roles, such as sister, brother, daughter, son, etc. (Edmiston, 2008). Although both children pictured themselves in everyday roles, they also explored a range of alternative identities, using the transformative power of play and drawing to achieve those identities. These findings relate to Wood and Attfield's (2005) definition of dramatic play, which involves: imitation, make-believe, imagination, creativity and symbolic activity. I would argue that all these features are relevant in respect of the children's meaning-making through their drawings.

Figure 6.6 Red Dragon (4 years, 8 months)

Conclusion

Power, agency, control, and transformation were key themes in terms of *what* meanings were attached to Elizabeth and Red Dragon's self-drawings. In creating their self-drawings, the children appeared to author imagined selves and scenarios – who they wanted to be and what they wanted to do within their socio-cultural contexts. Vygotsky (1976: 539) says that play involves the 'illusory realization of unrealisable desires', and this evidence supports the view that drawing offers children ways of communicating these desires. The meaning that the children attached to their self-drawings can be viewed as a record of the children's 'intellectual play' (Moyles, 1989).

In order to understand *how* the children communicated the meanings of their drawings, talk – or 'telling' (Wright, 2007: 43) – was essential. The meanings that I co-constructed with the children in our discussions were triangulated with the data that I gained from the interviews with their parents and Faye. If I had based my analysis on the drawings alone, without seeking the children's perspectives, or any input from their parents or Faye, I would not have known the specific contexts in which the children's drawings were made; nor gained an understanding of the apparent significance of the drawings to Elizabeth and Red Dragon.

In terms of *influences*, Elizabeth and Red Dragon's self-drawings appeared to be shaped by their socio-cultural contexts. The vast majority of the drawings were produced spontaneously, and as such we can be more confident that they reflected the children's personal interests and experiences, related to family, friends, hobbies, books, television and popular culture. Although gender differences have been identified in previous studies (e.g. Anning and Ring, 2004), the uniqueness of Elizabeth and Red Dragon's drawings should also be recognised; and I argue the same in reference to all children's drawings. In particular, the content of the drawings becomes meaningful when used as a prompt for discussion.

Wood and Attfield (2005) suggest that children play with 'what if …?' and 'as if …?' scenarios in relation to: roles and identities, rules, games, materials, possibilities, knowledge, language, concepts, ideas and stories. In exploring and making sense of their identities through drawing, Elizabeth and Red Dragon played with 'what if …?' and 'as if …?' scenarios with great skill. By combining everyday experiences with imagination, the children used their self-drawings to create powerful and playful authoring spaces (Edmiston, 2008). The full potential of drawing as an authoring space can only be realised if children have the opportunity to *talk* about their drawings and to communicate their meanings and intentions. Only then can the significance of power, agency, control and transformation become visible.

Reflective tasks

- Talk to some children about their drawings ...

  Identify some focus children in your setting and collect a few examples of their self-drawings (that you have not previously talked to them about). Ask the children if they would like to discuss their drawings. It may be helpful to do this with a small group of children to put them at their ease. There is always a danger that children think the adult wants the 'right' answer as opposed to what they really think, so bear this in mind when asking questions. Did you learn anything new?

- Consider children's drawing behaviour and interests ...

  Have you seen examples of spontaneous self-drawings from all of the children in your setting? If not, why do you think this might be? It may be helpful to undertake an audit of what resources are continually available for drawing; how much time do children have available for drawing; do adults ever sit with children as they draw? (It should be acknowledged that adult presence often conveys high status in children's minds about activities.) Discuss with colleagues.

- Consider opportunities for authoring ...

  In what ways do you think you can support the authoring of children's identities through play and drawing in your setting? Discuss with colleagues.

Acknowledgements

Emese Hall would like to thank all of her willing participants: Faye, the children, and their parents – without whom her research would not have been possible.

Further reading

Ahn, J. and Filipenko, M. (2007) 'Narrative, imaginary play, art, and self: intersecting worlds', *Early Childhood Education Journal* 34(4): 279–89.

Edmiston, B. (2008) *Forming Ethical Identities in Early Childhood Play*. Abingdon: Routledge.

References

Ahn, J. and Filipenko, M. (2007) 'Narrative, imaginary play, art, and self: intersecting worlds', *Early Childhood Education Journal* 34(4): 279–89.

Anning, A. (2003) 'Pathways to the graphicacy club: the crossroad of home and pre-school', *Journal of*

Early Childhood Literacy 3(1): 5–35.

Anning, A. and Ring, K. (2004) *Making Sense of Children's Drawings*. Maidenhead: Open University Press.

Boyatzis, C.J. and Albertini, X. (2000) 'A naturalistic observation of children drawing: peer collaboration processes and influences in children's art', in C.J. Boyatzis and M.W. Walson (eds) *Symbolic and Social Constraints on the Development of Children's Artistic Style*, pp. 31–48. San Francisco: Jossey-Bass.

Brooks, M. (2005) Bringing a Vygotskian Socio-cultural Lens to Young Children Drawing: Engaging, Collaborating and Communicating. Research paper presented at the Art and Early Childhood conference, Froebel College, Roehampton University, July.

Clement, R. (1992) 'The classroom reality of drawing', in D. Thistlewood, S. Paine and E. Court (eds) *Drawing Research and Development*, pp.121–30. Harlow: Longman.

Côté, J.E. and Levine, C.G. (2002) *Identity Formation, Agency and Culture: A Social Psychological Synthesis*. Mahwah, NJ: Lawrence Erlbaum.

Cox, S. (2005) 'Intention and meaning in young children's drawing', *International Journal of Art and Design Education* 24(2): 115–25.

De Ruyter, D. and Conroy, J. (2002) 'The formation of identity: the importance of ideals', *Oxford Review of Education* 28(4): 509–22.

Edmiston, B. (2008) *Forming Ethical Identities in Early Childhood Play*. Abingdon: Routledge.

Greig, A., Taylor, J. and Mackay, T. (2007) *Doing Research with Children*, 2nd edn. London: Sage.

Hall, E. (2009) The Communicative Potential of Young Children's Drawings. Unpublished thesis for the degree of PhD, University of Exeter

Hawkins, B. (2002) 'Children's drawing, self-expression, identity and imagination', *Journal of Art and Design Education* 21(3): 209–19.

Helwig, C.C. (2006) 'The development of personal autonomy through cultures', *Cognitive Development* 21: 458–73.

Hughes, P. (2001) 'Paradigms, methods and knowledge', in G. MacNaughton, S.A. Rolfe and I. Siraj-Blatchford (eds) *Doing Early Childhood Research: International Perspectives on Theory and Practice*, pp. 31–55. Maidenhead: Open University Press.

Kelly-Byrne, D. (1989) *A Child's Play Life: An Ethnographic Study*. New York: Teachers College Press.

Lenz-Taguchi, H. (2006) 'Reconceptualizing early childhood education: challenging taken-for-granted ideas', in J. Einasdottir and T.T. Wagner (eds) *Nordic Childhoods and Education: Philosophy, Research, Policy, and Practice in Denmark, Finland, Norway and Sweden*, pp. 257–87. Greenwood, CT: Information Age Publishing.

Lewis, A. and Lindsay, G. (2000) 'Emerging issues', in A. Lewis and G. Lindsay (eds) *Researching Children's Perspectives*, pp. 189–97. Buckingham: Open University Press.

Marsh, J. (2000) '"But I want to fly too!" Girls and superhero play in the infant classroom', *Gender and Education* 12(2): 209–20.

Matthews, J. (1999) *The Art of Childhood and Adolescence: The Construction of Meaning*. London: Falmer Press.

Matthews, J. (2003) *Drawing and Painting: Children and Visual Representation*. London: Paul Chapman.

Mayall, B. (1994) 'Children in action at home and in school', in B. Mayall (ed.) *Children's Childhoods Observed and Experienced*, pp. 114–27. London: Falmer Press.

Mayall, B. (2000) 'Conversations with children: working with generational issues', in P. Christensen and A. James (eds) *Research with Children: Perspectives and Practices*, pp. 120–35. London: Falmer Press.

Millard, E. and Marsh, J. (2001) 'Words with pictures: the role of visual literacy in writing and its implication for schooling', *Reading* 35(2): 54–61.

Moyles, J.R. (1989) *Just Playing? The Role and Status of Play in Early Childhood Education*. Buckingham: Open University Press.

Pollard, A. (1996) *The Social World of Children's Learning: Case Studies of Pupils From Four to Seven*. London: Cassell.

Thompson, C.M. (1999) 'Action, autobiography and aesthetics in young children's self-initiated drawings', *The International Journal of Art and Design Education* 18(2): 155–61.

Vygotsky, L. (1976) 'Play and its role in the mental development of the child', in J.S. Bruner, A. Jolly and K. Sylva (eds) *Play: Its Role in Development and Evolution*, pp. 537–54. Harmondsworth: Penguin.

Whitehead, M. (1999) *Supporting Language and Literacy Development in the Early Years*. Maidenhead: Open University Press.

Wood, E. (2005) 'Young children's voices and perspectives in research: methodological and ethical considerations', *International Journal of Equity and Innovation in Early Childhood* 3(2): 64–76.

Wood, E. and Attfield, J. (2005) *Play, Learning and the Early Childhood Curriculum*, 2nd edn. London: Paul Chapman.

Wright, S. (2007) 'Young children's meaning-making through drawing and "telling": analogies to filmic textual features', *Australian Journal of Early Childhood* 32(4): 33–48.

Supporting a Playful Approach to Drawing

Kathy Ring

The aims of this chapter are to:

- develop practitioners' understanding of the powerful role that drawing can play for young children as a tool for making meaning
- provide guidance in developing practice for supporting young children's drawing through its continuous provision in the early years setting.

Previous research (Anning and Ring, 2004; Ring, 2003, 2006), reported the misconceptions of teachers about drawing and the way these misconceptions influenced their practice to the detriment of the child's experience. Ring (2003) found that young children were discouraged from using drawing as a tool for making meaning in everyday routines and rituals. Practitioners tended to prioritise conventional and formalised writing whilst drawing lacked recognition and celebration by teachers as one of a range of tools used by young children to make meaning. Common difficulties for the children included: not having constant access to paper and drawing tools; drawing being limited to a small 'mark-making' area where children were surrounded by letters and formats for writing; and over-direction from adults in relation to expected outcomes, combined with lack of praise and recognition for creativity and originality.

Another finding from this earlier research was that, for many teachers and children, replacing the term 'drawing' with 'mark-making' had separated it from play. My view was that this was a problem that needed to be addressed. I designed a three-day course where training and action research were intertwined to address both theoretical understanding and pedagogical practices. Over the last six years, 60 early years teachers (three cohorts of 20), have undertaken small-scale action research projects which have focused upon developing strategies for supporting and valuing drawing in their settings. The outcomes of these studies are reported in this chapter.

The importance of a playful approach to drawing

> Playing with ideas is not just the highest form of intellectual activity; it is also the most fundamental. It is where we all begin: to wonder, to think and to become independent rational beings. (Hope, 2008: 17)

The need to be playful is essential to human intellectual growth and emotional well-being. Whilst being playful, human minds use the capabilities developed in childhood to imagine, dream, create, consider and invent new ways of problem-solving. Playfulness is an important attitude of mind which is dependent upon the internal qualities that children bring to an activity. Playfulness develops over time as a result of experience and interaction and can continue to influence thinking and behaviour throughout our lives. Being playful allows children to ensure an activity is meaningful to them, and to cope with their need for personal freedom in spite of the social constraints which may arise from interaction with others (Hope, 2008; Howard, 2002; Parker-Rees, 1999). As Wood argues in Chapter 1, play and playfulness should be integral to provision and practice in educational settings.

Howard's (2002) study of children, aged between three and six years, focuses upon their perceptions of play, work and learning in educational settings. For these children, play took place in any location where there was no adult present, where there was an emphasis upon process rather than product, and importantly where they perceived they had choice and control. Work, in contrast, occurred at a table with an adult present. There was an emphasis on skill development and attainment, with little choice, and control was held by the adult. In order for practitioners to maximise the developmental potential of an activity and to be accepted as co-players, Howard emphasises the importance of the child perceiving an activity as play and consequently taking a playful approach, thereby harnessing intrinsic qualities such as motivation, enthusiasm, freedom from fear, willingness and engagement. In Chapter 9, Howard reinforces the point that understanding children's views about their classroom activities enables practitioners to provide activities that are perceived by children as play, rather than activities that 'look like play' to adults.

Not all the activities which practitioners label as 'creative' lead to children's creative development and to an expression of meaning. For example, asking young children to paint or draw an adult-prescribed object or person, with adult-prescribed colours and media, on an adult-prescribed coloured, shaped and sized piece of paper – and with maybe just a little help from the adult 'so that parents will recognise what it is' – leaves little scope for the child's creativity or meaning-making. Where supposedly creative outcomes are determined by the adult, they tend to leave the child looking to the adult for approval, and generally lack the vigour that accompanies a response that has greater significance and meaning for the child (Ring, 2003). Drawing and other modes of meaning-making are the creative outcomes of the child's playfulness and therefore belong to the child, as evidenced by Hall in Chapter 6, and Worthington in Chapter 8.

Drawing arises out of young children's exploration of the world through their body movement and tool use and their growing recognition that they can leave their mark or impression upon the world (Matthews, 1999). In early years settings, the availability of materials, objects, language and actions carry a wide range of potential meanings. The child constructs or builds meaning within the boundaries that are set by everyday routines and rituals.

With experience, children assimilate increasingly complex symbolic tools, allowing the child to work with ideas and information more fluently. Both drawing and writing emerge from children's exploratory behaviour, gesture, speech and social play. Young children's drawing is part of their playful, meaningful and multi-modal engagement with the world. It supports their ability to hold ideas in the mind and to communicate those ideas with others and with themselves, which suggests that these experiences and opportunities should be available to them in their educational settings (Kress, 1997; Pahl, 1999).

Figure 7.1 illustrates the complexity of the interrelationship between play and drawing and shows their development to be a cumulative process for the developing child.

Dyson (1993) highlights the interrelationship of gesture, speech, play, drawing and writing for the young child. She recognises the importance of speech in allowing children to represent meaning, to share their ideas with other people and to engage in increasingly more deliberate, better planned and more playful activity. This kind of collaborative, playful talk supports the evolution of drawing itself and links with intellectual growth Dyson (1993). Hope (2008) also recognises the power of drawing to externalise thinking. For some children, the power of movement and action upon objects can be better represented and extended through drawing than through words:

By objectifying inner thoughts and images, the drawing enables these to be observed by the thinker. The imagination becomes visible and takes form. Changing and developing ideas now have something tangible on which to work, allowing review and reflection, return another day and with other ideas both new and old, which can be incorporated with the ideas recorded. The common thread is the need to record visually and graphically that which could not be considered, manipulated or communicated by words alone. (Hope, 2008: 5)

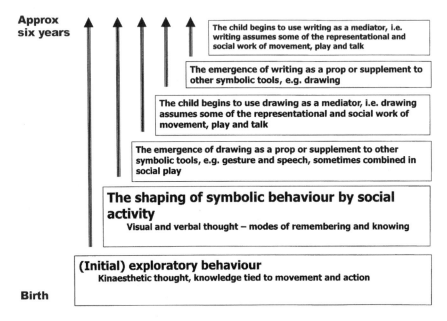

Figure 7.1 The situated nature of drawing within a continuum of children's use of symbol systems (Ring 2003, developed from Dyson, 1993)

The research: supporting teachers in an action-research training programme

This Local Authority (LA) funded programme was attended by lead early years practitioners who were taking part in the Early Years Foundation Stage Communication, Language and Literacy Pilot (2006–8). The need for practitioners to develop greater understanding of young children's use of increasingly complex symbolic tools, i.e. their transitions across play, drawing and writing, was recognised by the LA to be important. They were also concerned with reports that young boys were not choosing to draw and the project sought to address this through this professional development programme.

The programme was formulated around four principles of practice that have been validated through research:

- to work *with* practitioners to help them understand and engage with personal uncertainties about drawing and their role in supporting drawing. This would involve their participation in data collection, interpretation and analysis of findings, so that they could increase their impact upon practice. (Noffke and Somekh, 2005)

- to *foreground visual methods*, for example, collecting digital images, videotape and booklets of annotated drawings alongside narrative in order to provide the teacher-researchers and the trainer/researcher (myself) with context-related images and narratives and rich data for joint analysis (Weber, 2008)

- to take a *longitudinal* approach with the initial action-research group forming the first phase of the project, followed by a second longer phase of in-depth study where I would be working more closely with a smaller number of interested practitioners

- to take an *interpretive* approach, the primary goal being to understand the complexities involved in how practitioners develop and interpret their role in supporting young children's drawing in early years settings.

The intention of the action-research programme was to support practitioners in understanding and interpreting their role in supporting young children's use of drawing. My intention in researching the learning processes of the participants was to uncover the complexities involved in the action-research process. It was important that the research design allowed those complexities and possible contradictions to be brought into view. Across the three days of the course, this was facilitated through the ongoing exchanges of views between participants, working as a focus group, and the trainer-researcher. Records were kept in note form as part of the proceedings. My role was that of an empathetic and critical friend who began by exchanging theoretical knowledge for knowledge of everyday practice. I gradually became part of a collaborative team, as theory became embedded in participants' understanding of what they observed and interpreted. The use of participatory action research supported the focus on what the practitioners did, what they meant and what they valued, and the discourses in which they understood and interpreted their world (Kemmis and McTaggart, 2005). The overall project was structured as follows and shows how the participants and I collected our respective data sets.

As the practitioners came together on the three days of the course (Stage 1) to reflect upon their individual spiral of self-reflective steps, they were involved in:

- *planning* a change in their provision for drawing

- *acting* and *observing* the process and consequences of the change
- *reflecting* on these processes and consequences
- *replanning*
- *acting* and *observing again*
- *reflecting* again, and so on. (Kemmis and McTaggart, 2005: 563)

It was stressed to participants that their work as action-researchers would be experimental and exploratory and that they would be engaged in a 'fluid, open and responsive' process (Kemmis and McTaggart, 2005: 563). The validity of the research findings was increased by taking a multi-method approach to the collection of data, as detailed in Figure 7.2, and through constant comparison of data and findings across practitioners. Comparison was also made with findings from a further two cohorts of practitioners carrying out similar training/research projects. These practitioners were drawn from a range of local authorities across the north of England.

Stage 1 20 participants	Initial and final questionnaires	Completed by individual practitioners as part of the training course and focusing upon their beliefs about drawing and the practices in their settings
	Notes of content of structured discussions in sessions	Completed by practitioners working in groups as part of the training course
	Booklets of annotated children's drawings and digital prints of children's drawing in context	Completed by individual participants in own settings, recording evidence of changes in practice and changes in child drawing behaviours
Stage 2 10 self-selected participants	Digital images accompanied by practitioner and researcher narratives	Collected as the practitioner walked the trainer-researcher through their setting, pointing out evidence of change in provisioning or child behaviours in relation to drawing (described below)
	Semi-structured interviews	Completed by individual participants and trainer-researcher in practitioners' settings. Interviews structured by the annotated drawings and digital prints collected in the booklets and focused on change in practice and its impact within the setting

Figure 7.2 Data collection methods

Visual images and narrative methods were integral to the research design. The responses by participants to both drawings and digital images made them an appropriate choice for this study where research participants were involved as collaborators or co-researchers, and the lines between the researcher and the researched were, at times, blurred. Within the project, visual images were:

- produced by the participants and the researcher as data

- used as data or springboards for reflecting and theorising

- used to elicit or provoke other data

- used for feedback and documentation of the research process

- used as a mode of interpretation and/or representation. (Weber, 2008: 47)

It was recognised that much of the usefulness of the visual evidence depended on the researcher's skill in drawing data from the images to form the basis of interpretations about what was happening in relation to changing practice and its impact (Rieger, 1996). There was a need to engage with issues of personal and procedural reflexivity. In acknowledging that there are diverse ways of viewing visual data, i.e. different audiences and viewing positions other than the researcher's (Prosser and Loxley, 2008), the focus group was particularly effective in enabling images to be shared and to elicit responses across the participants, researcher and others knowledgeable in the field of early years education, art education and visual research methodology.

During Stage 2 with the 10 self-selected participants, 'Walk, talk and snap' was developed as a tool for the collection of images and narrative. It involved the action-researcher and the trainer-researcher in walking through the participant's setting and engaging in audio-taped discussion, debate and analysis of the impact of change. 'On the spot' analysis took place as the practitioner and researcher made joint decisions about images to be 'captured' via digital photography. Sampling criteria for an image or event were defined as:

- a change in provision perceived as significant for facilitating altered or new child drawing behaviours

- children engaged in short sequences of action, with or without communication with others, illustrating the variety of child behaviours that might be considered to be drawing or emerging drawing behaviours, e.g. pulling sticks across soil to leave a line

- children and practitioners engaged in short sequences of communicative action, which illustrate the variety of behaviours which might be considered as supporting drawing, e.g. a child adapting the content of a drawing to fit in with a friend's drawing narrative and, by doing so, keeping up the momentum of the drawing play.

The foregrounding of visual images in research, from data collection to dissemination of findings, raises ethical issues. The use of visual imagery, circulated as electronic rather than hard copy, is a sensitive issue for parents, practitioners and researchers. Control over the use of the image is limited once placed on a website. In publishing images showing young children, care was taken to ensure anonymity. Permissions were gained from parents/guardians and, whenever possible, from the children, for those images which did show faces and were to be used in the dissemination of research findings.

Findings – implications for practice

Data analysis identified two central themes associated with the changes in practice necessary to allow children to engage playfully and meaningfully in drawing. These themes are:

1. Making continuous provision for playful drawing.

2. Developing greater awareness of how to support children's playful drawing.

Teachers' narratives are used to exemplify their changing thinking and practice in the light of their engagement with the work of Dyson (1993) and Kress (1997), and their understanding of drawing as one of many symbolic tools used by young children to make meaning.

Making continuous provision for playful drawing

Whilst working hard to raise literacy attainment, a particular concern of the participants was the well-being and self-esteem of the youngest in the academic year group, the summer-born children. They had particular concerns about summer-born boys whose physical maturity, especially the bones and muscles controlling the fine motor movements of the hand, made 'conventionally acceptable' drawing and writing difficult. Whilst most of the girls were happy to draw, the consensus was that young boys generally chose not to draw and associated drawing with the difficulties of holding and making a mark with a pencil.

As they began their observations, several action-researchers immediately recognised boys' lack of involvement in drawing. They also recognised their own previous assumption and acceptance that boys generally did not want to draw. There had been little consideration of what type of provision might encourage young boys to find drawing enjoyable. Practitioners' analysis of drawing was that it usually took place inside, seated at a table and was limited and confined by the amount of space in which to draw and the small size of the paper provided. In relation to boys' perceptions of activities as 'play' or 'work' (Howard, 2002), there was little in the practitioners' provision for boys, with their general preference for big movements in a large space, to recognise as play. Whilst the girls incorporated drawing into their roles as 'teacher' or 'school girl', the boys who did draw were often less physically active and/or had older sisters and had fitted in to their modelled drawing routines. Changing the scale on which children could draw, by using the walls and the floor, and removing adults' suggestions for the content of what was drawn, was found to make drawing accessible to boys and girls. In discussions with me, practitioners commented on the new kinds of involvement by boys in their settings:

> I think they've explored scale a lot more because of the different paper and things that we've had. We've always had some bigger paper, but there's more of it everywhere and particularly with the big whiteboard that's up on the wall inside. Now that wasn't there before and that's come from the changes we made and that's really made a big impact. They all use it. They use it in different ways really – the younger children to explore mark-making and particularly large motor movements that they just don't get on a table and with a smaller tool. It particularly helps those children that have got immature palmar grasps. They're able to just use their whole arm. (Foundation 1 and 2 [F1&2] action-researcher)

> For a change I just put some big sticks of charcoal out because it's just so easy to draw with, isn't it, and they did enjoy that. A lot of them do it, but particularly the boys. They just love to get down on there on their tummies and draw directly onto the paper and it does just give them that extra bit of support with their forearm. This child is very young and he's only just beginning to show interest in mark-making. Now whether he would have chosen to draw if it had been small bits of paper outside or it had been more restrictive, whether he would have been attracted to it … (F1 action-researcher)

From the analysis of annotated drawings, digital images and narratives across settings, the impact of making continuous provision for drawing on a large scale, indoors and outdoors, was that all children were able to engage in drawing activity that was emotionally satisfying, and increased their sense of well-being and their freedom of expression. As a consequence, drawing became seen as more child-appropriate and became a favoured activity chosen by many or even most children. The same provision was used differently by children dependent on age and/or level of experience, and degree of previous exploration.

It was noted and discussed that close body contact with materials supported children in feeling the movement of their bodies, e.g. drawing with fingers in sand or paint or on the interactive whiteboard. Boys associated being on the floor or standing at the whiteboard with playfulness and ownership of ideas and were particularly attracted to large-sized paper and to drawing implements that made large marks and flowed across the surface easily. Being able to draw on a large scale also led to gross and fine motor activity being combined as a child was able to use large arcs of movement alongside movements that were small, tightly controlled and detailed. Small group collaboration occurred because of the provision of both space and materials and this led to the sharing of ideas and to the increased use of narrative and story making alongside drawing. Whilst the younger children particularly benefitted from being able to use whole-arm action and from seeing older children modelling drawing, all children gained confidence working together on one large sheet of paper as this allowed responsibility for the outcome and for ownership to be shared.

After this initial success, the action-researchers moved on to ensure that provision for playful drawing was accessible within other areas of provision, as the following comments show:

> Having paper in the construction area means there is a mixture of activity. Some of the drawings might be linked to construction and used to represent ideas either before or after building but also they obviously just use it for drawing. It is important that they are able to pin it up on the board themselves and it is immediate. (F2 action-researcher)

> The book area has now been situated next to the mark-making area. The effect is a very fluid one, with children moving freely between the two areas. The mark-making area has been better and more carefully organised to give a much wider range of choice in materials for mark-making and surfaces to make marks on. It has had a big impact upon the children's drawings. (F2 action-researcher)

> I selected 'The Gingerbread Man' as the focus text for our shared book work one week. Later on that week, Luke selected a notebook from the mark-making area and a thick pen and seated himself on a beanbag with 'The Gingerbread Man' text propped up on another one. He systematically went through every page and drew his own image based on the one that was shown in the book. He used a separate page for each image. He talked to himself about the story whilst he was doing this. Later on that day he went back to the mark-making area and rummaged through one of the 'enhancement' trays. He selected a piece of sugar paper for a front cover and took them out into the corridor where 'The Workshop' is situated. Luke got the sticky tape dispenser down from the shelf, tore every drawing from the notebook and then fixed them into the piece of sugar paper to make a front cover. He showed every adult in the setting his work. (F2 practitioner)

Making continuous provision for playful drawing accessible across several areas allowed more children to draw on a regular basis. Importantly, in relation to Kress' (1997) recognition of the importance of multi-modal meaning-making, children used drawing to carry and transform their thinking across areas of provision. We noted a strong interrelationship for children between drawing and the provision of 'junk modelling' or 'workshop' materials including scissors, glue, tape, paper and pens. This supported children in working across 3D and 2D, which in turn supported greater fluidity of thinking and possibilities for playfulness, creativity and the development of imagination. Children's thinking and communicative possibilities were also transformed through their use of scissors, e.g. cutting out or cutting up a drawing allowed it to take on 3D properties, to be transportable and/or take on different meanings. These transformational experiences may have supported the development of interconnections between the areas of learning and experience, as over time there was evidence of increased depth and richness in children's meaning-making.

Developing greater awareness in supporting children's playful drawing

As children began consistently to use drawing as a means of representing their ideas, the action-researchers gathered observations which, with their new and growing understanding, had enhanced significance for them. Although their focus was upon drawing, they began to see children's movement within Dyson's (1993) symbolic continuum (Figure 7.1). In their responses to children, they were giving messages which stemmed from genuine interest and gradually became secure enough in their understanding to hold back their previous pattern of response, which often cut across children's meanings, and to now allow time for children's fascinations to come to the fore. The following narratives are examples of their changes in thinking:

> You know, you do need to see the children and know the children and to have followed their interest to really engage and to understand their drawing. The child who we saw drawing at the table, he's so imaginative. He doesn't draw one thing. It's all interconnected and his ideas are just racing. Well it's important not to stop that flow. He uses things like the role-play areas and props and he'll use construction and develop his stories and ideas through those and outside as well. But the main thing he tends to go for will be the drawing. (F2 action-researcher)

> In the child-initiated activities they've got the freedom to move to different areas and explore a range of resources and opportunities. It gives them freedom to make links and develop their thinking. It's really important that they might go from a role-play area into mark-making or construction or whatever it is and continue that play in a different way. (F1&2 action-researcher)

> As child-centred planning evolves, observation, reflection and focus on the 'next steps' has become key – planning has become more flexible, responsive and 'open' to children's choices and use of resources, which in turn has opened up opportunities for children's creativity and for adults to develop a role as 'collaborators' in play and learning. (F1 action-researcher)

> I used to put limits on where children could take things. They had to keep certain things in certain areas but now I seem to have relaxed this. The children can keep their play theme going for much longer now because they can move from area to area taking things with them. (F1 action-researcher)

> At the heart of our philosophy and practice are well-being and involvement, and practitioners working alongside children in reflective co-construction of meaning. This has led us to be more open, less restrictive and increasingly aware of the need for sensitive, subtle and respectful interaction. (F1 action-researcher)

In summarising the development of their thinking, it was evident that these practitioners became more aware of the need to put the well-being of children at the heart of their practice in relation to drawing, and the pedagogical strategies that supported this perspective. Rather than fitting children into pre-specified goals, they considered that they knew more about their children and their fascinations. Their greater understanding of children's use of drawing as a tool for thinking and learning made them eager to share and value what children were now able to show them. Many were more confident in recognising and supporting children's use of narratives derived from popular culture and in ensuring their provocations connected with children's interests, thereby enabling children to access new knowledge, understanding, skills, attitudes and feelings.

Conclusion and suggestions for practice development

The participants in this project looked with a fresh eye at the children's use of drawing. Their new theoretical awareness allowed them to better understand how resources and adult–child interactions can support children in finding a sense of well-being, enjoyment, satisfaction and intellectual challenge from drawing. Many were taken on journeys by the children which left them wondering at the subtlety and competence of children's thinking. One participant commented that what had been 'black and white and certain for her', in terms of what she recognised as 'typical drawing activity and typical drawing provision', was now 'multi-coloured and open, ready for further discovery'. At times, her journey had been uncomfortable. However, she now understood that she needed to take a moment before speaking or acting in order to avoid a previously entrenched pattern of over-controlling the children and setting narrow boundaries for acceptable or expected behaviour in drawing. Her most significant discovery was that she had been wrong in thinking that some children choose not to draw. As the routines and rituals surrounding drawing within her setting changed, and became focused upon children's playful exploration and understandings of personal experience, so in turn drawing became incorporated into many children's everyday routines and became a key part of the meaning-making process.

I offer the following final points to support you in starting to think about your own understanding of and provision for drawing, and to further consider its relationship with learning and intellectual development.

Reflective tasks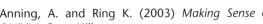

- Observe the children in your setting. Who draws? Where do they draw? When do they draw? How do they draw? What do they say when they draw? What do your findings tell you about the everyday routines and rituals in your setting and how they relate to drawing? If a colleague also carries out this task, compare your findings.

- Put a large sheet of paper on the floor. It can be indoors or outdoors. Provide some drawing tools that move fluidly across the paper and make large, bold lines, for example large felt tips, crayons or some softer tools such as pastels or charcoal. Sit on the floor and, if no child has the confidence to make the first mark on the paper, make a continuous wavy line on the page – do not be tempted to draw something that is a recognisable object. Note what happens next.

- Build up your observations and notes about children using drawing in your setting. What actions could you take to improve children's opportunities to:

  - develop an enthusiasm for and love of drawing

  - use whole-body action when drawing

  - observe, draw alongside and collaborate with their peers

  - use drawing tools that move fluently across the page or space or material and leave a strong visible impact

  - explore drawing, make their own choices and become engrossed

  - feel secure enough to experiment and take risks with drawing, and build up their drawing skills and behaviours pleasurably within safe, secure, unpressurised conditions.

Further reading

Anning, A. and Ring K. (2003) *Making Sense of Children's Drawings.* Maidenhead: OUP/McGraw-Hill.

Bruce, T. (2004) *Cultivating Creativity in Babies, Toddlers and Young Children.* London: Hodder and Stoughton.

Gandini, L., Hill, L., Cadwell, L. and Schwall, C. (eds) (2005) *In the Spirit of the Studio: Learning from the Atelier of Reggio Emilia.* New York: Teachers College Press.

Kolbe, U. (2001) *Rapunzel's Supermarket.* Byron Bay, Australia: Peppinot Press.

References

Anning, A. and Ring, K. (2004) *Making Sense of Children's Drawings*. Maidenhead: OUP/McGraw-Hill.

Dyson, A.H. (1993) 'From prop to mediator: the changing role of written language in children's symbolic repertoires', in B. Spodek and O.N. Saracho (eds) *Yearbook in Early Childhood Education: Language and Literacy in Early Childhood Education, Vol. 4*, pp. 21–41. New York: Teachers College Press.

Hope, G. (2008) *Thinking and Learning Through Drawing*. London: Sage.

Howard, J. (2002) 'Eliciting children's perceptions of play using the Activity Apperception Story Procedure', *Early Child Development and Care* 172(5): 489–502.

Kemmis, S. and McTaggart, R. (2005) 'Participatory action research', in N.K. Denzin and Y.S. Lincoln (eds) *The Sage Handbook of Qualitative Research*, 3rd edn. London: Sage. pp. 559–603.

Kress, G. (1997) *Before Writing: Rethinking the Paths to Literacy*. London: Routledge.

Matthews, J. (1999) *The Art of Childhood and Adolescence: The Construction of Meaning*. London: Falmer Press.

Noffke, S. and Somekh, B. (2005) 'Action research', in B. Somekh and C. Lewin (eds) *Research Methods in the Social Sciences*. London: Sage. pp. 89–96.

Pahl, K. (1999) *Transformations: Making Meaning in Nursery Education*. Stoke-on-Trent: Trentham Books.

Parker-Rees, R. (1999) 'Protecting playfulness', in L. Abbott and H. Moylett (eds) *Early Education Transformed*. London: Falmer Press. pp. 61–72.

Prosser, J. and Loxley, A. (2008) *Introducing Visual Methods*. ESRC National Centre for Research Methods Review Paper NCRM/010.

Rieger, J. (1996) 'Photographing social change', *Visual Sociology* 11(1): 5– 49.

Ring, K. (2003) Young Children Drawing at Home, Pre-School and School: The Influence of the Socio-cultural Context. Unpublished doctoral dissertation, School of Education, University of Leeds.

Ring, K. (2006) 'Supporting young children drawing: developing a role', *International Journal of Education through Art* 2(3): 195–209.

Weber, S. (2008) 'Visual images in research', in J.G. Knowles and A.L Cole (eds) *Handbook of the Arts in Qualitative Research*, pp. 41–54. Thousand Oaks, CA: Sage.

Play is a Complex Landscape: Imagination and Symbolic Meanings

Maulfry Worthington

> **The aims of this chapter are to:**
> - show the complexity of children's thinking as they explore, make and communicate meanings through complex signs within their imaginative play
> - explore the relationship between the semiotic potential of play (children's meaning-making) and *children's mathematical graphics*
> - consider the value of making and analysing observations of child-initiated play episodes, in deepening professional knowledge and pedagogy.

This chapter presents the findings from the first phase of an ethnographic study for doctoral research. The main focus is on the ways children explore meanings through making 'signs' or mental tools within their play, signs that include 'visual, textual and artefactual' practices (Pahl, 2002: 145) that are the precursor of symbolic languages such as writing (Vygotsky, 1978). Vygotsky recognised that 'Superficially, play bears little resemblance to the complex, mediated form of thought and volition it leads to. Only a profound internal analysis makes it possible to determine its course of change and its role in development' (1978: 104). In this study, empirical data are drawn from observations of children aged 3–4 years in two nursery schools in England. Analysis of their imaginative play has uncovered their complex meanings and communicative modes.

The first section explores the theoretical framing of the study. The second section explores the practice of making observations of children's self-initiated play, and what 'readings' of the data are possible in terms of identifying children's meaning-making and their semiotic practices. The findings indicate that observation and analysis of play by practitioners can lead to a deepening of professional knowledge and pedagogy, suggesting that research and critical reflection play a significant role in professional development.

The research

Background

The study builds on previous research into young children's graphicacy in mathematics (Carruthers and Worthington, 2005, 2006), and links with the work of Hall in Chapter 6 and Ring in Chapter 7. My aim is to explore the theory 'that make-believe play, drawing and writing can be viewed as different moments in an essentially unified process' (Vygotsky, 1978: 116) and to trace the emergence of *children's mathematical graphics*. Young children employ a range of means and use various media and resources to represent and communicate their internal, mental representations by creating external 'signs': these are semiotic resources rich with meaning potential. The terms 'signs' and 'symbols' are often interchanged: symbolic languages such as written mathematics include symbols such as '+' and numerals, and 'text' is generally understood to refer to written texts. However, in the literature on children's symbolic play, 'signs' and 'texts' also refer to the meaning potential of various 'modes', including language, models, gestures, arrangements of artefacts and graphical representations. A direct relationship exists between children's ability to make meanings in play and to use marks and symbols to signify meanings: just as physical tools enable us to solve physical problems, semiotic activities result in *symbolic tools* that can be used to resolve particular mental problems.

Studies of meaning-making (semiotics) have revealed the social significance of meanings, and research into the development of young children's meaning-making underscores the complexity of their symbolic actions and representations. These studies suggest that children's meanings may not always be readily available to adults, especially if there is little time to observe and understand children's imaginative play, and therefore emphasise the need for profound internal analysis of children's imaginative play.

Imaginative play

Whilst there is no consensus about a definition of play in early childhood education, in Vygotsky's view: 'Action in the imagination sphere, in an imaginary situation ... all appear in play and make it the highest level of pre-school development' (1978: 102). The word 'imagination' originates from the Latin *imago*, meaning 'to form an image' or 'to represent' and 'is at the roots of human thinking' (Van Oers, 2005: 5). Van Oers proposes that 'imagination is a basic element for individual empowerment within play and for the development of critical cultural agency' that promotes development (2005: 7–8).

The role of play was seen by Vygotsky 'as a leading factor in development': he emphasised connections between behaviours in play that are 'accomplished by movement in the field of meaning – which subordinates all real objects and actions to itself. Behaviour is not bound by the immediate perceptual field. This movement in the field of meaning predominates in play' (1978: 101). Vygotsky argued that 'each step' supports the role of imagination in cognition, resulting in cognition becoming 'more complex and richer' (1987: 349). As 'children continuously weave in and out of play' they transfer "real world" knowledge, skills and understandings from other areas of their lives. Play is also rich with meanings that children create for themselves' (Wood and Attfield, 2005: 7).

Research on role play reveals a range of different purposes and outcomes for children's learning and development. For example, Broadhead (2004) focuses on supporting social skills and cooperation through play and acknowledges the benefits of open-ended role play (2004: 130). Rogers and Evans (2008) provide similar perspectives, enlarging on the children's views and providing methodologies for studying this aspect of play. Role play also enables children to explore narratives: for example, through her sensitive observations and reflections, Gussin-Paley (2005) shows that as play scenarios develop, children's own narratives can support psychological, intellectual and social development.

Vygotsky's research into children's symbolic play explored some of the ways in which they make meanings. In more recent years, research by Kress (e.g. 1997) into children's semiotic explorations has shown the significance of 'multi-modal' play in which children make meanings in many ways and with diverse materials. This research led to Pahl describing multi-modal play in which children's meanings are embodied in visual media such as drawings, written texts and arrangements of items, models and cut-outs as 'visual, textual and artefactual' practices (2002: 145). These signs are 'always transparent to their makers ...' and, at the same time, 'more or less opaque to readers' (Kress, 1993: 180). This is especially pertinent in relation to children's self-initiated sign-making with found objects, models, cut-outs and drawings in play, in which the child selects 'those characteristics which he regards as most important for him in the thing he wants to represent ... the relation which united form and meaning is one of analogy' (Kress, 1997: 93). As Hall argues in Chapter 6, children's drawings can also be seen as 'authoring spaces' in which they reveal their identities and unique meanings.

Methodological approaches and research methods

The aim of my research is to explore Vygotsky's theory 'that make-believe play, drawing and writing can be viewed as different moments in an essentially unified process' (Vygotsky, 1978: 116), and to trace *children's mathematical graphics* from their emergence in imaginative play. In this study, *imaginative* play is interpreted from a 'multi-modal' perspective (Kress, 1997) and is underpinned by Vygotsky's work (1978). The first phase of this research focuses on young children's imaginative play and includes role play, junk models and cut-outs, drawings and other forms of graphicacy. The research began during the year in which the children were three and four years old, in their final year in two nursery settings. Both nursery settings are in the south-west of England. One is a maintained nursery located within an inner-city Children's Centre and the other a small, private nursery in a rural area. The nursery schools provide a 'play-based' curriculum that spans birth to five years of age (DfES, 2007).

The research draws on ethnographic theory and involves immersion through observation in the field of study in order to construct pictures of the children's cultural and perceptual world. Ethnography is applied to a wide range of social contexts such as classrooms and depends on 'participant observation, triangulation, interviewing and qualitative analysis – essentially, interpretation – in order to arrive at an understanding of the observed patterns of behaviour engaged in by those being studied' (Burns, 2000: 394–5). Since ethnographic research concerns people, ethical considerations which include gaining informed consent of everyone involved, ensuring confidentiality and being open with the findings of the research are central tenets.

The research also explores socio-cultural influences on the children's representations and how these contribute to their developing semiotic modes. This chapter draws on some of the data collected for the first phase of this research and was collected from a total of 16 children, of whom 12 were boys and four were girls. For the purposes of this chapter, I have analysed examples from the data using categories of *functions of the imagination* (Van Oers, 2005).

The qualitative data is drawn largely from written observations and photographs of children's imaginative play and graphicacy. Observations were made both by the practitioners and by the researcher to ensure reliability and were discussed collaboratively. The observations are supported by other 'rich data', including questionnaires, interviews and regular discussions with the nursery teachers and practitioners. The practitioners were partners in the research and during the year were given several publications on play which, with the observations, became a focus of collaborative discussions (teachers, practitioners and researcher).

Understanding imaginative play

Van Oers proposes that play is 'a process of continuous recontextualization' through which children develop towards more abstract forms of activities (1998: 141). During a research programme investigating children's play, he acknowledged that reflections and discussions of their data 'showed that the notion of imagination was more complex than it looked at the beginning'. The researchers 'encountered many new and unexpected productions of children that could be related to creativity', identifying 'emergent qualities of the phenomenon of imagination in the play activities of young children' (Van Oers, 2005: 8/5): this led the researchers to identify two categories of *functions of the imagination* that were based on their empirical research. Van Oers argues that the 'potentials of imagination' are the emergence of abstract and divergent thinking.

Using the examples gathered for the current study, a systematic analysis of observations of imaginative play episodes was undertaken using Van Oers' *functions of the imagination* (2005). However, when discussing and assigning examples to the two original categories, it became clear that some of my observations did not fit neatly into either of the categories. Following further discussion with an independent researcher and with the practitioners, I originated a third category, *imagination as an act of dynamic change*, enabling me to extend the existing research. In order to ensure inter-rater reliability, I invited the independent researcher to assess examples. A small percentage of observations (4%) were rejected, either because they were ambiguous or because we failed to reach agreement.

Functions of the imagination

By 'conceptualising imagination …' and 'trying to understand the novelties in children's activities or verbal narratives ', Van Oers (2005) found that the 'products' of imaginative play (i.e. images or 'signs') served particular functions in the play of children aged four to seven years. The characteristics of these three categories are described below and set out in Appendix 8.1.

Imagination as etcetera-act

This *function* 'serves the goal of abbreviating an ongoing sequence of actions, referring to the invisible, by suggesting – with the help of some symbolic means – that a given series or rule can be continued' (Van Oers, 2005: 8). Van Oers provides the following example to illustrate this category: six-year-old Inge explained her drawing of a boat on the sea, adding 'I did not draw all the fishes, you know; there are also two traffic lights, a red and a green one. The fishes also see the crosses'. Inge used speech to explain aspects she implied but had not drawn. Van Oers explains that Inge 'combined different elements from her everyday experience into a new configuration ... illustrating Vygotsky's combinatorial view on imagination' (2005: 8–9). Van Oers considers *imagination as etcetera-act* as a form of abstraction, of abstract thinking.

Analysing imaginative play episodes in the current study revealed several episodes of *imagination as etcetera-act*. However, since they are from children younger than those described by van Oers, they reveal aspects of children's abstract thought that emerge at an earlier point in their development. For example, three-year-old Joshua made scribble marks on paper with a green pen and making several cuts across it remarked: 'doggie' (Figure 8.1): it appeared he intended his cut-out to signify its head and body, and the tiny piece, its tail. This example includes sufficient visual information for Joshua to communicate his intention, whilst the lack of detail (face, ears and legs) can be said to 'refer to the invisible' and his cut-out may have allowed him to make a more explicit sign than a drawing.

Hamzah was drawing in the graphics area: after a while, he turned to the adult observing nearby, explaining he had drawn 'cars'. Later, he added two black dots beneath the row of brown dots (on the left) and finally drew a rectangular outline with 'wheels' and a 'driving wheel' at the foot of the page (Figure 8.2). Although Hamzah only spoke one word to communicate his meaning, we can see that he had captured what was, to him, the most significant feature of cars (i.e. their wheels), which, in an abbreviated representation, allowed him to communicate his symbolic intention. Kress includes a similar example of a three-year-old's interest as 'condensed' meaning: 'For him a car, clearly, was first and foremost defined by the criterial characteristic of having wheels ... representing these features of *car,* namely wheels, or 'wheelness' (1997: 11).

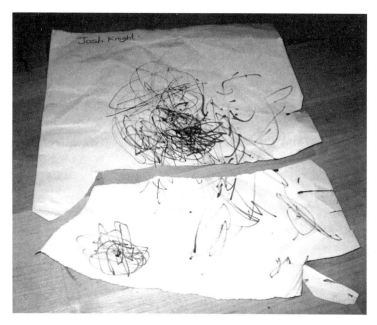

Figure 8.1 Joshua's doggie

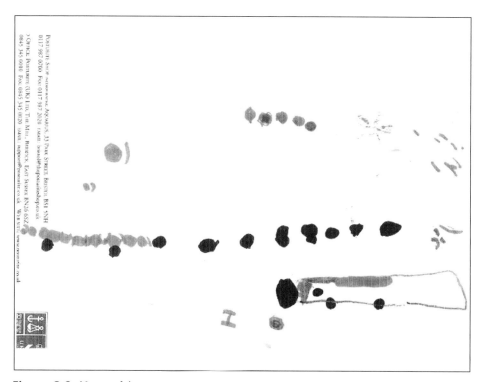

Figure 8.2 Hamzah's cars

It can sometimes be difficult for adults to understand a young child's intention when they represent their ideas. Nathan chose an envelope and, screwing up some purple and green paper, he tucked the pieces beneath its flap and secured it with masking tape. He explained he'd made 'an astronaut' and, announcing 'blast off', lifted it above his head to make it 'fly to the moon'. He then showed how, by lifting the masking tape, the 'astronaut' could get out of his space suit (the envelope). The materials Nathan had chosen allowed him to communicate his intended meanings and we can see that he combined some elements from his everyday experience of dressing and undressing, to signify new meaning. The lack of visual details in his astronaut was balanced by his actions and words and was sufficient to ensure that others understood his meaning.

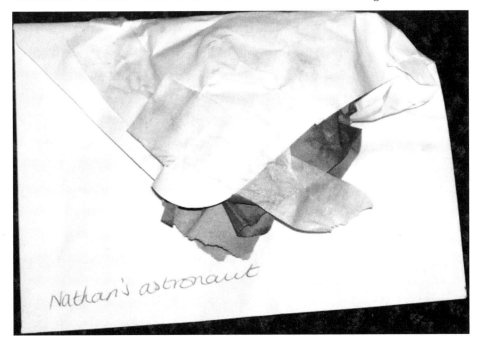

Figure 8.3 Nathan's astronaut

These examples suggest that young children's images are personal expressions of internal (mental) representations which, through external representation, allow them to communicate personal meanings to others. Their symbolic tools have an economy that captures some of the essential elements, here, for example, of a dog, of cars or an astronaut in his suit. Rather than the child's words illuminating the invisible, we are sometimes left to continue the children's own 'rules' ourselves.

Imagination as an act of generating alternatives

In this *function*, children make 'alternative representations of objects, situations and actions. It consists of how the world *could* be ... mental constructs, which picture the world differently from how it is commonly seen' (Van Oers, 2005: 9). Van Oers proposes that Vygotsky's description of a child substituting a stick for a horse is an example of this *function*, developing 'out of social interaction and exteriorization of the positions of different people, eventually resulting in divergent thinking' (2005: 9).

Case study

Sophie was playing with several friends and hid various artefacts in a box of hay they found. Felicity held out a toy wheel, naming it as a 'chocolate cake' and others followed her lead, naming various cylindrical objects as 'chocolate' and 'strawberry' cakes. Sophie suggested they have a picnic and handed out wooden blocks as 'ice-creams' and gave a large sea shell 'to eat' to an adult nearby. Lifting the shell to her mouth, the adult paused, asking if she should eat it, adding 'it's very rough and might hurt my mouth'. Sophie hesitated, watching warily as the adult put her finger inside the shell and licked it, then smiling remarked that it tasted 'delicious'. It was clear that Sophie was anxious to see if the adult understood the 'rules' implied in their spontaneous game: would she spoil it by saying that she couldn't eat a seashell? Did she understand that for that moment it was important that all the players in the game shared the same 'rule' – that the objects they employed signified food? The players in the game needed to have a shared understanding of the rules and meanings in this play: the adult's action (pretending to scoop out some ice-cream and eat it), her use of language, her tone of voice and smile as she commented 'delicious' allowed meanings to be negotiated and confirmed that the adult understood and was able to share in their pretence and sustain play. Finally, as if to affirm acceptance of the adult as a full player in their game, Omar reached for the shell and said, 'Let's have some!'

In the next example, Nathan used one sign to explore two different meanings. Nathan's mum had made a 'caterpillar'-shaped birthday cake for his recent fourth birthday. Nathan drew a horizontal line with zigzags as his 'birthday cake' *(not shown)* and turning his paper over, repeated the same lines and zigzags, now referring to them as 'writing' (Figure 8.4). For his representation of his cake, the zigzag appeared to suggest the shape (and possibly the movement) of a caterpillar. Duplicating the same marks, Nathan then used them to represent something of the appearance of writing, or perhaps the movement of a hand as someone writes. Exploring these dual meanings through one sign also enabled him to further explore the flexibility of signs and the way in which there needs to be shared

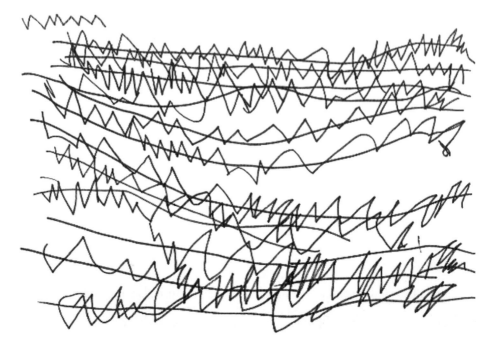

Figure 8.4: Nathan's writing

understanding in order to communicate meanings to others. Pahl describes a child exploring a range of meanings as she transforms her model:

> Her mind was internally 'gluing together' different concepts ... The things that are linked in the mind have become linked in the material world ... Using one idea the children are driven by internal links within them to explore other possibilities. This reflects both the children's inner thoughts and their interest in how the object looks ... These meanings then develop as they move from one concept to another. (1999: 20–1).

Working with young children can sometimes challenge our understanding of their symbolic representations and it is important that we tune into the child's personal meanings and as they create signs and tools. Children need to communicate their meaning in order to establish shared rules and co-construct meanings. Their meanings have to 'make sense' in the context of their imaginative worlds, although this may not always make sense to an outsider who does not have access to shared and negotiated meanings.

Figure 8.5 shows Finley's representation using junk materials: he explained this was 'the sea and a whale' and that the clear plastic was 'rubbish in the sea' that will injure creatures living there. Staff at his nursery knew that Finley had a keen interest in animals and often talked about them: the previous week, the television had featured news about floating 'islands of plastic refuse' in the Pacific Ocean and it is possible that he may have heard adults discussing this.

Figure 8.5 Finley's whale

Imagination as an act of dynamic change

As we observed the children's play, a number of examples revealed an aspect of imagination that was significantly different from the *two functions of imagination* above. The children's representations embodied complex ideas and actions that placed the child or children as central players, able to exert a direct influence on what happened next in their play and led to an additional 'function': *imagination as an act of dynamic change.*

The data showed that boys particularly drew on their love of adventure and gadgets. Their experiences and interest included new media and technologies, such as televisions and remote controls, computers, game consoles and electronic toys; combined with popular culture and 'superheroes' such as 'Nintendo', 'Power Rangers' and American wrestling which all exerted strong influences on children's play (Marsh, 2006). The children assigned specific powers to the signs they created, using these to 'operate' their imagined technologies to effect change.

Mason was pressing the buttons on a real calculator, yelling excitedly, 'Yeah! Fighting games! Video games!' He reached for a small spiral-bound notebook and made marks on the first page before tearing it off; 'this is a *different* calculator with computer games on!' Mason's interest triggered other play episodes of 'paper calculators' that involved several other children over an extensive period. His friend Alfie made marks on a notepad saying, 'Lots of fighting!' and a week later, Mason announced, 'I've made a calculator. I'm putting Batman on it – black and green'. The boys involved in this play returned to it many times over a period of two terms and although during this time there was little attempt to write numerals on their paper calculators, several of them, including Mason, had written numerals for other purposes during this period. Many of the children made rapid marks, either drawing 'buttons' on their calculator, or (as here) using scribble-marks, and combined these graphic representations with talk. Exploring layers of meanings over an extended period allowed the children's understanding to evolve over time.

Figure 8.6 Mason's paper calculator

A later example from Mason showed that he was now a champion of this '21st century' play. Next to him at the writing table, Leola was making vertical snips around a folded piece of yellow card. Mason watched Leola and finding a piece of yellow card, folded and snipped similar cuts around its perimeter. Next, he wrote letters and numerals, reading 'sk' '714bp10' and, lifting it to his face, explained it was 'a spy gadget ... "sk", is 'to keep the password safe. To switch it on you have to say "714bp10"'. I asked if there was a way to switch his 'spy gadget' off and picking it up, he replied excitedly, 'Yeah! You have to read it backwards!', promptly reading, '10 pb417'. Nathan had invested his special gadget with technological powers and drew on his considerable knowledge of passwords and controls.

Figure 8.7 Mason's spy gadget

These play episodes suggest 'a construct of fantasy (that) may represent something substantially new ... once it has been externally embodied, that is, has been given material form, this crystallized imagination that has become an object begins to actually exist in the real world, to affect other things' (Vygotsky, 2004: 20–1). The observations reveal how young children's understanding of new media and technologies populate their imaginative play and suggest that communication (about the function of their technologies) is essential to establishing shared meanings and actions in such imaginative play episodes.

In all the examples, the children's brief verbal explanations could be understood in the context of their sign-making: for example, cutting his paper allowed Joshua to arrange the pieces into a new arrangement to communicate his meaning. In other contexts (as in Sophie's picnic and the paper calculators), children made greater use of talk to negotiate and co-construct meanings about their signs. Sometimes the affordances of open-ended junk materials and actions provided the most satisfactory modes to communicate meaning, as in Nathan's astronaut. In contrast, marks made with pens (for drawing and writing) offered the most appropriate media for Hamzah and Nathan to signify their meanings and revealed the emergence of graphical symbols that will develop into symbolic written languages such as writing and written mathematics.

Discussion

This analysis of imaginative play has uncovered some of the children's complex meanings and communicative modes as they created, adapted and co-constructed signs to fulfill specific semiotic needs. The categories developed by Van Oers provided a valuable tool to help understand the children's imaginative play and led to a new function, *imagination as an act of dynamic change*.

Created within their imaginative play, Van Oers argues that the 'products' of such semiotic activities gradually evolve 'in close relationship to the function it serves *in different contexts*' (2005: 9; italics added), proposing that 'the etc-form (abstraction) and the alternatives producing form (divergent thinking)' are closely linked. Analysing an example of a child's plan (a 'schematisation') of a castle he had built, Van Oers found it included 'new functional ways of representing quantities' and reflecting 'on sign-meaning relationships through an alternative way of representing the numeral' (2005: 12): in this and other examples, he identified the 'beginnings of mathematical imagination' (Van Oers, 2005: 11).

I would argue that these same functions can also be traced throughout *children's mathematical graphics* and directly support children's emerging understanding of the standard, abstract written language of mathematics. For example:

- *Imagination as an etcetera*-act (abstraction) is revealed when children use 'implied symbols' in their personal representations of calculations.

- *Imagination as an act of generating alternatives* (divergent thinking) is evident when children use alternative (personal) ways of representing numerals or mathematical symbols such as '+', and when they use their own ways of representing calculations or data.

- *Imagination as an act of dynamic change* appears to support children's understanding of the way in which mathematical signs (operators) are used to effect change within calculations. This is particularly evident when children use 'narrative action' – for example, representing arrows or hands to signify the action (operation) of subtraction as 'taking away'.
(See Carruthers and Worthington [2006] for further details).

It is important to emphasise that children's imaginative play should be valued for the many rich experiences it provides young children at the moment in which they are involved. However, the findings here also suggest that the 'potentials of imagination' support the gradual evolution of *children's mathematical graphics* in ways that we are only beginning to understand.

Implications for pedagogy

Play is a complex landscape: children's thinking and the complexity of their ideas and signs deserve closer attention if we are to understand and truly value their meaning-making. This perspective is reinforced by the contributors to this book.

The data have revealed the importance of understanding children's symbolic communicative competences, and have provided insights into their early meaning-making as symbolic written languages emerge, revealed through a 'profound, internal analysis'. The findings underscore the significance of imagination and highlight the relationship between adults' involvement and understanding, and the power of imaginative play for making meanings in diverse contexts.

Many of the examples explored in this study were gathered through teachers' and practitioners' observations of children's self-initiated play and showed that the pedagogical feature that appeared to contribute most to imaginative play was the adults' focus on children's *meanings*. The implications for practice are that detailed observations of children's play provide an invaluable tool to support adults in their understanding of children's play and meaning-making; as Drummond argues, 'the act of seeing gives way to the act of understanding' (2003: 66). Collaborative discussions that focus on observations with colleagues enable adults to make sense of children's imaginative play and semiotic explorations and often reveal surprising insights into their thinking and their ability to construct, co-construct and communicate complex and abstract ideas. Significantly, the findings also imply that pedagogical support and interest in children's meaning-making and communicative practices can support their emerging understanding of the written language of mathematics. This highlights the need for practitioners' discussions to embrace the full range of children's early semiotic representations and consider the interrelationship between imagination and mathematics. Such analysis of imaginative play can enable practitioners to explore and appreciate this complexity, and extend our understanding beyond the reductive lens of the curriculum goals of the Early Years Foundation Stage.

One of the key pedagogical challenges for practitioners is how they might use observations as a form of enquiry that allows them to understand and support this complexity through deepening understanding of their pedagogical roles and strategies. The findings from the research explored in this chapter show that paying close attention to children's semiotic activities and co-construction of events and meanings in children's imaginative play can support practitioners in gaining greater insights into play and the beginnings of symbolic languages.

Reflective tasks 〰️

- Collect examples of observations of imaginative play from your own settings, including children's models, drawings and writings. It would be helpful if other colleagues could also undertake this to facilitate team discussions.

- Using the *functions of the imagination* explored in this chapter, analyse your observations in relation to children's meaning-making and symbolic representations. How much has this added to your understanding of the potential of imaginative play for meaning-making by children in their early years setting?

- Compare your observations with colleagues and discuss their potential for using formative assessment as a basis for supporting children's development in relation to meaning-making and symbolic representations.

- This may also lead you to consider together how you can further focus on children's own meanings and provide more open-ended opportunities for play of this kind by the children.

Appendix 8.1 Characteristics of 'functions of the imagination'

Category	Indicators/characteristics
Imagination as etcetera-act	• Refers to the invisible • Suggests that – with the help of some symbolic means – a given series or rule can be continued • Combines different elements from everyday experience into a new configuration • Abbreviates an ongoing sequence of events
Imagination as an act of generating alternatives	• Making alternative representations of objects, situations and actions • Picturing how the world *could* be • Using an object to signify something else • Using common elements from their environments that were part of a previous experience
Imagination as an act of dynamic change	• Representations embody complex ideas and actions and place the child as a central player • Combines elements from their experience • Reflects interest in new media and technologies • Children assign special powers to their imaginary technologies, 'operating' them to effect change

Further reading

DCSF (2009) *Children Thinking Mathematically: PSRN Essential Knowledge for Early Years Practitioners.* London: DCSF.

Pahl, K. (1999) *Transformations: Meaning Making in the Nursery.* Stoke-on-Trent: Trentham Books.

Marsh, J. (ed.) (2006) *Popular Culture, New Media and Digital Literacy in Early Childhood.* London: RoutledgeFalmer.

Van Oers, B. (2005) 'The potentials of imagination', *Inquiry: Critical Thinking across the Disciplines* 24(4): 5–17.

Texts given to practitioners involved in the research

Carruthers, E. and Worthington, M. (2006) *Children's Mathematics, Making Marks, Making Meaning*, 2nd edn. London: Sage.

Children's Mathematics Network: www.childrens-mathematics.net
This website focuses on children's mathematical graphics and includes some children's examples with features referred to here in the discussion.

Kress, G. (1997) *Before Writing: Re-thinking the Paths to Literacy.* London: Routledge.

Pahl, K. (1999a) 'Making models as a communicative practice – observing meaning making in a nursery', *Reading* November: 114–19.

Pahl, K. (1999b) *Transformations: Meaning Making in the Nursery.* Stoke-on-Trent: Trentham Books.

References

Broadhead, P. (2004) *Early Years Play and Learning: Developing Social Skills and Cooperation.* London: RoutledgeFalmer.

Burns, R. (2000) *Introduction to Research Methods.* London: Sage.

Carruthers, E. and Worthington, M. (2005) 'Making sense of mathematical graphics: the development of understanding abstract symbolism', *European Early Childhood Education Research Association Journal* (EECERA) 13(1): 57–79.

Carruthers, E. and Worthington, M. (2006) *Children's Mathematics: Making Marks, Making Meaning,* 2nd edn. London: Sage.

Department for Education and Skills (DfES) (2007) *Practice Guidance for the Early Years Foundation Stage.* London: DfES.

Drummond, M.J. (2003) *Assessing Children's Learning,* 2nd edn. London: David Fulton.

Gussin-Paley, V. (2005) *A Child's Work: The Importance of Fantasy Play.* Chicago: University of Chicago Press.

Kress, G. (1993) 'Against arbitrariness: the social production of the sign as a foundational issue in critical discourse analysis', *Discourse and Society* 4(2): 169–91.

Kress, G. (1997) *Before Writing: Rethinking the Paths to Literacy.* London: Routledge.

Marsh, J. (ed.) (2006) *Popular Culture, New Media and Digital Literacy in Early Childhood.* London: RoutledgeFalmer.

Pahl, K. (1999) *Transformations: Meaning Making in the Nursery.* Stoke-on-Trent: Trentham Books.

Pahl, K. (2002) 'Ephemera, mess and miscellaneous piles: texts and practices in families', *Journal of Early Childhood Literacy* 2(2): 145–66.

Rogers, S. and Evans, J. (2008) *Inside Role-Play in Early Childhood Education.* London: Routledge.

Van Oers, B. (1998) 'The fallacy of decontextualization', *Mind, Culture and Activity* 5(2): 135–42.

Van Oers, B. (2005) 'The potentials of imagination', *Inquiry: Critical Thinking across the Disciplines* 24(4): 5–17.

Vygotsky, L.S. (1978) *Mind in Society: The Development of Higher Psychological Processes.* Cambridge, MA: Harvard University Press.

Vygotsky, L.S. (1987) 'Imagination and its development in childhood', in W. Rieber and A. Carton (eds) *The Collected Works of L.S. Vygotsky, Vol. 1.* New York: Plenum Press. pp. 339–50.

Vygotsky, L.S. (2004) 'Imagination and creativity in childhood', *Journal of Russian and East European Psychology* 42(1): 7–97.

Wood, E. and Attfield, J. (2005) *Play, Learning and the Early Childhood Curriculum,* 2nd edn. London: Paul Chapman Publishing.

Worthington, M. (2009) 'Fish in the water of culture: signs, and symbols in young children's drawing', *The Psychology of Education Review* 33(1): 37–46.

Making the Most of Play in the Early Years: The Importance of Children's Perceptions

Justine Howard

The aims of this chapter are to:

- illustrate what separates play from other modes of action, using children's own perceptions of their play
- demonstrate the crucial role of early years practitioners in shaping children's perceptions of play, maximising subsequent opportunities for learning and being accepted as a cooperative play partner
- illustrate that approaching tasks playfully enhances young children's learning and development
- highlight how understanding play as an approach to tasks can empower practitioners, giving them confidence in advocating their play practice
- provide insights into our theoretical understanding of play and research methodologies for use with young children.

It has been proposed that play is a hallowed concept for teachers of young children (Pellegrini and Boyd, 1993). However, children learn in many different ways and, despite decades of play research, it has proved difficult to determine that play has unique developmental qualities, and to isolate the benefits of play from other causal determinants. Although the necessity of providing an operational definition of play has been debated, there is still no consensus. From an academic perspective, a generic definition ensures that researchers have a common understanding of play (Garvey, 1991) but when translated into practice, definitions can often limit children's experiences to those that look like play or that meet particular criteria (Wood and Attfield, 2005). Attempts to define play include categorical approaches (Piaget, 1951; Smilansky, 1968), criteria (Rubin et al., 1983) and continuum (Pellegrini, 1991). Common to these definitions is that they pay minimal attention to the dynamic and contextual nature of play and are based on an adult frame of reference rather than the views of children.

Guha (1988) suggests there is a difference between children's play at home and their play in school, which is evidenced by Brooker in Chapter 2 in the context of cultural diversity. Similarly, Saracho (1991) points out that play can mean different things to different people in different contexts. These perspectives highlight the situational specificity of play and, consequently, the need to consider the views of the players when deciding what it means to engage in play. In considering play as an approach to a task, Moyles (1989) distinguishes the internal affective qualities of play and the outward manifestation of these qualities in observable play behaviour. Categorical, criteria and continuum approaches to defining play usefully describe some (but not all) play behaviours, but do not necessarily capture the affective qualities that separate it from other modes of action. To get to the heart of why play is so important for children's development, we need to know when and why they choose to engage in play, and in what ways they subsequently benefit. This chapter describes a series of studies that focus on children's perceptions of play, the experiences that influence the development of these perceptions, and how participating in an activity when it is seen to be play is beneficial for children's learning and development. The research describes the cues that children use to determine whether an activity is play, the ways in which classroom experience shapes these cues, and how their presence or absence influences children's performance on problem-solving tasks. Understanding children's views about their play can be formative and diagnostic, by providing a powerful means for practitioners to plan environments and learning opportunities where children adopt a playful mode of action that has a positive impact on task performance.

Why study children's perceptions of play?

Wood and Attfield (2005: 7) have warned that 'in the urge to categorise and define play we may be in danger of overlooking the fact that children have their own definitions of play'. Considering that most research interest in play stems from educational, developmental and therapeutic perspectives, it is surprising that there have been few attempts to elicit information about what children themselves see as being play or not play. Manning and Sharp proposed that 'there is no distinction between play and work in the infant mind ... [and that children] ... concentrate all their faculties on the one activity in which they are engaged' (1977: 12). Research which has attempted to understand children's views of their play has added a new and contrary dimension, namely that children can and do differentiate between the various activities in which they are engaged, and that the type of environment they experience influences the development of their views. Children have a clear awareness of the difference between play and work, and distinguish whether an activity is associated with learning (Keating et al., 2000).

Using interviews, King (1979) revealed how children made a clear distinction between play and work. Play was generally referred to as children's self-initiated activity whereas work involved teacher presence or direction. Karrby (1989) found that young children tended to describe play as involving pretence, following a certain theme and being governed by self-determined rules. Activities that were described as not play involved specific goals (such as making a clay model) or simple experiences (such as swinging or chasing). Conversely, when Rothlein and Brett (1987) asked children what they thought of when they heard the word 'play', around one-third of their responses related to outdoor activity (where swinging and chasing would be most likely to occur). In comparing child-centred environments with formal, directed environments, Karrby (1989) found that children who had experienced structured classroom environments tended to associate learning with teacher-directed activity and failed to recognise play as a learning opportunity. This play–work distinction, prompted by teacher presence or direction, was also found by Robson (1993) who proposed that the children had learned through their classroom experiences to associate play with their self-initiated activity and formal work with teacher direction. Wing (1995) also found that children saw freely chosen and self-directed activities as play, and activities that involved adult initiation and direction as work. These children also reported that play was less likely to be evaluated by the teacher as being right or wrong.

Reflection point

How do you define play? Why do you think you define play in this way? What has influenced your idea of what play is? Has your definition of play changed over time? Why?

The studies of children's views previously described were based on adult observations of children at play and interviews with children either engaged in play or reflecting on previous play activity. Whilst using interviews alongside observations allows children to share their views and participate in the research process, there are some important considerations to bear in mind, particularly when working with young children. Whilst young children are capable of sharing their ideas, research methods must be developmentally appropriate in order to ensure that their views are reported accurately and ethically. If interviews are conducted whilst the child is 'on-task', they can be distracting and alter the course of the activity. If done retrospectively, they require reflection on prior activities and may place developmentally advanced cognitive demands on the child. In some cases, these reflective interview studies involved children as young as two years old (e.g. Rothlein and Brett, 1987). In reflecting on past activities, the child is required to: (1) remember the task; (2) place her/himself back in the situation; (3) decide whether or not this was play or not play; and (4) justify this decision. The time required to interview and observe individual children also means that sample size in these studies is relatively small. The difficulties associated with conducting such interviews have led to the development of a more systematic methodology which uses visual methods, as described in the following section.

The Research: Understanding Children's Perceptions of Play using the Activity Apperception Story Procedure (AASP)

The AASP (Howard, 2002) is based on the School Apperception Story Procedure (SASP) developed by Jones (1995). It is a two-part procedure that enables the researcher to elicit young children's perceptions of their activities using a photographic sorting procedure and focused discussion around these photographs. The use of photographs is consistent with the notion that children aged 3–6 years are more likely to associate photographic representation with reality (Kose et al., 1983). There are 26 photographs in the AASP that depict artificially 'set up' classroom activities such as sand, water or reading and writing, and the photographs are paired so that certain cues are present or not present within each picture. These cues were based on previous studies of children's perceptions of play and theoretical descriptions of play, and included space and constraint (whether an activity occurred at the table or on the floor), adult presence (present or not present), positive affect (whether the activity was fun or serious) and activity type (play or academic materials). For example, one pair of photographs shows a group of children completing a number task at the table, (a) with an adult present, and (b) with no adult present. Another pair shows two children completing jigsaw puzzles, (a) on the floor, and (b) at the table. Table 1 shows additional pairs of photographs and the cues these are based on.

Table 9.1   AASP pictorial cues and example scene descriptions

Cue used	Example photograph pair
Positive affect	Child in the water tray, *concentrating and pouring*
	Child in the water tray, *laughing and splashing*
Space and constraint	Child completing number activity *at the table*
	Child completing number activity *on the floor*
Adult presence	*Children alone* in the home corner
	Children and teacher in the home corner
Activity type	Child showing *book* to the teacher
	Child showing *Lego model* to the teacher

In part one of the AASP, children sort the photographs into brightly coloured post boxes according to whether or not they believe the activity depicts 'play' or 'not play'. The categorical sorting element of the task is grounded in the literature that suggests children respond well to game-like procedures (e.g. Royeen, 1985; Sturgess and Ziviani, 1996). Part two of the procedure allows the researcher to check the consistency of previous choices and asks children to discuss their choices for a smaller number of the photographs. The method is more reliable than interviews and observations in that it systematically elicits children's views in a game-like procedure that is developmentally appropriate with minimal cognitive load.

One hundred and eleven children aged between three and six years completed the original AASP procedure (Howard, 2002). The mean age of the sample was 4:11 and the children were located within six different pre-school, nursery and primary settings. Reliability was measured via the consistency of choices between part one and part two of the procedure. There was a high level of consistency (91.5%). Use of the pictorial cues was taken as a measure of validity in that the cues present in the photographs were attended to by the children when making their decisions. Across the whole sample, more children categorised the activity as play when the photograph showed the activity occurring on the floor rather than on the table, without rather than with teacher presence, when positive affect (e.g. enjoyment) was depicted and where the task involved 'play-like' rather than 'academic' materials (e.g. sand and water rather than reading or writing). As well as attending to the depicted cues, analysis of justifications for categorical decisions in part two of the procedure revealed that children spontaneously offered additional cues that had been unanticipated in the design of the AASP, or could not be pictorially represented. For example, children justified decisions by referring to pretence ('it's play because they are only pretending'), distinguishing play from work ('it's not work because they are only playing'), the inclusion of toys ('toys aren't work'), skill or difficulty ('it's hard work'), choice ('they can choose because they've finished their work') and the fact that the activity was occurring in the school context ('because you learn when you go to school'). There were interesting differences in the use of these cues according to the type of early years setting. Children in primary school classes rather than day nursery settings were more likely to emphasise skill development in work and free choice in play. They were less likely to associate play with learning. Children who had experienced a strong contrast between play and formal activity in their classes, and where teachers engaged infrequently in play, more readily used adult presence and table-top activities as a cue to these examples being 'not play'.

A further study employing the AASP procedure analysed children's play choices according to social context within an educational setting (Howard et al., 2006). In this study, the same procedure was followed but for the purposes of analysis, the cards were grouped according to the social context they depicted. Social contexts included solitary activity, paired activity and group activity, either with or without adult presence. Ninety-two children (mean age 4:9) participated in the study and findings revealed that children made more 'play' choices where there was no adult presence and where cooperative or group activities, rather than solitary activities, were depicted.

The findings from the two studies that have utilised the AASP method (Howard, 2002; Howard et al., 2006) provide insights into young children's perceptions and definitions of play within an educational setting, and support the findings of previous interview and observation studies. Children appear to define play according to the choices they are afforded, positive affect, where an activity takes place and with whom. In addition, the type of classroom experiences appears to play an important role in the development of their views. However, the design of the AASP involved complex statistical analysis as the number of cards for each cue was not constant. A further criticism was that the photographs were not of the children's actual classrooms but rather 'set up' to replicate activities that may occur, which required a degree of hypothetical thought on the part of the children. These considerations led to developments in the research method. The RAP (Revised Apperception Procedure; Howard et al., 2008) has improved the developmental appropriateness of the original method by using photographs of children's *actual* classrooms. In this study, six activities were chosen to be representative of what the children experienced across the school day. These were blocks, literacy, reading, art, puzzles and computer use. A series of photographs were taken for each activity, including one or more possible cues as to the nature of the task. The cues for each activity included: whether an adult was present or not, whether the activity occurred alone or in a group and whether the activity occurred inside, outside, at the table or on the floor.

The sorting part of the procedure was consistent with the two previous AASP studies described earlier in the chapter, but in the Revised Apperception Procedure, children were not required to justify their choices. Instead, to measure the reliability of the findings, a sample of 15 children repeated the photograph-sorting procedure some time after the initial presentation. There was a high level of consistency in their categorical decisions (90.9%). A total of 72 children aged three to six years participated in the RAP (mean age 4:3). The children were from a nursery, reception and year 1 class within the same school. Consistent with findings from the AASP, children made more play choices where activities were on the floor rather than at a table, outside rather than inside and without rather than with teacher presence. Certain activities were also perceived as more play-like than others. Of significance were the overall trends within the data that further supported the importance of age and experience in the development of perceptions. Younger children had broader perceptions of play, whereas older children appeared to have learned to distinguish play from more formal activities according to where and with whom they took place, and whether they were considered voluntary or teacher-directed.

Reflection point 〰

What messages do you think your environment sends to children about play? Do you think the children in your class would be more likely to see play as something that occurred on the floor rather than at the table? Would they be more likely to see an activity as play if you (or another adult) were not present?

Do children perform differently on tasks when they see them as play?

Whilst we can see how children are learning and developing in their play, trying to establish that play makes a key contribution to their learning is more of a challenge. To do this, we need to demonstrate that children perform differently when they are engaged in play compared to more formal learning situations. The following section considers research that compares children's performance in playful and formal learning situations. This comparative approach to studying the benefits of children's play has been adopted by Whitebread (Chapter 10) in his research into play, metacognition and self-regulation. A key difference is that the learning situations described below are those determined by children's cues to 'play' or 'not play'. The research is based on the proposition that whether children regard an activity as play or not play will impact on their behaviour.

So far, this chapter has presented three studies that focus on children's own perceptions of play, two using the AASP (Howard, 2002; Howard et al., 2006) and one using the RAP (Howard et al., 2008). These studies provide a series of cues that children use to define play, some of which can be altered in experimental conditions to determine the relationship between playful practice and performance. The cues to play (as used by the children) that can be altered include where an activity takes place, with whom the activity takes place and the level of choice afforded with regards to participation.

Howard et al. (2004) hypothesised that children who practised a task playfully (when cues to play were present) would show significantly superior performance when compared to children who practised a task formally (when cues to not play were present). The study followed a pre-test, post-test design where 30 children aged 3–5 years (mean 4:9) were initially tested on a familiar problem-solving task that involved timing how long it took to complete an age-appropriate jigsaw puzzle. Following this pre-test measure, children were assigned either to a playful or formal 10-minute practice session. Consistent with the cues revealed by studies of children's perceptions of play, in the playful condition, children were asked if they would like to have a go with some more puzzles on the floor (without adult presence or involvement). In the formal condition, children were asked to sit at the table and complete some more puzzles (with adult presence but not involvement). The conditions represented the cues of space and constraint (table vs floor), adult involvement (teacher present vs teacher not present) and choice and control (being told to complete the practice or invited to do so). Following the practice sessions, children were then re-tested on the original task (post-test). Despite there being no significant difference in performance at the pre-test stage, children who practised in the playful condition demonstrated significantly higher improvement at the post-test stage than those who practised formally. Both groups of children improved on the task but the children who practised the task playfully improved more, in that they completed the task significantly faster. Thomas et al. (2008) adopted a similar design but with an additional post-test following a one-week delay. Findings here were of particular interest in that after the delay, the improved performance of children who experienced playful practice was significantly greater than for those who practised formally, indicating an important residual effect as Figure 9.1 shows:

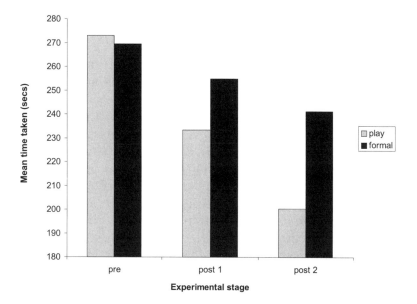

Figure 9.1 Children's performance on task following playful or formal practice at immediate and delayed post-tests (Thomas et al., 2006) (Reproduced with permission from *Psychology of Education Review* © The British Psychological Society.)

These studies provide empirical support for the relationship between playful practice and improved performance. In addition, they demonstrate the importance of understanding the cues children use to define play as their mode of action. Therefore, it can be argued that, by providing a playful environment, practitioners can facilitate the development of cues for action that have the potential to promote learning across multiple domains. Children learn in a number of ways but it would appear that regarding an activity as 'play' amplifies learning potential.

Why does a playful approach improve performance?

Although play is not the only enjoyable way for children to learn, there appear to be characteristics inherent in play that separate it from other activities. Children are more enthusiastic and willing to participate in play activities (King, 1979) and the lack of external goals and level of control afforded to children during play create an environment where children are able to try out their ideas within self-maintained boundaries (Moyles, 1989). The fact that the boundaries in play are set, regulated and modified by children themselves, means that play promotes and protects self-esteem and maintains children's attention. Taking a playful approach to task (i.e. regarding an activity as play) facilitates learning and development via enthusiasm, motivation and self-preservation.

Howard and Miles (2008) have developed a theory to explain why a playful approach to task leads to improved performance, based on the cues children use to define play and findings from studies investigating the relationship between play and learning. Their 'threshold and fluency theory' assumes that playfulness manifests itself in the guise of lower behaviour thresholds (i.e. the level of confidence needed in a behaviour before it is enacted), and consequently leads to children showing greater behaviour fluency when they feel playful. Metaphorically, lowering the threshold required for a behaviour to be considered for execution renders the child an 'arrow-rich archer'. Rather than having a single arrow with which to hit a target, their quiver is full, allowing multiple shots. The theory suggests that a wider range of behaviours will be exhibited by a child who is playful than when the same child is not playful. Figure 9.2 shows the theory in diagramatic form. The letters A, B, C and D represent potential behaviours that might be trialled. Whether children perceive an activity as playful or not playful has the potential to influence their decision. A perception of playfulness leads to more behaviours being trialled. This increased behavioural fluency, as a result of lowered thresholds, can explain why children perform better in problem-solving tasks when they have practised these tasks under playful rather than formal conditions (Howard et al., 2004; Thomas et al., 2006).

The theory builds upon and operationalises the theoretical ideas of Sutton-Smith (1979) and Bruner (1974), who suggest that play is effective in promoting flexible and adaptive thinking. The suggestion within the threshold and fluency theory, that play as an approach to task can provide threshold information that guides behaviour and influences subsequent learning outcomes, is supported by detailed observations of children engaging in playful or formal practice situations. McInnes et al. (2009) conducted extensive analyses of children's behaviour when participating in formal and playful practice conditions. Using micro-observational software (Noldus Observer Pro), they found that children participating in playful practice conditions demonstrated more purposeful problem-solving behaviours and were more deeply engaged in the task. In the formal practice condition, children were easily distracted and tended to persevere with incorrect problem-solving strategies.

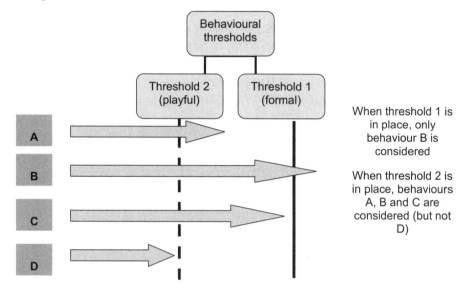

Figure 9.2 The threshold and fluency theory of play (Howard and Miles, 2008)

> **Reflection point** 〰
>
> Observe the children in your class whilst they complete a directed activity and a play activity. Do you notice anything different in their behaviour? Is what you see consistent with the findings presented here? Do you notice any other differences? Why do you think that children might behave differently in play and formal situations?

Making the most of play: practitioner research in the classroom context

Research studies across a range of early years settings have revealed that whilst practitioners work within the same curriculum guidance, there are differences in the experiences they provide for children (Sylva et al., 1999). Whilst settings can be similar in the variety of activities they offer and the adult support available for children, they function differently. There are many ways to structure the environment and a range of factors will influence the way in which each practitioner goes about this task, such as the size of the room or the amount and type of resources available. In addition, practitioners have their own perspectives on play and particular interaction styles. The research that has been described so far in this chapter, suggests that there are certain cues that children appear sensitive to when making play judgements. In addition, it appears that practitioners have a certain level of control in terms of the development of this sensitivity. Findings from the Apperception studies suggest that children use cues from their classroom environment and the interactions they have had with others when forming perceptions of play. In these previous studies, when children had experienced an environment where play was the principal activity, the majority of photographic stimuli were defined as play regardless of the cues that were depicted, suggesting that they perceived playfulness in a range of activities. In more formal environments, where play and work were clearly distinguished throughout the day, children thought play was most likely to occur without adult presence, on the floor rather than at a table and involving traditional play materials (Howard, 2002). This suggests that children make decisions based on their experiences. In environments where play was clearly separate from work activity, children were less likely to value play as a learning activity. Therefore, it can be argued that how practitioners plan the classroom environment is important in shaping the approach children take to their daily activities. Perceived playfulness is maximised when children are afforded control, when adults engage in all types of activity and when activities are not constrained by where they take place. Essentially, play is maximised when practitioners communicate that it is of equal value to other activities.

> ## Reflection point 〰
> How do you think play is presented in your class? Do you communicate that play is of equal value to other activities? If yes, how have you achieved this? If not, why not, and how might you go about changing this?

The photographic sorting procedure (AASP) provides a systematic means of identifying children's perceptions of play. The following section describes how it has been used as a formative and diagnostic measure to reflect on the playfulness of an early years classroom in a small-scale study by a reception class teacher, funded by the General Teaching Council of Wales.

Westcott and Howard (2007) asked children in one reception class in South Wales to complete the AASP procedure. Fourteen children were asked to sort photographs of their daily activities into post-boxes, according to whether or not they thought they were play, and were then invited to discuss the reasons for their choices. The class teacher was enthusiastic about the role of play for development in the early years and had made decisions about her classroom environment and curricula materials based on recent research into play and development. The classroom environment had been structured to centralise play and communicate its importance as follows:

- activities occurred in all areas of the classroom, both indoors and outdoors

- adults interacted with children across a range of activities

- activities were self-chosen and not timed

- observations of play were used to record achievement

- academic tasks were integrated into play.

Findings supported the researchers' prediction, that because of the centrality of play within the classroom, children would be insensitive to the cues. The children had a broad perception of play that spanned almost all classroom activities, social contexts and locations. They were just as likely to categorise an activity as play if a teacher was present or if it occurred at the table. In relation to teacher involvement, the children made justifications for their choices, such as '[that is play because] … she is helping them to do it' or 'the teacher is having a play with them'. This demonstrates that the teacher had been accepted as a cooperative play partner (Rich, 2002). Because the teacher had planned for play activities to occur in all areas of the classroom at any time of the day, children made few categorical decisions that were based on where an activity took place. In addition, children perceived play in all of the activities depicted within the stimuli (art, puzzles, blocks, number activity and television) with the exception of books. This finding provoked professional reflection and the modification of classroom practice, and a number of ways to increase the playfulness of early literacy activities were introduced. Rather than a book corner, a social tented area was constructed where story 'chests' could be shared. Story props were introduced with character role play and dressing-up materials. The location of storytime was varied, for example reading and enacting appropriate stories outside.

This small-scale, practice-based study demonstrates the value of continued professional development schemes that encourage cooperation between researchers and practitioners. The Activity Apperception Story Procedure enabled the teacher to evaluate classroom practice and gave her confidence in the experiences she was providing for the children. The study also demonstrated how important practitioners are in determining children's perceptions of play through the experiences they provide.

> ## Reflection point 〰️
>
> Try asking the children in your class about their activities. You could try taking photographs of the children involved in various activities and use these as prompts for discussion. What cues do the children appear to be attending to? Are some things seen as more play-like than others? What changes might you make and why? Do you think you are accepted as a play partner?

Children can differentiate play from other activities: approaching an activity as either 'play' or 'not play' leads to an increased behavioural repertoire and superior performance. Playfulness can be seen as a trait that remains constant across different situations, or as an approach to task that can be influenced by the environment. Findings from studies of children's perceptions appear to support the latter position in that the type of environment children have experienced influences the development of their perceptions, their approach to task and their subsequent performance. The role of environmental and emotional cues in the development of children's perceptions and subsequent behaviour can be explained by theories of conceptual development that focus on the development of scripts. Children develop scripts for action, that are based on their experiences and these scripts are then used to guide future behaviour (Rogoff, 1990). Whilst the studies described here focused on children in early years settings, Brooker's research (Chapter 2) shows the ways in which children's perceptions are influenced by familial interactions and beliefs which reflect social and cultural diversity. By reflecting on how children are interpreting their experiences at home and in early years settings, practitioners can ensure that their play provision is considered to be 'play' by the children themselves.

Understanding children's perspectives can inform the ways in which practitioners plan curricula that centralise play (McInnes et al., 2009), and help them to develop the integrated pedagogical approaches that are described above, and by Wood in Chapter 1 and by Broadhead in Chapter 3. This chapter demonstrates the role of children as active participants in research, and the ways in which their perceptions can contribute to reflective practice. Being aware of the subtle cues that contribute to children's categorical decisions about what is and what is not considered to be play can enable practitioners to create and maintain playful learning environments, and to be accepted as cooperative play partners by the children. Early years educators are arguably the most important play professionals in children's lives. The experiences they provide shape children's views of their classroom activities which in turn influence their approach to task, subsequent behaviour and potential learning outcomes.

Further reading 📖

Ashiabi, G.S. (2007) 'Play in the preschool classroom: its socioemotional significance and the teacher's role in play', *Early Childhood Education Journal* 35(2): 199–207.

Canning, N. (2007) 'Children's empowerment in play', *European Early Childhood Education Research Journal* 15(2): 227–36.

Howard, J. (2002) 'Eliciting young children's perceptions of play, work and learning using the activity apperception story procedure', *Early Child Development and Care* 127: 489–502.

McInnes, K., Howard, J., Miles, G.E. and Crowley, K. (2009) 'Behavioural differences exhibited by children when practising a task under formal and playful conditions', *Educational and Child Psychology* 26(2): 31–9.

References

Bruner, J.S. (1974) 'Child's Play', *New Scientist* 62: 126–8.

Garvey, C. (1991) *Play*, 2nd edn. London: Fontana.

Guha, M. (1988) 'Play in school', in G. Blenkin and A. Kelly (eds) *Early Childhood Education,* pp. 15–46. London: Paul Chapman.

Howard, J. (2002) 'Eliciting young children's perceptions of play, work and learning using the activity apperception story procedure', *Early Child Development and Care* 127: 489–502.

Howard, J. and Miles, G. (2008) Incorporating Empirical Findings that Link Play and Learning into a Behavioural Threshold and Fluency Theory of Play. Paper presented as part of a symposium at the BPS Psychology of Education Section conference, Milton Keynes, November.

Howard, J., Miles, G. and Griffith, J. (2004) Effectiveness of Practice in Playful and Formal Environmental Conditions. Paper presented at the BPS Education Sector conference, Glasgow, October, 2004.

Howard, J., Jenvey, V. and Hill, C. (2006) 'Children's categorisations of play based on social context', *Early Child Development and Care* 176(3&4): 379–93.

Howard, J., Miles, G. and Parker, C. (2008) Understanding Children's Perceptions of Play using the Revised Apperception Procedure: Implications for Practice in Early Years Settings. Paper presented at EECERA conference, Norway, April, 2008.

Jones, R. (1995) *The Child–School Interface*. London: Cassell.

Karrby, G. (1989) 'Children's conceptions of their own play', *International Journal of Early Childhood Education* 21(2): 49–54.

Keating, I., Fabian, H., Jordan, P., Mavers, D. and Roberts, J. (2000) '"Well, I've not done any work today. I don't know why I came to school". Perceptions of play in the reception class', *Educational Studies* 26(4): 437–54.

King, R. (1979) 'Play: the kindergartners perspective', *Elementary School Journal* 80(2): 81–7.

Kose, G., Beilin, H. and O'Connor, J. (1983) 'Children's comprehension of action depicted in photographs', *Developmental Psychology* 19(4): 636.

Manning, K. and Sharp, A. (1977) *Structuring Play in the Early Years at School*. London: Ward Lock Associates.

McInnes, K., Howard, J., Miles, G.E. and Crowley, K. (2009) 'Behavioural differences exhibited by children when practising a task under formal and playful conditions', *Educational and Child Psychology* 26(2): 31–9.

Moyles, J. (1989) *Just Playing: The Role and Status of Play in Early Childhood Education*. London: Open University Press.

Pellegrini, A. (1991) *Applied Child Study: A Developmental Approach*. Mahwah, NJ: Lawrence Erlbaum Associates.

Pellegrini, A. and Boyd, B. (1993) 'The role of play in early childhood development and education: issues in definition and function', in B. Spodek (ed.) *Handbook of Research on the Education of Young Children*, pp. 105–21. New York: Macmillan.

Piaget, J. (1951) *Play, Dreams and Imitation in Childhood*. London: Routledge and Kegan Paul.

Rich, D. (2002) 'Catching children's stories', *Early Education* 36: 6.

Robson, S. (1993) '"Best of all I like choosing time": talking with children about play and work', *Early Child Development and Care* 92: 37–51.

Rogoff, B. (1990) *Apprenticieship in Thinking: Cognitive Development in Social Context*. New York: Oxford University Press.

Rothlein, L. and Brett, A. (1987) 'Children's, teachers' and parents' perceptions of play', *Early Childhood Research Quarterly* 2: 45–53.

Royeen, C.B. (1985) 'Adaptation of likert scaling for use with children', *Occupational Therapy Journal* 5: 59–65.

Rubin, K.H., Fein, G.G. and Vandenberg, B (1983) 'Play', in P.H. Mussen and E.M. Hetherington (eds) *Handbook of Child Psychology, Vol. 4*, pp. 693–774. Basel: S. Karger.

Saracho, O. (1991) 'Educational play in early childhood', *Early Child Development and Care* 66: 45–64.

Smilanksy, S. (1968) *The Effects of Sociodramatic Play on Disadvantaged Preschool Children*. New York: Wiley.

Sturgess, J. and Ziviani, J. (1996) 'A self-report play skills questionnaire', *Australian Occupational Therapy Journal* 43: 142.

Sutton-Smith, B. (ed.) (1979) *Play and Learning*. New York: Gardner Press.

Sylva, K., Melhuish, E.C., Sammons, P., Siraj-Blatchford, I. and Taggart, B. (1999) *The Effective Provision of Pre-School Education (EPPE) Project: Technical Paper 6 – Characteristics of the EPPE Sample*. London: DfES/Institute of Education, University of London.

Thomas, L., Howard, J. and Miles, G. (2006) 'The effectiveness of playful practice for learning in the early years', *Psychology of Education Review* 30(1): 52–8.

Westcott, M. and Howard, J. (2007) 'Research into practice: creating a playful classroom environment', *Psychology of Education Review* 31(1): 27–34.

Wing, L. (1995) 'Play is not the work of the child: young children's perceptions of work and play', *Early Childhood Research Quarterly* 10: 223–47.

Wood, E. and Attfield, J. (2005) *Play, Learning and the Early Childhood Curriculum*, 2nd edn. London: Paul Chapman.

10

Play, Metacognition and Self-regulation

David Whitebread

The aims of this chapter are to:

- illustrate how play, particularly open-ended pretend or symbolic play, contributes to learning by supporting children's development of metacognitive and self-regulatory skills, which are crucial in the development of higher-order skills involved in learning, thinking, problem-solving and creativity
- explain the nature and significance of metacognition and self-regulation for young children's learning
- provide guidelines for early years practitioners that will support them in offering playful experiences to promote metacognition and self-regulation in young children.

The research

Metacognition and self-regulation in young children

Within cognitive developmental psychology, there is a considerable body of research evidence related to the development of children's 'metacognitive' skills. These are concerned with the child's developing self-awareness and control of their own mental processing. In the seminal study of Flavell et al. (1966), young children under the age of seven years were found to be capable of carrying out a taught memory strategy (rehearsal) when asked to remember a list of items, but, despite this success, were incapable of producing this strategy for use spontaneously when presented with a further list. This led to Flavell's (1979) development of a model of 'metamemory' and Brown's (1987) model of metacognition. In Brown's model, metacognition was characterised as consisting of three interrelated elements:

- *metacognitive experience*: the online monitoring or self-awareness of mental processing, and reflections upon it (for example, when reading late at night and suddenly realising our eyes are passing over the page, but nothing is being understood)

- *metacognitive knowledge*: the knowledge which is gradually accumulated, as a consequence of metacognitive experience, about one's own mental processing, tasks and cognitive strategies for dealing with tasks (for example, when we recognise that asking someone to draw a map would be useful when they are giving us directions)

- *metacognitive control*: the deployment of mental strategies which are developed and used increasingly appropriately in relation to tasks (for example, when we decide how to go about doing a mental calculation), based on our metacognitive knowledge and online monitoring of progress on the task.

This notion of metacognition has been enhanced by the more general concept of self-regulation, which derives from the work of Vygotsky (1978, 1986). For Vygotsky, the development of children's learning was a process of moving from other-regulation (or performing a task while supported by an adult or peer) to self-regulation (performing a task on one's own). In subsequent research and theory, there has been a broadening of notions of self-regulation from the purely cognitive concerns of Vygotsky, Flavell and Brown to include emotional, social and motivational aspects (cf. Baumeister and Vohs, 2004).

The consequences of young children developing early metacognitive and self-regulatory abilities have been shown to be profound. Blair and Razza's (2007) study of 3–5-year-old children from low-income homes in the USA, for example, showed that aspects of self-regulation accounted for unique variance, independent of general intelligence, in early maths and reading measured approximately a year later. Over a longer timescale, Schweinhart and Weikart (1998) followed a group of disadvantaged children who were randomly allocated to attend one of three pre-school programmes, one of which, High/Scope, encouraged children to develop a range of self-regulatory skills by following a pattern of plan-do-review, which crucially supports children in planning, taking responsibility for, and reflecting upon their own learning. Initially, all three groups showed an increase in IQ. However, a follow-up study when the subjects had reached the age of 23 showed that the High/Scope group were performing to a significantly higher level on a range of 'real-life' measures (e.g. rates of arrest, emotional problems, home ownership and salary).

In order to understand why self-regulatory abilities might impact so significantly on learning, and particularly school learning, over the long term, it is worth considering the nature of the cognitive processes involved. There are two important distinctions between different kinds of learning. First, there is the distinction between what might be termed 'incidental' learning and deliberate or 'intentional' learning, such as that which we engage in within educational settings. We all effortlessly learn and remember an enormous amount of information 'incidentally' in our everyday lives, but to learn and remember something intentionally requires effort, and involves us in a range of 'metacognitive' activities such as planning, selecting cognitive strategies and evaluating our own learning.

The second distinction is between cognitive activities which are practised and well understood (and which, consequently, are increasingly automaticised) and those required when the task involves problem-solving and being creative. In his influential 'triarchic' theory of human intelligence, Sternberg (1985) distinguished between three kinds of cognitive processes: 'knowledge acquisition components' through which we initially acquire information, skills and strategies; 'performance components' which enable us to implement learnt cognitive procedures and strategies; and 'metacomponents' – higher-order processes used to select and coordinate the activities of the other two components in relation to the task in hand and to plan, monitor and evaluate task performance. These 'metacomponents' distinguish able learners, who can apply existing knowledge and skills to new situations, problems and tasks, from children who struggle when presented with anything new.

Self-regulation, development and play

Consideration of these two distinctions in relation to different aspects of learning makes it clear that metacognitive or self-regulatory processes are likely to be particularly significant when cognitive tasks involve effortful attempts to learn intentionally, and when they require us to solve problems or to be creative. As Bruner (1972) argued, it is these higher-order cognitive skills, which he referred to as 'flexibility of thought', which are uniquely human and which are supported by the extended period of human childhood, and by the playful activities in which children engage during this period.

The impact of play on cognition has been mostly researched using variants of Sylva et al.'s (1976) classic study of children's problem-solving abilities. Typically, in these experiments, one group of children was 'taught' how to use a set of objects to solve a particular problem, while a second group were simply given the opportunity to play with the same objects. Consistently, the two groups subsequently performed equally well in solving the problem. However, in the 'taught' group, there tended to be an 'all or nothing' pattern of responses, with the children either succeeding immediately or giving up. By contrast, the children who had the experience of playing with the objects were more inventive in devising strategies to solve the problem and persevered longer if their initial attempts did not work. Subsequent work by Pellegrini and Gustafson (2005), in which observational data were collected of 3–5-year-old children over a school year, demonstrated that the amount of playful exploration, construction and tool use in which children engaged predicted their subsequent performance on a problem-solving task similar to that used by Sylva et al. (1976). Similar findings are reported by Howard in Chapter 9.

Much of the recent work concerned with children's play, and particularly that related to educational contexts, has been inspired by the influential theoretical ideas developed by Vygotsky (1978). These contain two further insights about the cognitive mechanisms by which play might contribute to effortful, intentional learning, problem-solving and creativity. First, he relates play to children's developing sense of control and self-regulation of their own learning. During play, children create their own zone of proximal development by setting their own level of challenge, and so what they are doing is always developmentally appropriate (to a degree which tasks set by adults will never be). Specifically, neo-Vygotskian work has also explored the development of cognitive self-regulation and control relating to particular types of play. Vygotsky's contention that sociodramatic play has a significant role in the development of self-regulation has been supported by a range of research, mostly focusing on attentional and emotional self-regulation (Berk et al., 2006; Elias and Berk, 2002; Karpov, 2005).

Second, Vygotsky argues that play makes a crucial contribution to the development of symbolic representation. Human thought, culture and communication are founded on the unique human aptitude for using various forms of symbolic representation, which include drawing and other forms of visual art, visual imagination, language in all its various forms, mathematical symbol systems, musical notation, dance and drama. The different play contexts in which symbolic representations occur are described by Broadhead in Chapter 3, Hall in Chapter 6, and Worthington in Chapter 8. Play is recognised as the first medium through which children explore the use of symbol systems, most obviously through pretence. Play becomes a transition from the 'purely situational constraints of early childhood' to the adult capability for abstract thought (Vygotsky, 1978: 98). Lacking these tools, the argument follows, children require the support of real situations and objects with which the ideas are worked out through play.

A range of studies has provided empirical support for Vygotsky's argument regarding the link between pretend play and the development of symbolic representational abilities in children. Dyachenko (1980; reported in Karpov, 2005) showed that the ability of 5–6-year-old children to retell a story was significantly enhanced by the use of representational objects such as sticks and paper cut-outs, and that their ability to retell a story without the use of these objects was subsequently enhanced. Berk et al. (2006) reported a series of observational studies of 2–6-year-old children in which they recorded the incidence of 'private speech'. In Vygotskian theory, young children's tendency to talk to themselves, or self-commentate, while they are undertaking a task, is of great significance, as he argues that such speech is an important step in the processes by which children learn to represent ideas to themselves in language, and learn to use language to self-regulate their activities. Berk and her colleagues found particularly high levels of private speech and verbal self-regulation among 2–6-year-old children during open-ended, make-believe or pretend play.

The C.Ind.Le project

My research in this area has been of two complementary kinds, and bears upon the issues of adult involvement in children's play and of the relationship between play and open-ended, problem-solving or creative activities. Evidence in relation to the first issue emerged from the Cambridgeshire Independent Learning in the Foundation Stage (C.Ind.Le) project (Whitebread, 2007; Whitebread et al., 2005, 2007), which explored the extent to which self-regulatory skills could be encouraged amongst 3–5-year-old children within Foundation Stage settings.

This two-year project involved 32 Foundation Stage practitioners and their nursery or reception classes. The practitioners were invited to participate based on their excellent practice and openness to pedagogical innovation. They developed playful activities to provoke metacognitive or self-regulatory behaviours. These activities required the children to solve a problem or be creative (for example, constructing a model), with children working individually (for example, dressing some dolls) or in collaborative groups (for example, playing a card or board game, or producing a collaborative drawing); some activities were constructed to involve peer tutoring (for example, teaching a friend how to plant a sunflower seed); some activities included adult participation (for example, with a group of children teaching a puppet to count). A guiding principle was that all activities were negotiated and all child initiatives were encouraged. Often, the activities were taken by the children in quite different directions to those envisaged by the practitioner. While video-recording these designed activities, spontaneous, entirely child-initiated activities were also recorded; as is often the case, these activities usually involved the children in setting themselves goals or problems. 'Events' were recorded both inside classrooms, and in outside play areas; across all areas of the Foundation Stage curriculum; and involving a wide range of different play types, including construction, object play, pretence and role play.

An analysis of 582 video-recorded activities which contained self-regulation was undertaken. Of these, 376 (64.6%) were child-initiated, while only 114 (19.6%) were adult-initiated and 92 (15.8%) were jointly initiated. Further, while only 21 (3.6%) involved a whole class working together, and 116 (19.9 %) involved individual children working on their own, an impressive 445 events (76.5%) involved children working in pairs or in small groups. Finally, these 582 events were analysed for the degrees of both collaboration and talk, according to whether there was none, whether it was intermittent or extensive. Figures for the numbers of events showing no collaboration and talk were 155 (26.6%) and 44 (7.6%) respectively; for intermittent levels, the figures were 148 (25.4%) and 144 (24.7%); and for extensive levels, they were 279 (47.9%) and 394 (67.7%).

Taken together, these findings suggested that, within the three to five age range, we were finding extensive evidence of metacognitive or self-regulatory behaviours which most frequently occurred during learning activities which were initiated by the children, involved them in working in pairs or small groups, and which entailed extensive collaboration and talk. However, as the figures above show, around one in five of the recorded events involved children working alone, and within these there were many examples of private speech. Figure 10.1 reports a simple, but clear, example of Ruby using private speech to help herself carry out the task of placing the correct number of candles on a pretend birthday cake for her sister.

As has been reported elsewhere in the literature, we did, however, find that the adult practitioners, who had been selected to be part of the project because of their generally excellent practice, struggled to participate effectively in the children's play. Analysis of the 582 events in terms of adult involvement revealed that, as the level of adult involvement increased, the rate of behaviours showing evidence of metacognitive knowledge (i.e. what children were able to say about

Ruby has placed a large lump of play dough in the top of a plastic mug. She explains to two other children, who are engaged in their own dough-related activities at the same table, that she is making a birthday cake. She has stuck three drinking straw 'candles' in the top of the dough 'cake'.

Observed activity	Analysis
Ruby: *Pointing to each drinking straw candle in turn, matching one candle to one counting word*: 1, 2, 3 candles.	In this observation a familiar strategy, counting, is applied to a new situation. The cognitive process is supported by the non-verbal gesture of pointing. *Control and regulation: applies a previously learned strategy to a new situation, in this case supported using a non-verbal gesture*
Ruby now adds further drinking straw candles, one at a time. At each addition, she says the next number word in the counting sequence: 4 candles, 5 candles, 6 candles, 7 candles, 8 candles, 9 candles	There is no evidence to suggest that these utterances are directed at any other member of the group and so may be interpreted as a self-commentary, in which the verbalisation is related to the degree to which performance is progressing towards a goal. *Monitoring: self-commentates*
After adding the ninth candle, Ruby holds her hands either side of the completed cake in a cradling gesture. She smiles broadly. There! This is for my sister ... And she'll love it!	The pleasure in having completed the cake is evident in the tone of this utterance, an interpretation supported by the use of facial expression. *Emotional/motivational monitoring: expresses awareness of positive emotional experience of a task* The second element to the utterance also indicates that the outcome of the task has been evaluated in relation to the intended goal, and has been deemed to be successful. *Reflection and evaluation: evaluating the quality of performance*
Ruby starts to pick up the dough cake by gripping the straw candles. Almost immediately, she puts the cake down again and changes her grip, placing her hand around the plastic mug in which it is has been constructed. In this manner, she carries the cake away from the table.	The activities observed here suggest that through cognitive monitoring an initial, ineffective strategy is changed to a more successful one. *Control and regulation: changes strategy as a result of monitoring*

Figure 10.1 Birthday candles

their own learning) increased slightly (usually in response to adult questioning), but the rate of behaviours showing children regulating the cognitive or emotional/motivational aspects of the activity itself markedly decreased.

There were, however, some excellent examples of practitioners who managed to participate in, or support, the children's playful activities without completely taking over the regulatory role. In one event, for example, a practitioner supported a three-year-old boy in attempting to put on a fireman's jacket. The child's friend had already donned a policeman's jacket and helmet, and was waiting to play, so he was keen to put on the jacket as quickly as possible, but was having difficulty. This is clearly a situation in which he could easily have become frustrated, angry and upset. It would have been easy for the nursery teacher to have quickly put the jacket on him to avoid this potentially distressful situation. If she had done this, however, she would have removed the problem for the child and the opportunity for the child to regulate his own emotions so that he could complete the task successfully for himself. All together, from the child's initial attempt to the point where he finally succeeded in putting on the jacket correctly, the event lasted well over three minutes. During this time, at no point did the nursery teacher touch the jacket. What she did, however, was provide attention (talking to him about the problem and focusing her attention on him throughout), provide emotional support (smiling throughout, laughing positively and playfully when the jacket fell to the floor, encouraging him enthusiastically and expressing delight at each successful move), and provide clear visual guidance (demonstrating 'putting your arm in like this'). These strategies enabled the boy to finally put the jacket on by himself. The delight on the boy's face and his obvious sense of achievement made it clear that this simple event had been transformed by the practitioner's pedagogical skills into a powerful learning experience in self-regulation. The lessons that this boy had learnt in terms of perseverance, emotional control and self-efficacy became self-evident over the next two weeks, when he put on the fireman's jacket as soon as he arrived in the nursery.

Experimental studies

Alongside this observational study, I have also been involved with colleagues in carrying out two experimental studies based upon and developing the study by Sylva et al. (1976) (Lander, 2007; Whitebread and Jameson, 2005). The focus in both these studies was to investigate the kind of learning that the experience of playful activities would support. In both studies, children experienced a 'taught' and 'play' condition, but the impact of these experiences was explored in relation to creative or problem-solving tasks likely to draw upon self-regulatory and metacognitive processes, rather than simple recall or non-strategic tasks.

In the first study (Whitebread and Jameson, 2005), rather than practical problem-solving, we were interested to see if the same kind of pattern observed between play and taught conditions would emerge in relation to the different area of children's oral and written storytelling. We chose a sample of able and older children, partly to counter the common misconception that play is mostly beneficial to less able or younger children. This sample consisted of 35 Year 1 and Year 2 children (aged five to seven years) with an average IQ (as measured by Ravens Progressive Standard Matrices IQ Test) of 131, which is within the top two per cent of the population. Every child in the group had a reading age at least six months above his/her chronological age.

Following the general structure of the original Sylva et al. (1976) study, and inspired by the earlier Dyachenko study (1980; reported in Karpov, 2005), the children were asked to produce oral and written stories after they had been read a story and had experience of story dolls and props under 'play' (10 minutes free play with the dolls and props in small groups), 'taught' (where the adult modelled other stories using the dolls and props for 10 minutes, but the children were not allowed to handle them) and 'control' (where the children were shown photocopied sheets of story characters, but offered no further help) conditions.

The analysis of the children's written stories arising from the three conditions showed that in the 'play' condition, the children included more conflicts and resolutions than in the control condition, and about the same number as in the 'taught' condition. However, in the 'play' condition, more of these conflicts and resolutions were different from those in the original story than in either of the other two conditions, and their stories were of higher quality (as measured by National Curriculum levels) than in the 'taught' condition.

The analysis of the children's oral storytelling showed that in the 'play' condition, the children showed more confidence (measured on a five-point scale from 'extremely unconfident and anxious' to 'extremely confident' based on observational analysis of their behaviour during task completion) than in either of the other two conditions. This difference appears to have been mostly attributable to a greater number of children lacking confidence after the 'taught' condition. After the 'play condition', the children also showed more confidence in the oral storytelling activity than their teachers had observed in their regular classroom activities. It is important to note that this was a repeated measures design, and so these results are for the same 35 children experiencing different pedagogical practices.

In the second study (Lander, 2007), a repeated measures design was also used with a sample of 16 nursery school children aged three to four years. This study aimed to examine the impact of 'play' and 'taught' conditions, but this time with a spatial task involving a magnetic shapes game and, following an interesting study by Pepler and Ross (1981), involving a closed or 'convergent' task with only one correct solution and an open, 'divergent', more creative task with an infinite number of possible different solutions. The closed task involved the child in completing a pattern from which there were missing shapes, and the open task involved using the shapes to make a picture of the child's free choice, having been shown an example picture of a man constructed by the researcher.

The results showed a significant difference between the times the children persevered on the tasks depending on the preceding condition. They persevered longer on the open task when this was preceded by the play condition. There was also a significantly greater level of originality on the open task when a play condition preceded the task, compared to a taught condition. While the level of involvement of the children (measured using the Leuven Involvement Scale for Young Children (LIS-YC) developed by Laevers, 1994) in the taught/open and play/closed conditions decreased from the condition to the task, and remained the same in the taught/closed condition, it significantly increased in the play/open condition. While this is a small-scale study, the results clearly support the position that playful experience is particularly effective in preparing children for effortful, problem-solving or creative tasks which require a higher level of metacognitive and self-regulatory performance. The detailed analysis of children's behaviour in playful and formal situations described by McInnes et al. (2009) further supports these findings. In this study, children in playful situations demonstrated more problem-solving strategies, higher levels of involvement and less distraction, than when in a formal situation.

Implications for pedagogy

There is a considerable body of evidence within the psychological literature supporting the role of play, and particularly pretend or symbolic play, which might involve objects or other children, in particular kinds of learning. This research is of particular significance for play within educational settings, as it appears to have its most significant impact in relation to effortful, intentional learning involved in the development of problem-solving and creativity skills. This chapter has reviewed some of this evidence and related theory and has presented some of the authors' own studies focusing on the involvement of play in supporting the development of metacognitive and self-regulatory skills, including private speech, verbal self-regulation and representational abilities, which are particularly significant in intentional learning.

These perspectives are important for advancing theoretical understanding about the relationships between play and learning, and providing guidelines for practitioners in supporting play in educational settings, in ways which are likely to be productive for children's learning, particularly in their self-regulated learning (Whitebread, 2007; Whitebread and Coltman, 2007). The four principles derived from the C.Ind.Le study of emotional warmth and security, children's initiation and feelings of control, cognitive challenge through problem-solving and creativity, and talk about learning (including private speech and collaborative talk), are all applicable and highly relevant to organising and supporting play in educational settings.

Emotional warmth and security – attachment

The importance of children experiencing emotional warmth and security is well-established in the research literature. Secure emotional attachments in young children have been found to be associated with a range of positive emotional, social and cognitive outcomes and, as noted earlier, are closely linked to the amount and sophistication of children's play. The evidence also suggests that this emotional security is the product of the child experiencing early relationships which are emotionally warm, sensitive and predictable (see Durkin, 1995).

Within the C.Ind.Le project, we collected many examples of adults providing emotional support when a child had a problem, in ways which enabled a child to persevere with a task which they might otherwise have abandoned (e.g. putting on the fireman's jacket). They enabled the child to learn that perseverance can be a pleasurable experience and lead to a successful outcome. Often, in the absence of this kind of support, either the element of perseverance is lost as adults complete the task for the child, or pleasure is replaced by frustration and the task is abandoned.

Reflection point 〜

To what extent are the following strategies, which provide emotional warmth and security in the classroom environment, integral to your practices? Do you:

- show an interest in the children as people, and share aspects of your own personal life?
- act playfully and have fun, showing enjoyment of the children's natural playfulness?
- provide a model of emotional self-regulation, talking through emotional difficulties, including your own (for example, when something happens which annoys you), with the children?
- show that you appreciate effort and enthusiasm at least as much as what the children produce or achieve?

Feelings of control

Closely related to this need for emotional security is the need for feelings of control. Research has established that from birth we enjoy feeling in control of our environment and, as Vygotsky argued, a significant aspect of play is that it gives children control of their own learning. Feeling in control of their environment and their learning is fundamental to children developing confidence in their abilities, and the ability to respond positively to setbacks and challenges.

Often in early years settings, young children are inspired by a particular experience and will want to follow this up in some way, perhaps through play, or other self-initiated activities. Early years practitioners need to have the confidence to allow flexibility for a child (or group of children) to pursue ideas and interests. The evidence from the C.Ind.Le project indicated the importance of creating opportunities for child-initiated activities that enhance children's sense of ownership of and responsibility for their own learning. More broadly, consulting children about the environment, the rules and procedures in the setting, the nature and layout of the provision, is beneficial both for their development as self-regulating learners, and to inform their teachers about the 'received curriculum' as experienced by the children. Howard's research in Chapter 9 demonstrates the value of eliciting children's views about what constitutes play, and shows that children's choice and control over their activities is particularly important if an activity is to be seen as play rather than work.

Reflection point 〰

To what extent are the following strategies, which are helpful in giving children this feeling of control, integral to your practices? Do you:

- make sure that children have access to a range of materials for their own playful purposes?
- give children the opportunity to make choices about activities?
- discuss classroom rules and routines, the classroom layout, and the provision within your setting with the children, and take on board their ideas?
- involve the children in the design, development and maintenance of role-play areas, displays, etc.?
- adopt a flexible approach to timetabling which allows children to pursue an activity, including playful activities, to their satisfaction, avoiding unnecessary interruptions?

Cognitive challenge

The third underlying principle of good practice which encourages self-regulatory and independent learning, is the presence of cognitive challenge. In Vygotsky's theories of learning, the most effective learning has been shown to take place when the child is working (or playing) in their zone of proximal development, and managing to carry out a task with some assistance from an adult, or their peers, which they would not have been able to do without assistance. Children spontaneously set themselves challenges in their play and, given a choice, will often choose a task which is more challenging than one chosen by an adult. The high incidence of metacognitive and self-regulatory behaviours observed in the playful events recorded and analysed in the C.Ind.Le project are a testimony to this element of challenge. Providing children with achievable challenges, and with appropriate assistance, are powerful pedagogical strategies for encouraging positive attitudes to learning, and the children's independent ability to create and take on their own challenges.

> **Reflection point** 〰
>
> To what extent are the following strategies, which promote cognitive challenge, integral to your practices? Do you:
>
> - require children to plan activities?
> - consider whether activities planned to be carried out individually could be made more challenging as a collaborative group task?
> - ask genuine, open-ended questions that require higher-order thinking, e.g. why, what would happen if, what makes you say that?
> - give children opportunities to organise activities themselves, avoiding too early adult intervention?

Articulation of learning

Finally, it is clear that if children are going to develop awareness of their own mental processing, the processes of thinking and learning need to be made explicit by adults, and the children need to learn to talk about and to represent their learning and thinking. As noted earlier, Vygotsky and others have highlighted the significance of children's spontaneous private speech in developing their self-regulatory abilities. This aspect of developing verbal self-regulation is stimulated by playful and open-ended activities (Berk et al., 2006).

Within the C.Ind.Le project, many practitioners developed pedagogical strategies to stimulate children's reflections and held extended conversations with them about their learning. These included, for example, taking digital photographs of the children playing or engaging in a task, and then reviewing them with the children on a laptop computer. In situations where they had not been an active participant in the children's imaginative play, they were able to ask genuine questions and stimulate the children to reflect upon their thinking and decision-making during the activity.

Reflection point

To what extent are the following strategies, which are effective in stimulating children to talk about their learning, integral to your practices? Do you:

- encourage children to play, solve problems or carry out activities in pairs or small collaborative groups?

- plan for and encourage peer tutoring, where one child teaches another?

- involve children in self-assessment?

- make learning intentions explicit when tasks are introduced or discussed, either while the children are engaged in the task, or afterwards in a review session?

- model a self-commentary, which articulates thinking and strategies (for example, when making a junk model and selecting materials)?

It is argued here that the notion of self-regulation, properly understood, has helped practitioners when they are considering their pedagogical roles and strategies in children's play. The findings from the studies reported here support Wood's argument in Chapter 1 for integrated pedagogical approaches, and for playful, co-constructive engagement between children and adults. As Howard demonstrates in Chapter 9, children's acceptance of adults as cooperative play partners requires skill and sensitivity, but a clear understanding of the importance of self-regulation in children's learning significantly helps teachers of young children to interact more productively in playful contexts.

Further reading

Berk, L.E., Mann, T.D. and Ogan, A.T. (2006) 'Make-believe play: wellspring for development of self-regulation', in D.G. Singer, R.M. Golinkoff and K. Hirsh-Pasek (eds) *Play Learning: How Play Motivates and Enhances Children's Cognitive and Social-Emotional Growth*, pp. 74–100. Oxford: Oxford University Press.

Bronson, M.B. (2000) *Self-regulation in Early Childhood*. New York: The Guilford Press.

Guha, M. (1987) 'Play in school', in G.M. Blenkin and A.V. Kelly (eds) *Early Childhood Education*, pp. 61–79. London: Paul Chapman.

Vygotsky, L.S. (1978) 'The role of play in development', in *Mind in Society*, pp. 92–104. Cambridge, MA: Harvard University Press.

Whitebread, D. and Jameson, H. (2005) 'Play, story-telling and creative writing', in J. Moyles (ed.) *The Excellence of Play*, 2nd edn, pp. 59–71. Maidenhead: Open University Press.

References

Baumeister, R.F. and Vohs, K.D. (eds) (2004) *Handbook of Self-Regulation: Research, Theory and Applications.* New York: The Guilford Press.

Berk, L.E., Mann, T.D. and Ogan, A.T. (2006) 'Make-believe play: wellspring for development of self-regulation', in D.G. Singer, R.M. Golinkoff and K. Hirsh-Pasek (eds) *Play Learning: How Play Motivates and Enhances Children's Cognitive and Social-Emotional Growth*, pp. 74–100. Oxford: Oxford University Press.

Blair, C. and Razza, R.P. (2007) 'Relating effortful control, executive function, and false belief understanding to emerging math and literacy abilities in kindergarten', *Child Development* 78: 647–63.

Brown, A.L. (1987) 'Metacognition, executive control, self-regulation and other more mysterious mechanisms', in F.E. Weinert and R.H. Kluwe (eds) *Metacognition, Motivation and Understanding*, pp. 65–116. Hillsdale, NJ: Lawrence Erlbaum.

Bruner, J.S. (1972) 'Nature and uses of immaturity', *American Psychologist* 27: 687–708.

Durkin, K. (1995) 'Attachment to others', in *Developmental Social Psychology: From Infancy to Old Age.* Oxford: Blackwell.

Elias, C.L. and Berk, L.E. (2002) 'Self-regulation in young children: is there a role for sociodramatic play?', *Early Childhood Research Quarterly* 17: 216–38.

Flavell, J.H. (1979) 'Metacognition and cognitive monitoring: a new area of cognitive developmental inquiry', *American Psychologist* 34: 906–11.

Flavell, J.H., Beach, D.R. and Chinsky, J.M. (1966) 'Spontaneous verbal rehearsal in a memory task as a function of age', *Child Development* 37: 283–99.

Karpov, Y.V. (2005) 'Three- to six-year-olds: sociodramatic play as the leading activity during the period of early childhood', in *The Neo-Vygotskian Approach to Child Development*, pp. 139–70. Cambridge: Cambridge University Press.

Laevers, F. (ed.) (1994) 'Defining and assessing quality in early childhood education', *Studia Paedagogica* 16. Leuven, Belgium: Leuven University Press.

Lander, R. (2007) *Investigating the Effects of Play on Children's Problem Solving and Creativity.* Unpublished MPhil thesis, University of Cambridge.

McInnes, K., Howard, J., Miles, G.E. and Crowley, K. (2009) 'Behavioural differences exhibited by children when practising a task under formal and playful conditions', *Educational and Child Psychology* 26(2): 31–9.

Pellegrini, A.D. and Gustafson, K. (2005) 'Boys' and girls' uses of objects for exploration, play and tools in early childhood', in A.D. Pellegrini and P.K. Smith (eds) *The Nature of Play: Great Apes and Humans*, pp. 113–35. New York: Guilford Press.

Pepler, D.J. and Ross, H.S. (1981) 'The effects of play on convergent and divergent problem solving', *Child Development* 52(4): 1202–10.

Schweinhart, L.J. and Weikart, D.P. (1998) 'Why curriculum matters in early childhood education', *Educational Leadership* 55(6): 57–60.

Sternberg, R.S. (1985) *Beyond IQ: A Triarchic Theory of Human Intelligence.* New York: Cambridge University Press.

Sylva, K., Bruner, J.S. and Genova, P. (1976) 'The role of play in the problem-solving of children 3–5 years old', in J.S. Bruner, A. Jolly and K. Sylva (eds) *Play: Its Role in Development and Evolution*, pp. 55–67. Harmondsworth: Penguin.

Vygotsky, L.S. (1978) 'The role of play in development', in *Mind in Society*, pp. 92–104. Cambridge, MA: Harvard University Press.

Vygotsky, L.S. (1986) *Thought and Language.* Cambridge, MA: MIT Press.

Whitebread, D. (2007) 'Developing independence in learning', in J. Moyles (ed.) *Early Years Foundations: Meeting the Challenge*. pp. 220–38. Maidenhead: Open University Press.

Whitebread, D. and Coltman, P. (2007) 'Developing young children as self-regulated learners', in J. Moyles (ed.) *Beginning Teaching Beginning Learning*, 3rd edn, pp. 154–68. Maidenhead: Open University Press.

Whitebread, D. and Jameson, H. (2005) 'Play, story-telling and creative writing', in J. Moyles (ed.) *The Excellence of Play*, 2nd edn, pp. 59–71. Maidenhead: Open University Press.

Whitebread, D., Anderson, H., Coltman, P., Page, C., Pino Pasternak, D. and Mehta, S. (2005) 'Developing independent learning in the early years', *Education 3–13* 33: 40–50.

Whitebread, D., Bingham, S., Grau, V., Pino Pasternak, D. and Sangster, C. (2007) 'Development of metacognition and self-regulated learning in young children: the role of collaborative and peer-assisted learning', *Journal of Cognitive Education and Psychology* 3: 433–55.

Conclusion: Understanding Playful Learning and Playful Pedagogies – Towards a New Research Agenda

Pat Broadhead, Elizabeth Wood and Justine Howard

It is always a challenge to convey complex ideas in accessible ways, and the diversity of play scholarship makes this challenge even greater. Play is a complex landscape: understanding how play connects with children's learning deepens the complexities even further. As the studies in this book have shown, play has particular qualities and characteristics because it is shaped by many different influences that begin in homes and continue into early years educational settings. Educators need to understand the playing child as a learner, their own roles in relation to playful learning, and the interconnections across these two dimensions of playful learning and playful pedagogies. This also involves understanding what children are doing in their play, the significance of their meanings and intentions for their learning and development, and how educators can create spaces and places for deep learning through play.

To further develop professional knowledge about these two dimensions, we need to interconnect the disciplinary perspectives that can create a more holistic understanding of the benefits of play. Play has been studied from educational, sociological, psychological, health-related, anthropological and historical perspectives, although not, to any great extent (even in education), within early years educational settings. The 'hallowed concept of play' is also imbued with powerful ideological claims that exerted strong influences on practice, particularly during the 1960s. The research studies in this book advocate moving away from outdated ideologies, and from the traditional emphasis on child development as the main reference point for pedagogy, learning and curriculum provision. In contrast, the authors have provided an interdisciplinary focus by reporting studies that are theoretically located within socio-cultural, biocultural and psychological approaches to researching play and learning in the early years in different settings. They offer contrasting perspectives and interpretations, which are derived from the theoretical and methodological framing of their research, justify their findings and support the claims that are being made (both individually and collectively) in support of re-conceptualising learning through play.

In this conclusion, we draw together some key issues and compelling ideas for readers, and offer potentially new and theoretically informed ways of thinking about and responding to play. Our aim has not been to urge educators to take ownership of children's play within educational settings but to liberate it from external pressures such as targets, outcomes and effectiveness agendas. As Hakkarainen (2006) points out, play is an intrinsically motivated process with outcomes and developmental effects that are not always immediately visible. This is a challenge to educators who, for the last 20 years or so, have been encouraged to measure anything that moves and to 'prove' what play does for children in relation to defined learning outcomes. A further challenge is to perceive play in educational settings as a bridge into a world of understanding children's learning (Broadhead, 2004), particularly because, as Howard (2009) proposes, early years practitioners are arguably the most important play professionals in young children's lives.

To facilitate this view of play as a bridge into a world of children's learning, this conclusion proposes the following issues for consideration. These are based on a cumulative synthesis of the preceding chapters. We ask you to consider:

- the young child's right to make choices in their early learning environment, and their ability to do so, based on their own culturally influenced interests and experiences within and beyond their early years settings

- the educator's responsibility to create and sustain an environment in which choice is facilitated, so as to promote maximum opportunity for playful learning through individual and group activity.

The child's right to make choices within their early years setting in support of their own playful learning

Although the concept of choice (alongside freedom, ownership, autonomy and control) remains central to integrated pedagogical approaches, we argue here for a critical approach to what this actually means. 'Choice' can be a conservative and narrow experience, where children repeat familiar tasks, which may not support or advance their learning. As Wood (2007) has pointed out, the choices that children make can sometimes be at the expense of opportunities for learning for other children. Whilst young children can be altruistic, play is highly motivational and children make a substantial commitment to it. They will protect it from interference where they can, for example by excluding those they see as less expert than themselves, or those that aren't members of an established friendship group, if they feel that the progress of their play will be disrupted. In relation to social justice, individual and group choices can also be influenced by perceptions of difference and diversity, so that children can be included or excluded on the basis of ability, social class, culture, ethnicity, gender, language, race and sexual orientation (Genishi and Goodwin, 2008). Choice is also about exercising and contesting power structures and relationships, which is perhaps one of the most challenging issues for practitioners, especially where children's choices do not fit neatly into the available provision, or into the rules and structures.

When considering the child's right to make choices, we are not talking about educators being 'child-centred', or about 'starting with the child' in relation to curriculum provision. We have not used these concepts in this book, because they have been misinterpreted and over-used, and their pedagogical meaning has been obscured by past ideologies. Nor have we advocated using these concepts for capturing the complexities around children making choices in support of their playful learning. An important determinant of choice is the child's own perception of what 'choice' might mean within educational settings. The research presented by Howard in Chapter 9 highlights how powerful the illusion of choice can be in determining the nature of children's play activity. We argue that predominantly developmental notions of learning and autonomy need to be replaced by a deeper understanding of choice as a socio-cultural phenomenon that interconnects the child's inner self with their peers and their early years environment, through individual and collective motivation. Children's choices are also driven by social and cultural diversity, and reflect their knowledge and understanding of their everyday worlds, which have been influenced substantially by home-based beliefs and practices around play (Gaskins and Miller, 2009). Taking a critical and more complex perspective on children's choices requires educators to understand the impact of the educational environment and pedagogical routines on those choices, and the repertoires of choices that children make. And herein lie the deep pedagogical responsibilities described by Elizabeth Wood in Chapter 1.

None of the authors advocate 'leaving children to it' in terms of their developing abilities to make choices, neither have they privileged 'planned and purposeful play', where adults aim to develop children's capacities for making choices (and especially those choices that are sanctioned by adults' plans and purposes). Instead, the authors offer a more complex mosaic of play, including: how children learn to self-regulate through play (Whitebread); how they can take risks and still stay safe, and how their self-selected physical activity links with learning (Tovey, Jarvis); how they perceive the world of play and their own relative autonomy within that world and what that means in terms of intrinsic motivation (Howard); how their cooperative engagements are also cognitively challenging (Broadhead); and how their capacities to express inner meanings can be highly evolved and multi-modal (Ring, Hall, Worthington). Each of these chapters illustrates the crucial importance of adult's professional knowledge and understanding of flexible pedagogical approaches, and the different types of participation and engagement that they need to encourage in their provision.

It may seem contentious that we have not advocated play as 'the child's world', or as the best and most natural play way of learning. Instead, we have taken the socio-cultural perspective that knowledge is created in many different collective, relational spaces. In order to sustain a knowledge-creation metaphor (as discussed by Elizabeth Wood in Chapter 1), we have argued collectively for a deeper understanding of children's repertoires of choice and participation in play: the ways in which children share ideas and goals with one another in their play communities and, when they choose to do so, with adults; how they challenge one another and set and solve problems together; and how they learn through co-constructive engagements in order to expand their repertoires of skills and knowledge. Drummond (1996: 339) describes this as 'their powers to do, to think, to feel, to know and understand, to represent and express', but goes on to question why educators have traditionally under-estimated these powers, and the ways in which they become manifest in high-quality play-learning environments. Why is it that these tensions and contradictions continue to exist in play provision?

Early childhood education has been influenced by many different ideologies, theories, movements and, more recently, by national policy frameworks and government-sponsored research. Whilst we have been critical of the power of uncontested truths and ideologies, we also need to remember that we once had a theoretically based, educational play tradition in the UK which derived from the empirical work of, for example, Susan Isaacs and Margaret McMillan, and their followers. Ideas about playful learning and teaching were discussed and debated by different stakeholders and were embedded in thinking, understanding and practice. This knowledge was developed though pre- and in-service programmes so that professional understanding developed with experience, and with critical engagement in the theory–practice relationship. This educational play heritage was substantially eroded by the culture and climate of educational reform from the late 1980s onwards (Broadhead, 2004), to the extent that the status of play in education has been at its lowest point in the last 20 years. The introduction of the national play policy (DCMS, 2006; DCSF/DCMS 2008), has emphasised play development in the wider community with an associated development in the status of playworkers. There have been no parallel developments within education and, for many students in teacher education programmes, there is inadequate emphasis on the theoretical understanding and application of playful pedagogies. Even where students do address these areas, they may still experience dislocations between theory and practice, as illustrated by Elizabeth Wood in Chapter 1. In this book, we argue for re-establishing a culture of knowledge creation and critical reflection around playful learning within and beyond early years settings. Such a culture needs to be informed by research evidence which is accessible to practitioners, so that the tensions and contradictions that exist between theory, policy and practice can be debated and addressed. As the authors in this book have demonstrated, developing a theory of playful learning is a significant endeavour for two reasons: first, to promote research-informed practice, and second to promote research-informed policy-making in which play is given status for its power and potential. Such endeavours would help to sustain a knowledge-creation metaphor for professional learning and development.

The adult's responsibility for facilitating choices within playful learning

Developing a theory of playful learning must be accompanied by a theory of playful pedagogies. As the authors have shown, playful learning communities involve playful adults as well as playful children. This represents a significant (and overdue) recognition that adults have key roles in creating and sustaining playful learning environments, enabling participation and engagement for all children, and considering diversity, equity and social justice. In this regard, Liz Brooker's research was critical to framing the subsequent chapters because she demonstrates that children bring their own cultural heritages, languages and identities into early years settings as their primary reference points, and looks at the implications this has for their learning and development. With age and experience, peer relationships, the culture of the setting and the curriculum are added into this cultural mix, so that children learn to build and connect their funds of knowledge and experience, through adult-led and child-initiated activities. However, the challenge for practitioners is to acknowledge that the culture of the setting might not be readily understood by children, which in turn influences their choices, participation and engagement in play activities. When children have the right opportunities, they use their culturally shaped funds of knowledge to create and sustain their play themes, and in their joint problem-solving with peers and adults. These activities promote different expressive modes and multi-modal communications, which are important for children who are learning English as an additional language, or who have special educational needs. We argue that if playful experiences are to be rich with learning potential, the child's right to choose involves integrating familiar cultural experiences, and extending their repertoires of choice and participation as their play skills and social skills progress. Thus, the concept of 'choice' is not wholly individual, but relational and contextual, involving peers and adults as co-players.

Each of the previous chapters has illustrated how playfulness is linked to learning via all aspects of children's development – cognitive, social, physical and emotional, and via their home and curriculum experiences, all of which contribute to their well-being. Whilst this is not a new concept, the authors have drawn on research evidence to illustrate how these links can be made in early years educational settings. However, the relationship between theory, research, policy and practice, remains problematic – there is no 'SatNav' to guide practitioners, and the minimum standards laid down in national policy documents do not, in themselves, guarantee high-quality education. The tensions and challenges that practitioners face are influenced by national policy frameworks, because they are not adequately underpinned by theory and research evidence about play, learning and pedagogy. Thus, there are significant challenges in developing integrated pedagogical approaches: this does not just require practitioners to use different approaches to supporting playful learning, but to develop the capacity to underpin their pedagogical choices with their professional knowledge and conceptual understanding of play and its relationship to learning. Although practitioners must attend to policy because this forms the basis of inspection and accountability frameworks, and defines constructs of 'effective practitioners', this raises the question of where and how they acquire the knowledge to be 'effective practitioners', when effectiveness is narrowly defined in relation to learning outcomes. The authors have demonstrated the value of practitioner-led and collaborative research in their own settings, and, in particular, the value of observations as a research and pedagogical tool. The cycle of observation, reflection, critical discussion and professional action can help practitioners to build their own theories, by developing personal understandings of what is involved in playful learning, how this is manifest in their settings, and how they can best support this through integrated pedagogical approaches. Successful integration relies on different forms of adult involvement, including non-participant observation, focused interactions, direct teaching and sustained engagement as a co-player.

Several chapters have been informed by observational studies, including the ways in which children play together, and the artefacts, tools and symbols that they create through their playful engagements. Observation sits at the heart of understanding the links between play and learning, and the significance of playful meanings and intentions for young children. By studying these processes, we gain insights into their learning, their misconceptions, their repertoires of choice and participation, and their diverse ways of interpreting their social and cultural worlds. Educators can use these insights to engage with children in extending their knowledge, skills and understanding, and in supporting progression and continuity. Consequently, we argue that observation, critical reflection and joint interpretation are at the heart of research into children's playful learning, and at the heart of effective practice. Effective practice is ethical practice, because it involves understanding the educator's responsibility for enabling children to make choices in the indoor and outdoor environments, and to exercise those choices in ways that respect inclusion, diversity and social justice (Genishi and Goodwin, 2008).

We acknowledge that putting observation at the heart of practice requires a significant shift in practitioners' skills and knowledge. Practitioners often think that if they are observing, they are not working; or, if they are not sure what they are observing, then it becomes difficult to interpret meaning and significance. Hence, we do not advocate brief observations as a means of assessing specific learning outcomes, where practitioners rely on tick lists and post-it notes. Instead, we do advocate sustained observations of their play and meaning-making activities, which includes listening to conversations between peers in order to better understand their ideas, imaginings and intentions, and engaging in conversations with children about their play. These pedagogical strategies will enable practitioners to use **children's** interests and ideas as starting points for conversations, so that the **adult's** intentions are grounded in a responsive approach that offers enrichment and development of children's knowledge, skills and understanding. In supporting playful learning, adults need to become deep, reflective thinkers, so as to locate children's play choices and activities within a wider theoretical framework of the nature of playful learning. The skills of interpreting meaning from observation need to be acquired and refined through professional development opportunities. Such a model locates observation as integral to critically examined action, which can focus on adults' as well as children's actions.

Adults also need to be deep thinkers in order to encourage children's involvement in making decisions about organising the learning environment, what materials and resources are available, and how these might be used. For example, the freedom to combine small-world play and large construction play can help children to progress from building a structure to creating imaginative worlds and scenarios. We have seen from several chapters that practitioners respond to the policy messages in ways that can stifle playful learning. This is most often seen where certain forms of play are banned or constrained, such as rough and tumble, and physical activities that may involve risk and danger, as discussed by Pam Jarvis and Helen Tovey. These authors have advocated eloquently for enabling such forms of play because of their potential benefits, and because the real risk to children's well-being lies in no-risk environments. This reminds us that well-being is not about keeping safe through lack of challenge, but learning about safety through assessing risks and hazards, testing personal boundaries, developing resilience and showing collective concern for others.

We have aimed in this book to present research studies and their findings in ways that can provide early years educators with the knowledge and confidence to articulate the relationship between play and learning, in terms of *what play does* and *what play means* for young children. We hope it encourages readers to challenge their own theories and practices, to engage in their own research, to try some new ideas and approaches, and to articulate the impact on children's playful learning that might arise from these innovations. We also strongly advocate for more research into playful learning within and beyond the early years.

As this book goes to press, we sense important shifts across early years and primary education. As described in the opening chapter, the research reported here is already proving influential in policy contexts, and through the work of the authors in teacher-education programmes, continuing professional development, and academic and professional publications. The recommendations of the Independent Review of the Primary Curriculum (DCSF, 2009) give due recognition to play, and promote more flexible pedagogical approaches into Key Stage 1. The degree of prescription in the primary curriculum is being reduced, and there are encouraging signs that teachers and children will have more scope for creativity, flexibility and playfulness in their practice. We believe that now is the time to embed playful learning and teaching within and beyond early childhood education, and to ensure that future initiatives promote rather than erode the status of play. Most of all, we want to promote a view of children as expert players and learners, who draw on the resources of their communities (human and material) to support and extend their play. The authors have illustrated the many ways in which children learn through play, from their peers, from adults and from meaningful action in their social and cultural worlds. In each chapter, the tasks and reflective questions have aimed to help educators to think critically about how they integrate their pedagogical approaches in ways that facilitate play alongside the requirements of the curriculum. Perhaps most importantly, we argue for more time: time for children to engage deeply and seriously in their play activities; time for children to develop and sustain their play themes and imaginative worlds; time for adults to observe, listen and engage with children's perceptions, ideas and interests; and time for them to learn from team-based reflections on their observations and interactions with children as skilled and capable players. We hope that the book will inform future reflections on play and learning, and contribute to the continuous professional development of practitioners, through stimulating dialogue, critical reflection and change processes. Most of all, we hope that the book will help practitioners to use the research evidence to justify the power of play, and the need for play and playfulness across the lifespan.

References

Broadhead, P. (2004) *Early Years Play and Learning: Developing Social Skills and Cooperation.* London: Routledge.

Department for Culture, Media and Sport (DCMS) (2006) *Time for Play.* London: DCMS.

Department for Children, Schools and Families (DCSF) (2009) *The Independent Review of the Primary Curriculum,* http://publications.teachernet.gov.uk [Accessed 12 June 2009]

Department for Children, Schools and Families and Department for Culture, Media and Sport (DCSF/DCMS) (2008) *Fair Play: A Consultation on the Play Strategy.* London: DCSF.

Drummond, M.J. (1996) 'Whatever next? Future trends in early years education', in D. Whitebread (ed.) *Teaching and Learning in the Early Years.* London: Routledge.

Gaskins, S. and Miller, P.J. (2009) 'The cultural roles of emotions in pretend play', in C. Dell Clark (ed.) *Transactions at Play. Play and Culture Studies, Vol. 9.* Lanham, MD: University Press of America.

Genishi, C. and Goodwin, A.L. (eds) (2008) *Diversities in Early Childhood Education: Rethinking and Doing.* New York: Routledge.

Hakkarainen, P. (2006) 'Learning and development in play', in J. Einarsdottir and J.T. Wagner (eds) *Nordic Childhoods and Early Education.* Connecticut: Information Age Publishing.

Howard, J. (2009) 'Play, learning and development in the early years', in T. Maynard and N. Thomas (eds) *An Introduction to Early Childhood Studies,* pp. 101–12. London: Sage.

Wood, E. (2007) 'Re-conceptualising child-centred education', *Forum* 49(1): 121–36.

Index